RETHINKING CAPITALISM

Economics and Policy for Sustainable and
Inclusive Growth

RETHINKING CAPITALISM

Economics and Policy for Sustainable and Inclusive Growth

Edited by
Michael Jacobs and Mariana Mazzucato

Wiley-Blackwell
In association with *The Political Quarterly*

Blackwell Publishing was acquired by John Wiley & Sons in February 2007. Blackwell's publishing programme has been merged with Wiley's global Scientific, Technical and Medical business to form Wiley-Blackwell.

Registered Office

John Wiley & Sons Ltd, The Atrium, Southern Gate, Chichester, West Sussex, PO19 8SQ, United Kingdom

Editorial Offices

350 Main Street, Malden, MA 02148-5020, USA

9600 Garsington Road, Oxford, OX4 2DQ, UK

The Atrium, Southern Gate, Chichester, West Sussex, PO19 8SQ, UK

For details of our global editorial offices, for customer services, and for information about how to apply for permission to reuse the copyright material in this book please see our website at www.wiley.com/wiley-blackwell.

The rights of Michael Jacobs and Mariana Mazzucato to be identified as the editors of the editorial material in this work have been asserted in accordance with the Copyright, Designs and Patents Act 1988.

First published in 2016 by John Wiley & Sons

Library of Congress Cataloging-in-Publication Data

Names: Jacobs, Michael, 1960- editor. | Mazzucato, Mariana, 1968- editor.

Title: Rethinking capitalism : economics and policy for sustainable and inclusive growth / edited by Michael Jacobs and Mariana Mazzucato.

Description: Chichester, West Sussex, United Kingdom : Wiley-Blackwell, in association with The Political Quarterly, 2016. | Includes bibliographical references.

Identifiers: LCCN 2016024733 | ISBN 9781119120957 (pbk. : alk. paper)

Subjects: LCSH: Capitalism. | Sustainable development. | Economic development--Environmental aspects.

Classification: LCC HB501 .R4295 2016 | DDC 330.12/2--dc23 LC record available at https://lccn.loc.gov/2016024733

Set in 10.5/12pt Palatino by SPS

Printed in the UK by Hobbs the Printer

1   2016

For

Calum, Natasha and Lucienne

and

Leon, Micol, Luce and Sofia

Acknowledgements

WE ARE indebted to Daniele Girardi, Caetano Penna, Frank Brouwer and Jeff Masters for their invaluable editorial work on key chapters of this book.

We are very grateful to Joni Lovenduski and Deborah Mabbett at *The Political Quarterly* for their support, and for the great help provided by Emma Anderson. Thanks to Sandra Fardon Fox, Lena Hawkswood and Rachel Smith at Wiley Blackwell, and to Kristy Barker and Sarah Price for copy editing and proof reading.

Mariana Mazzucato acknowledges support from a research grant from the Institute for New Economic Thinking (grant no. 5474) and from the European Community's H2020-Euro-Society-2014 call on 'Overcoming the crisis: new ideas, strategies and governance structures for Europe' (ISIGrowth grant no. 649186).

Contents

Notes on Contributors

Michael Jacobs is Visiting Professor in the School of Public Policy and Department of Political Science at University College London. An environmental economist and political theorist, his work has focused on the political economy of environmental change. His books include *The Green Economy: Environment, Sustainable Development and the Politics of the Future* (Pluto Press, 1991), *Greening the Millennium? The New Politics of the Environment* (ed., Blackwell, 1997), *The Politics of the Real World* (Earthscan, 1996) and *Paying for Progress: A New Politics of Tax for Public Spending* (Fabian Society, 2000). From 2004 to 2010 he was a Special Adviser to the UK Prime Minister, responsible for domestic and international policy on energy and climate change, and before that (2004–2007) a member of the Council of Economic Advisers at the Treasury. He has previously been General Secretary of the Fabian Society, Co-Editor of *The Political Quarterly* and a research fellow at Lancaster University and the London School of Economics.

Mariana Mazzucato is the RM Phillips Professor in the Economics of Innovation at SPRU at the University of Sussex. She has held academic positions at the University of Denver, London Business School, Open University and Bocconi University. Her book *The Entrepreneurial State: Debunking Public vs. Private Sector Myths* (Anthem, 2013) was on the *Financial Times'* 2013 Books of the Year list. She is winner of the 2014 New Statesman SPERI Prize in Political Economy and the 2015 Hans-Matthöfer-Preis, and in 2013 the *New Republic* called her one of the 'three most important thinkers about innovation'. She is an economic advisor to the Scottish government and the Labour Party, and is a member of the World Economic Forum's Global Agenda Council on the Economics of Innovation. Her current research is funded by the European Commission, the Institute for New Economic Thinking (INET), the Ford Foundation, NASA and the Brazilian Ministry for Science and Technology.

Stephanie Kelton is Professor of Economics at the University of Missouri-Kansas City. Her research expertise is in Federal Reserve operations, fiscal policy, social security, international finance and employment. She is best known for her contributions to the literature on Modern Monetary Theory. Her book, *The State, The Market and the Euro* (Edward Elgar, 2003) predicted the debt crisis in the eurozone. She served as Chief Economist on the US Senate Budget Committee and as an economic advisor to the Bernie Sanders 2016 presidential campaign. She was Founder and Editor-in-Chief of the top-ranked blog 'New Economic Perspectives' and a member of the TopWonks network of America's leading policy thinkers. She consults with policy-makers, investment banks and portfolio managers across the globe, and is a regular commentator on national radio and broadcast television.

L. Randall Wray is Professor of Economics at Bard College and Senior Scholar at the Levy Economics Institute. He is the author of *Money and Credit in Capitalist Economies* (Edward Elgar, 1990); *Understanding Modern Money: The Key to Full Employment and Price Stability* (Edward Elgar, 1998); and *Modern Money Theory: A Primer on*

Published by John Wiley & Sons Ltd, 9600 Garsington Road, Oxford OX4 2DQ, UK and 350 Main Street, Malden, MA 02148, USA

Macroeconomics for Sovereign Monetary Systems (Palgrave Macmillan, 2012, 2nd rev ed, 2015). He is also co-editor of, and a contributor to, *Money, Financial Instability, and Stabilization Policy* (Edward Elgar, 2006), and *Keynes for the 21st Century: The Continuing Relevance of The General Theory* (Palgrave Macmillan, 2008). His latest book is *Why Minsky Matters: An Introduction to the Work of a Maverick Economist* (Princeton University Press, 2016).

Yeva Nersisyan is Assistant Professor of Economics at Franklin and Marshall College. She received her BA in economics from Yerevan State University in Armenia in 2006, and her MA and PhD in economics and mathematics from the University of Missouri-Kansas City in 2013. She is a macroeconomist working in the post-Keynesian and institutionalist traditions. Her research interests include banking and financial instability, and fiscal and monetary theory and policy. She has published a number of papers on shadow banking, fiscal policy, government deficits and debt, financial fragility and instability, financial reform and retirement policy.

Andrew G. Haldane is the Chief Economist at the Bank of England and Executive Director, Monetary Analysis and Statistics. He is a member of the Bank's Monetary Policy Committee. He also has responsibility for research and statistics across the Bank. In 2014, *TIME* magazine named him one of the 100 most influential people in the world. Andrew has written extensively on domestic and international monetary and financial policy issues. He is co-founder of 'Pro Bono Economics', a charity which brokers economists into charitable projects.

William Lazonick is Professor of Economics at University of Massachusetts Lowell. He is co-founder and president of the Academic-Industry Research Network. Previously, he was Assistant and Associate Professor of Economics at Harvard University, Professor of Economics at Barnard College of Columbia University and Distinguished Research Professor at INSEAD. His book *Sustainable Prosperity in the New Economy? Business Organization and High-Tech Employment in the United States* (Upjohn Institute, 2009) won the 2010 Schumpeter Prize. His article, 'Innovative Business Models and Varieties of Capitalism' received the Henrietta Larson Award from Harvard Business School for best article in *Business History Review* in 2010. His article 'Profits Without Prosperity: Stock Buybacks Manipulate the Market and Leave Most Americans Worse Off' was awarded the HBR McKinsey Award for outstanding article in *Harvard Business Review* in 2014. He is currently completing a book, *The Theory of Innovative Enterprise*, to be published by Oxford University Press.

Stephany Griffith-Jones is Financial Markets Director, Initiative Policy Dialogue, Columbia University; Emeritus Professor, Institute of Development Studies, Sussex University, where she was Professorial Fellow; and Research Associate, Overseas Development Institute. An economist, she has led many major international research projects on international and domestic financial issues and has published widely, having written or edited over twenty books and numerous journal and newspaper articles. Her books include *Time for a Visible Hand: Lessons from the 2008 World Financial Crisis*, co-edited with Jose Antonio Ocampo and Joseph Stiglitz (Oxford University Press, 2010), and *Achieving Financial Stability and Growth in Africa*, co-edited with Ricardo Gottschalk (Routledge, 2016). She has advised many international organisations, including the European Commission, European Parliament, World Bank, Commonwealth Secretariat, IADB and various UN agencies and several governments and central banks, including those of the UK, Chile, Sweden, South Africa, Tanzania, Brazil and Czech Republic.

Giovanni Cozzi is Senior Lecturer in Economics at the University of Greenwich and a member of the Greenwich Political Economy Research Centre. He was formerly Senior Economist at the Foundation for European Progressive Studies (FEPS) in Brussels and Research Fellow at the Centre for Development Policy and Research at the School of Oriental and African Studies. His current research is on fiscal policies, the role of social and physical investment in promoting sustainable growth and employment and the role of development banks. Several of his research publications employ the Cambridge Alphametrics Model (CAM), a structuralist growth model, to project alternative macroeconomic scenarios and their policy implications.

Joseph E. Stiglitz is University Professor at Columbia University, the winner of the 2001 Nobel Prize in Economics and the John Bates Clark Medal. He was also one of the lead authors of the 1995 report of the Intergovernmental Panel on Climate Change, which shared the 2007 Nobel Peace Prize. He is Co-Chair of the High-Level Expert Group on the Measurement of Economic Performance and Social Progress at the OECD, Chief Economist of the Roosevelt Institute, and the Founder and Co-President of Columbia University's Initiative for Policy Dialogue. He was Chairman of the US Council of Economic Advisors under President Clinton and Chief Economist and Senior Vice President of the World Bank from 1997 to 2000. He held the Drummond Professorship at All Souls College Oxford and has taught at MIT, Yale, Stanford and Princeton. His books include *Globalization and its Discontents* (Penguin, 2002), *The Price of Inequality* (Penguin, 2012) and *The Great Divide: Unequal Societies and What We Can Do About Them* (Allen Lane, 2015).

Colin Crouch is a Professor Emeritus of the University of Warwick and external scientific member of the Max Planck Institute for the Study of Societies at Cologne. He is vice-president for social sciences of the British Academy. He is a former editor and former chair of the editorial board of *The Political Quarterly*. He has published within the fields of comparative European sociology and industrial relations, economic sociology and contemporary issues in British and European politics. His most recent books include *Post-Democracy* (Polity, 2004); *Capitalist Diversity and Change: Recombinant Governance and Institutional Entrepreneurs* (Oxford University Press, 2005); *The Strange Non-death of Neoliberalism* (Polity, 2011); *Making Capitalism Fit for Society* (Polity, 2013); *Governing Social Risks in Post-Crisis Europe* (Edward Elgar, 2015); *The Knowledge Corrupters: Hidden Consequences of the Financial Takeover of Public Life* (Polity, 2015); and *Society and Social Change in 21st Century Europe* (Palgrave Macmillan, 2016).

Dimitri Zenghelis is Co-Head, Climate Policy at the Grantham Research Institute on Climate Change and the Environment at the London School of Economics. In 2013–2014 he was Acting Chief Economist for the Global Commission on the Economy and Climate. He was recently Senior Economic Advisor to Cisco's long-term innovation group (2008–2013) and an Associate Fellow at the Royal Institute of International Affairs, Chatham House. Previously, he headed the Stern Review Team at the Office of Climate Change, London, and was a senior economist on the Stern Review on the Economics of Climate Change, commissioned by the then Chancellor Gordon Brown. Before working on climate change, he was Head of Economic Forecasting at HM Treasury. He has also worked at Oxford Economics, the Institute of International Finance, Washington DC, and Tokai Bank Europe, London.

Carlota Perez is Centennial Professor of International Development at the London School of Economics, Professor of Technology and Development at TUT, Estonia, and Honorary Professor at SPRU, University of Sussex. She is the author of *Technological Revolutions and Financial Capital: the Dynamics of Bubbles and Golden Ages* (Edward Elgar, 2002). She conducts interdisciplinary research on the changing impact of technical change on world development. She has always combined teaching and research with consultancy and civil service. As Director of Technological Development in the Ministry of Industry of Venezuela, she created the nation's first venture capital fund. As a consultant she has worked for business (including IBM, Cisco and PDVSA), several governments and various multilateral organisations (such as IADB, UNCTAD, CEPAL, OECD, the World Bank and the EU). Her current research project, on the role of the state in shaping the context for innovation, is being funded by the Anthemis Institute.

1. Rethinking Capitalism: An Introduction

MICHAEL JACOBS AND MARIANA MAZZUCATO

IN NOVEMBER 2008, as the global financial crash was gathering pace, the 82-year-old British monarch Queen Elizabeth visited the London School of Economics. She was there to open a new building, but she was more interested in the assembled academics. She asked them an innocent but pointed question. Given its extraordinary scale, how was it possible that no one saw the crash coming?[1]

Hereditary sovereigns are not normally given to puncturing the pretensions of those in charge of the global economy, or of the economists paid to understand it. But the Queen's question went to the heart of two huge failures. Western capitalism came close to collapsing in 2007–2008, and has still not recovered. And the vast majority of economists had not understood what was happening.[2]

This book is about both failures. On the one hand the capitalist economies of the developed world, which for two hundred years transformed human society through an unparalleled dynamism, have over the past decade looked profoundly dysfunctional. Not only did the financial crash lead to the deepest and longest recession in modern history; nearly a decade later, few advanced economies have returned to anything like a normal or stable condition, and growth prospects remain deeply uncertain. Even during the pre-crash period when economic growth was strong, living standards for the majority of households in developed countries barely rose. Inequality between the richest groups and the rest of society has now grown to levels not seen since the nineteenth century. Meanwhile continued environmental pressures, especially those of climate change, have raised profound risks for global prosperity.

At the same time, the discipline of economics has had to face serious questions about its understanding of how modern economies work. What made the financial crisis such a shock—in two senses—was not simply that very few economists had predicted its coming. It was that over the previous decade the mainstream view was that policy-making had essentially solved the fundamental problem of the business cycle: major depressions, it was believed, should now be a thing of the past. And economic policy since the crisis has been no more successful. The orthodox prescription of 'fiscal austerity'—cutting public spending in an attempt to reduce public deficits and debt—has not restored Western economies to health, and economic policy has signally failed to deal with the deep-lying and long-term weaknesses which beset them.

The core thesis of this book is that these failures in theory and policy are related. Mainstream economic thinking has given us inadequate resources to

Published by John Wiley & Sons Ltd, 9600 Garsington Road, Oxford OX4 2DQ, UK and 350 Main Street, Malden, MA 02148, USA

understand the multiple crises which contemporary economies now face. To address these crises, we need a much better understanding of how modern capitalism works—and why in key ways it now doesn't. A reappraisal of some of the dominant ideas in economic thought is required. And in turn this needs to inform a set of new directions in economic policy-making which can more successfully tackle modern capitalism's problems.

Each of the chapters of the book therefore addresses both a key economic problem and the orthodox economic way of understanding it. The authors offer a different and more sophisticated approach to economic analysis, and from this generate new policy solutions. To do this they draw on important schools of economic thought whose powerful understandings of capitalist systems have been largely forgotten or sidelined in mainstream debate. In each case their conclusion is that capitalism can be reshaped and redirected to escape its present failures. But this can only be achieved if the mental frameworks of economics are rethought, and new approaches to policy taken.

Capitalism and its discontents

In this Introduction we pull together some of the key ideas which animate the book. We first set out the evidence of Western capitalism's failures, explaining the three fundamental problems which define its current weak performance. After describing the approach taken to these problems by each chapter, we draw out some of the lessons for economic theory and analysis. We offer a critique of the orthodox notions of markets and 'market failure'. And we explain how a richer and deeper understanding of capitalism can generate more successful approaches to economic policy, aimed at achieving more innovative, inclusive and sustainable forms of growth and prosperity.

Weak and unstable growth

There is no escaping the starting point for this analysis. The financial crash of 2008, and the long recession and slow recovery which followed, have provided the most obvious evidence that Western capitalism is no longer generating strong or stable growth.

The scale of the crash can hardly be exaggerated. In 2009 real gross domestic product fell in thirty-four of thirty-seven advanced economies and the global economy as a whole went into recession for the first time since World War II.[3] In a single year, real GDP fell by 4.5 per cent across the euro zone (including by 5.6 per cent in Europe's strongest economy, Germany), 5.5 per cent in Japan, 4.3 per cent in the UK and 2.8 per cent in the United States.[4] Between 2007 and 2009, global unemployment rose by around 30 million, over half of which was in advanced economies, including an increase of 7.5 million people in the US.[5]

To prevent an even bigger crisis, governments were forced to put unprecedented sums of taxpayers' money into bailing out the banks whose lending practices had precipitated the crisis. In the US the Federal Reserve had at its peak $1.2 trillion of emergency loans outstanding to thirty banks and other companies. In the UK, the government's exposure for support provided to the banks in the form of cash and guarantees peaked at £1.162 trillion.[6] At the same time governments undertook major stimulus measures to try to sustain demand as private spending and investment collapsed. The huge drop in output and the rise in unemployment led to large increases in public deficits as tax revenues fell and the 'automatic stabilisers' of welfare payments and other public spending took effect. In 2009–2010 these deficits reached as much as 32.3 per cent in Ireland, 15.2 per cent of GDP in Greece, 12.7 per cent in the US, 10.8 per cent in the UK, 8.8 per cent in Japan and 7.2 per cent in France.[7]

The financial crash exposed fundamental weaknesses in the functioning and regulation of the global financial system. As former Chairman of the Federal Reserve Alan Greenspan grudgingly acknowledged in his testimony to Congress, there had been a 'flaw' in the theory underpinning the Western world's approach to financial regulation. The presumption that 'the self-interest of organisations, specifically banks, is such that they were best capable of protecting shareholders and equity in the firms' had proved incorrect.[8] Contrary to the claims of the 'efficient markets hypothesis' which underpinned that assumption, financial markets had systematically mispriced assets and risks, with catastrophic results.[9]

The financial crash of 2008 was the most severe since that of 1929. But as Carmen Reinhart and Kenneth Rogoff have pointed out, since most countries undertook financial liberalisation in the 1970s and 1980s, there has been a marked increase in the frequency of banking crises (see Figure 1).[10] Globally, in the period 1970 to 2007, the International Monetary Fund has recorded 124 systemic bank crises, 208 currency crises and 63 sovereign debt crises.[11] For modern capitalism instability has become, not the exception, but a seemingly structural feature.

Unsurprisingly, policy-makers have focused since the crash on improving the regulation of banks and seeking to increase the overall stability of the financial system.[12] But important though this is, it does not address the more fundamental failure of modern capitalist economies to generate enough public and private investment in the real economy to fuel growth and a sustained level of demand.

The financial crisis exposed the uncomfortable truth that much of the apparently benign growth which had occurred in the previous decade did not in fact represent a sustainable expansion of productive capacity and national income. Rather, it reflected an unprecedented increase in household and corporate debt (see Figure 2). Low interest rates and lax lending practices, particularly for land and property, had fuelled an asset price bubble which would inevitably burst. In this sense the pre-crisis growth of output can be judged only alongside its post-crisis collapse.

3

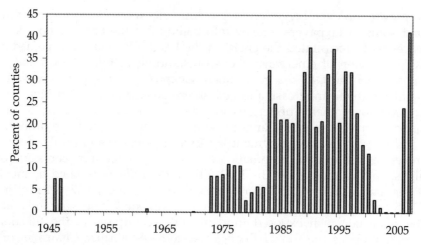

Figure 1: Percentage of countries experiencing a banking crisis (1945–2008) (weighted by their share of world income)

Note: Sample size includes all countries that were independent states in the given year.

Source: C. M. Reinhart and K. S. Rogoff, *This Time is Different: Eight Centuries of Financial Folly*, Princeton, NJ, Princeton University Press, 2009.

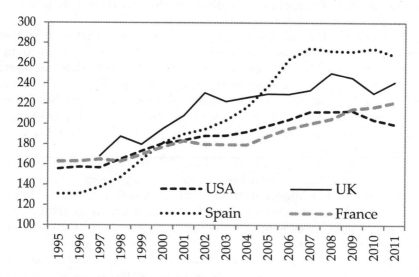

Figure 2: Outstanding private debt (% of GDP)

Source: OECD.stat (http://stats.oecd.org/index.aspx?queryid=34814 (accessed 12 April 2016)).

Since 2008, most Western economies have gradually returned to economic growth. But the recovery was the slowest in modern times. Output in the US, France and Germany did not return to pre-crash levels for fully three

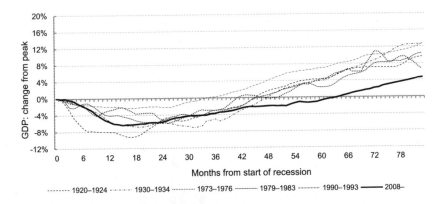

Figure 3: Comparing profiles of UK recessions and recoveries

Notes: Calculated from centred three-month moving averages of monthly GDP; the effect of the miners' strike in 1921 is excluded from the 1920–4 profile (the strike started on 31 March 1921 and ended on 28 June 1921). The effects of the miners' strike and the General Strike in 1926 are also excluded.

Source: National Institute of Economic and Social Research, *NIESR Monthly Estimates of GDP, 7th October, 2014,* London, 2014, p. 1, http://www.niesr.ac.uk/sites/default/files/publications/gdp1014.pdf (accessed 12 April 2016).

years. For the UK it took more than five (see Figure 3). Across most developed economies, unemployment has remained stubbornly above its pre-crisis rate. It was higher in 2014 than in 2007 in twenty-eight of thirty-three OECD countries for which comparable data is available (see Figure 4).[13] Even in countries where unemployment is lower than in 2007 or has been falling since its post-crisis peak, wages have been largely stagnant in real terms (see Figure 5). In the UK, where employment has grown, real wages suffered their sharpest decline since records began in 1964.[14]

Underpinning this weak growth pattern has been a dramatic collapse in private sector investment. Investment as a proportion of GDP had already been falling throughout the previous period of growth (see Figure 6). Since 2008 this has occurred despite the unprecedented persistence of near-zero real interest rates, bolstered in most of the major developed economies by successive rounds of 'quantitative easing', through which central banks have sought to increase the money supply and stimulate demand. Yet they have barely succeeded, as continuing low inflation rates have revealed.

The decline in investment is also related to the marked 'financialisation' of the corporate sector. Over the past decade or so, an increasing percentage of corporate profits has been used for share buybacks and dividend payments rather than for reinvestment in productive capacity and innovation. Between 2004 and 2013 share buybacks by Fortune 500 companies amounted to a remarkable $3.4 trillion. In 2014, these companies returned $885 billion to shareholders, more than their total net income of $847 billion.[15]

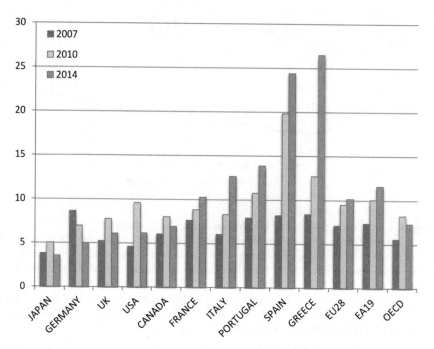

Figure 4: Unemployment rates, selected countries, 2007, 2010 and 2014
Source: OECD.stat (https://data.oecd.org/unemp/unemployment-rate.htm (accessed 12 April 2016)).

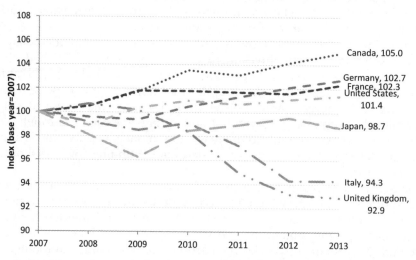

Figure 5: Average real wage index for selected developed countries, 2007–2013
Source: *ILO Global Wage Report 2014/15*, Geneva, International Labour Office, Geneva, 2015.

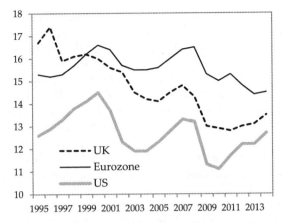

Figure 6: Investment (gross non-residential fixed capital formation) as a percentage of GDP

Source: Eurostat (http://ec.europa.eu/eurostat/data/database (accessed 12 April 2016)).

One critical result of the decline in investment is that productivity growth has also been weak relative to historic trends. In the decade prior to the crisis, labour productivity growth was below trend in almost all G7 countries, in some continuing a thirty-year decline. Since the financial crisis it has fallen further in most developed countries, including the US, Japan, France and the UK.[16] At the same time there appears to be some evidence that rates of productivity-enhancing innovation have also slowed down.[17] All this has led some economists to ask whether Western capitalism has entered a period of 'secular stagnation', in which a structural weakness of investment and demand leaves positive interest rates no longer able to support full employment. While such a prospect should not be regarded as somehow inevitable, it reflects a widespread concern that developed economies may face a long period of low growth and financial instability.[18]

Stagnant living standards and rising inequality

But weak and unstable growth is only part of modern capitalism's problem. One of the most striking features of Western economies over the past four decades is that, even when growth has been strong, the majority of households have not seen commensurate increases in their real incomes. In the US, real median household income was barely higher in 2014 than it had been in 1990, though GDP had increased by 78 per cent over the same period.[19] Though beginning earlier in the US, this divergence of average incomes from overall economic growth has now become a feature of most advanced economies.

There are in fact three separate trends here. In most developed countries, the total share of labour (salaries and wages) in overall output has fallen,

7

earnings have not kept pace with gains in productivity and the distribution of the reduced labour share has become more unequal.

Across advanced economies, the share of GDP going to labour fell by 9 per cent on average between 1980 and 2007, including 5 per cent in the US (from 70 to 65 per cent), 10 per cent in Germany (from 72 to 62 per cent) and fully 15 per cent in Japan (from 77 to 62 per cent).[20] Pay tended to track productivity until the 1970s. But since 1980, real hourly labour productivity in the US (non-farm) business sector has increased by around 85 per cent, while real hourly compensation has increased by only around 35 per cent.[21] Since 1999, the ILO calculates that across thirty-six developed economies, labour productivity has increased at almost three times the rate of real wage growth (see Figure 7).

At the same time as the labour share has been falling, more of it has been going to workers at the top of the earnings scale and less to those in the middle and bottom. Across advanced economies, higher-skilled workers claimed an additional 6.5 percentage points of the labour share between 1980 and 2001, whereas low-skilled workers saw their portion shrink by 4.8 percentage points.[22]

Meanwhile, those at the very top of the income distribution have done exceedingly well. In the US, between 1975 and 2012, the top 1 per cent gained around 47 per cent of the entire total of pre-tax increase in incomes (see Figure 8). In Canada over the same period it was 37 per cent, and in

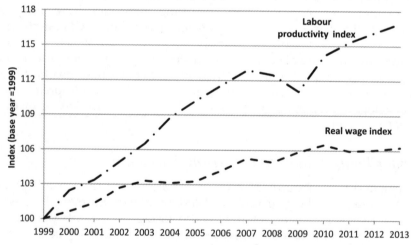

Figure 7: Trends in growth in average wages and labour productivity in thirty-six developed economies, 1999–2013

Note: Wage growth is calculated as a weighted average of year-on-year growth in average monthly real wages in thirty-six developed economies. Index is based on 1999 because of data availability.

Source: *ILO Global Wage Report 2014/15*, Geneva, International Labour Office, 2015.

Australia and the UK over 20 per cent.[23] In the US, the incomes of the richest 1 per cent rose by 142 per cent between 1980 and 2013 (from an average of $461,910, adjusted for inflation, to $1,119,315) and their share of national income doubled, from 10 to 20 per cent. In the first three years of the recovery after the 2008 crash, an extraordinary 91 per cent of the gains in income went to the richest one-hundredth of the population.[24] Overall, across the OECD over the past twenty years, the proportion of the labour share taken by the top 1 per cent of earners has increased by a fifth.[25]

At the same time, most developed countries have seen labour markets become more polarised and insecure. In the decade between the late 1990s and late 2000s, the proportion of low-paid workers increased in most advanced economies.[26] Since the financial crash unemployment has remained stubbornly high, particularly among young people. Across the OECD, unemployment in the 16–25 age group averaged 15 per cent in 2014, with rates of over a third in Spain, Portugal, Italy and Greece.[27] 'Non-standard' work (covering part-time, temporary and self-employed work, though not all of this is insecure) now accounts for around a third of total employment in the OECD, including half the jobs created since the 1990s and 60 per cent since the 2008 crisis. In 2013 almost three in ten part-time workers across the OECD were 'involuntary', meaning that they wanted to work full-time but could only find part-time jobs.[28]

The result of these trends has been a rise in inequality across the developed world. Between 1985 and 2013, the Gini coefficient measuring income inequality increased in seventeen OECD countries, was little changed in four and decreased in only one (Turkey).[29] Wealth inequality has grown even more than that of income, a result both of the shift in the distribution of earnings away from wages and towards profits and of the huge increase in land and property values. In the UK the share of national wealth owned by the top 1 per cent rose from 23 per cent in 1970 to 28 per cent in 2010. In the

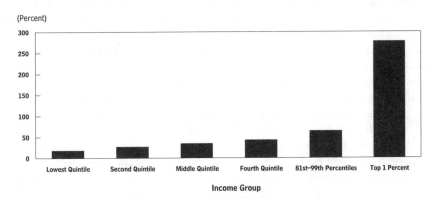

Figure 8: Growth in real after-tax income from 1979 to 2007, US
Source: Congressional Budget Office, *Trends in the Distribution of Household Income Between 1979 and 2007*, Congressional Budget Office Publication No. 4031, 2011, Summary Figure 1.

US it has risen from 28 to 34 per cent over the same period. In the US in 2010, the top 0.1 per cent alone owned almost 15 per cent of all wealth. In both countries, over 70 per cent of all wealth is now owned by a tenth of the population.[30]

Climate change and environmental risk

Underlying these recent trends in modern capitalism is another, deeper one. This is that of rising global greenhouse gas emissions, which have put the world at severe risk of catastrophic climate change.

Throughout capitalism's history economic growth has been accompanied by environmental damage, from the pollution of air, water and land to the loss of habitats and species, a constant subtraction from its successes in increasing welfare. In developed countries some of these problems have been partially tackled; but none has been solved. It remains too little acknowledged how dependent human societies are on the biophysical processes which underpin them, and how dangerous are the critical thresholds (or 'planetary boundaries') which many of these processes have now reached or are close to reaching.[31]

But climate change poses a unique kind of global threat. The cumulative effect of two hundred years of fossil fuel use in the developed world, now compounded by rapid growth in the emerging economies, means that, unless current emissions levels are drastically reduced, the world faces serious damage. At current emissions rates, the earth is on course for an increase in average global temperature of 3–4 degrees Celsius or more. Even above 2 degrees of warming, the Intergovernmental Panel on Climate Change warns that we can expect a much higher incidence of extreme weather events (such as flooding, storm surges and droughts), which may lead to a breakdown of infrastructure networks and critical services, particularly in coastal regions and cities; lower agricultural productivity, increasing the risk of food insecurity and the breakdown of food systems; increased ill-health and mortality from extreme heat events and diseases; greater risks of displacement of peoples and conflict; and faster loss of ecosystems and species.[32]

Broadly speaking, the evidence on this has been known for a quarter of a century.[33] But until very recently very little has been done to avoid it. The major reason is that the production of greenhouse gas emissions—particularly carbon dioxide—is so embedded in capitalism's historic systems of production and consumption, which have been built on the use of fossil fuels. In total 80 per cent of the world's energy still comes from oil, gas and coal. In developed economies, as a result both of structural deindustrialisation and recent climate-related policies, emissions are now declining. But part of this is simply due to the effective transfer of production to the developing world as globalisation has occurred.[34] Western economies are not yet reducing their emissions—either those they generate themselves or those embodied in the goods and services they import—at anything like the speed required to control global

10

warming (see Figure 9). Modern capitalism has in effect been storing up profound risks to its own future prosperity and security.

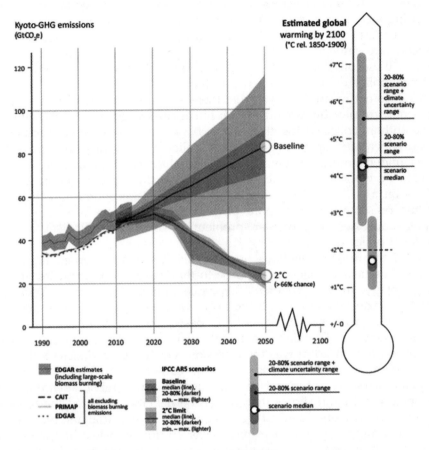

Figure 9: Global greenhouse gas emissions 1990–2050
Source: UNEP, *The Emissions Gap Report 2015*, Nairobi, United Nations Environment Programme, 2015, based on scenarios in the Intergovernmental Panel on Climate Change 5th Assessment Report, 2014, http://uneplive.unep.org/media/docs/theme/13/EGR_2015_301115_lores.pdf (accessed 12 April 2016).

Rethinking economic policy

In all these ways, therefore, the performance of Western capitalism in recent decades has been deeply problematic. The problem is that these failings are not temporary; they are structural. Regulators are now seeking to reduce the systemic risks created by financial market behaviour; but the complexity of the modern financial system has generated widespread concern that they cannot be eliminated. Strongly embedded incentives for both asset-holders and senior corporation executives create powerful tendencies towards

11

short-termism in both finance and industry. Low levels of investment, particularly in innovation, arise both from these incentives and from entrenched weaknesses in demand across the world's economies. Stagnant real wages and rising inequality spring from the structures of the labour market, corporate remuneration and ownership of land and wealth. High greenhouse gas emissions are embedded in the structures of energy and transport systems. None of these problems look likely to be solved by current approaches to economic policy in any developed country.

This does not mean, however, that there are no solutions. Western capitalism is not irretrievably bound to fail; but it does need to be rethought. For as the authors collected together in this book argue, the orthodox economic theory which underpins most current policy-making does not provide a proper understanding of how modern capitalism works, and therefore how to make it work better. They therefore base their prescriptions for new policies on a critique of the dominant approach to economics in their field and the presentation of a more powerfully explanatory alternative. Each chapter addresses a particular problem of modern capitalism and the associated policy debate.

One of the most contentious of those debates has concerned the role of fiscal and monetary policy in response to the financial crisis and the ensuing slow recovery. In their chapters, Stephanie Kelton, and Randall Wray and Yeva Nersisyan take issue with the orthodox prescription of fiscal austerity. Kelton's argument is that austerity is based on a fundamental economic misunderstanding. The claim that high deficits caused the recession turns the facts on their head: it was the recession which caused deficits to balloon, as the downturn slashed the tax revenues earned by governments and the automatic stabilisers of social security benefits and public spending went into operation. Kelton shows that in fact the deficits prevented the recession becoming much worse, generating demand just as the dramatic reduction in private consumption and investment was cutting it. Since all saving and borrowing in an economy (including its overseas sector) must by definition balance, increased public debt was an inevitable consequence of the huge retrenchment of private saving which occurred after the crash. By withdrawing demand from the economy in an attempt to get deficits down as quickly as possible, austerity policies have delayed recovery and, in the case of particularly hard-hit countries such as Greece, Spain and Portugal, largely prevented it. Very slow growth meant that deficits did not, in fact, fall as quickly as anticipated: austerity did not succeed even in its own objective.

Wray and Nersisyan go further. They argue that the orthodox view of macroeconomic policy stems from an incorrect understanding of the nature of money. Rather than being exogenously determined by the central authorities, as the orthodox view has it, money is effectively created whenever commercial banks lend, and thereby increase their borrowers' purchasing power. Money is endogenous to the real economy. Examining the operations of modern central banks, Wray and Nersisyan show that for a nation with its own currency, government spending is not constrained by the resources available from taxation or borrowing.[35] The euro zone in particular has suffered from its rules expressly designed to prevent weaker European economies from borrowing in the absence of their own currency. Quantitative easing meanwhile is a poor way of boosting aggregate demand. Fiscal policy, the authors argue, is a much more powerful and effective tool for stimulating growth.

Perhaps unsurprisingly, austerity policies have not succeeded in reversing the low levels of investment which have characterised Western economies for a long period. In their chapters, Andrew Haldane, William Lazonick, Mariana Mazzucato, and Stephany Griffith-Jones and Giovanni Cozzi address the economic sources of this problem.

Haldane asks if short-termism in financial markets may have reduced the willingness of firms to invest. Examining how far share prices reveal excessive discounting of future earnings, he finds an economically significant effect in the period since 1995 that was absent in the previous decade. Similarly, analysing the comparative behaviour of private and publicly quoted firms in distributing dividends, rather than retaining earnings for investment, he finds that UK private firms tend to plough between four and eight times more of their profits back into their business over time than publicly held firms. Overall, he concludes that short-termism appears to be making a material difference to corporate investment behaviour. He suggests various policy remedies, including greater transparency of long-term business strategy, changes in the ways senior executives are remunerated, reforms to shareholder governance and changes in the taxation regime to reward long-term asset holding.

Lazonick focuses on the orthodox economic theory of the firm. Neoclassical economists draw on a model of the firm as an optimising profit-maker constrained in its behaviour by the competitive markets in which it operates. But such a model cannot explain the phenomenon of innovation. Offering an alternative theory of the innovative enterprise—firms which generate improvements in productivity and more competitive goods and services, and are therefore the wellsprings of economic growth—Lazonick argues that the key is not the nature of the market, but the structure and organisation of the firm. Using the comparative example of Japanese and American industrial businesses in the second half of the twentieth century, he shows how different organisational and management methods generate different degrees of innovation, and therefore commercial success. He argues that only by studying real historical examples, rather than merely abstract theory, can economists properly understand how innovation and economic development occur.

Mazzucato's chapter picks up this theme. The orthodox economic view is that innovation is carried out by the private sector, and government policy should be restricted to basic scientific research. But Mazzucato shows that this is a misconception; in fact the modern state, particularly in the US, has

13

MICHAEL JACOBS AND MARIANA MAZZUCATO

been a driver of innovation in a whole range of fields. All the new technologies in the Apple iPhone, for example, were developed with government support. Detailing how reluctant private investors have become to finance innovation—contrary to the orthodox myth of 'venture capitalism'—she argues for an 'entrepreneurial state' investing in innovation to address major societal problems such as climate change and elderly healthcare. Given the risks that 'directing' innovation entails (choosing particular missions, technologies, sectors and firms to support), taxpayers should share in the rewards. She argues that state investment banks, such as Germany's KfW, can play a particularly important role in directing long-term 'patient' capital to higher-risk infrastructure and innovation.

Griffith-Jones and Cozzi then show what an investment programme based on these principles might achieve. Criticising the inadequate response of European Union policy-makers to the slow recovery after the financial crash, the authors propose a five-year investment stimulus package based on additional lending by the European Investment Bank (the EU's state investment bank). Taking issue with the orthodox economic view that public investment will ultimately 'crowd out' private, they argue that at very low interest rates, with a glut of capital looking for returns, the opposite is in fact the case: public investment will leverage greater private capital. They use a macroeconomic model to compare their investment package to 'business as usual': they find that not only would it increase European growth rates and employment, it would also reduce public deficits more rapidly.

The chapters by Joseph Stiglitz and Colin Crouch look at two of the major gaps between orthodox economic theory and the reality of modern capitalism. Stiglitz addresses the growth of inequality over the past thirty years. He takes on the neoclassical view that wages and salaries reflect the marginal productivity of workers, showing that the very high incomes of corporate executives in fact reveal a form of 'rent-seeking', in which rewards are extracted without relation to productivity or economic desert. Moreover he points out—again contrary to the orthodox view—that such inequality is not the price that has to be paid for greater economic prosperity, but actually retards growth. Stiglitz offers a range of policy measures which would reverse recent trends, including changes to executive compensation schemes, macroeconomic policies to reduce unemployment, greater investment in education and the reform of capital taxation. He concludes by insisting that economic policy indicators must do more than measure growth of GDP: its distribution and content also matter.

Crouch looks at the experience of privatisation and outsourcing. Over recent decades, a number of countries (notably the UK) have privatised nationalised industries and outsourced public services to market competition. These policies have followed the precepts of neoliberal economic theory, which argues that competition in markets will generate greater efficiency and consumer choice. But Crouch notes that this is not in fact what has happened. In practice, in both privatised industries and public service provision, oligopolies have been created, resulting in very little competition or consumer choice. What were intended to be market-based processes have become deeply politicised, a form of 'corporate neoliberalism' which runs contrary to the theory's original claims. He argues that corporate lobbying has now become so powerful that the principles of democracy itself are threatened.

The final two chapters of the book examine capitalism's environmental consequences. Dimitri Zenghelis shows why climate change poses such a challenge, not just to the economic system, but also to economics. The science of climate change means that greenhouse gas emissions must ultimately be reduced to near zero if the rise in global temperature is to be stopped. But almost all economic activity currently rests on the combustion of fossil-based carbon, the principal source of such emissions. So an almost complete structural transformation of energy, transport, land use and industrial systems will be required to tackle the problem. Zenghelis argues that in the analysis of such a task, the focus of neoclassical economics on marginal market failures is wholly inadequate. We need rather to understand the processes of technological innovation and structural change. These are influenced both by 'path-dependence'—through which historic investments constrain future change—and by economic expectations. Strong and consistent policy-making can help shift investment towards tipping points when innovation may be driven rapidly in a low-carbon direction.

Carlota Perez notes that structural change of this kind has happened before. From the original industrial revolution based on water power and mechanisation, through the ages of coal and steam, steel and railways, automobiles and mass production, and latterly information and communications technologies (ICT), the modern world has witnessed distinct waves of technological revolution. Each of these has followed a pattern, both in the diffusion of the new technologies and products and in the response of the financial system and government policy-making. Perez argues that there is now huge potential to combine the further development of ICT with environmental technologies which radically reduce the carbon and material content of production and consumption. The result would be a new wave of growth which would simultaneously reduce environmental damage, provide new sources of employment and potentially reduce inequalities. Arguing for a range of policies to accelerate such a transition, including a shift in the burden of taxation from labour and profit to energy and resources, Perez sees this both leading to, and drawing on, a redefined, greener vision of the 'good life', in both developed and developing countries.

Beyond market failure: towards a new approach

Each chapter of the book approaches its subject in a different way. In commissioning them we wanted to reflect a variety of perspectives, both on the nature of the problems of modern capitalism and in the economics required to address them. The authors are responsible only for their own

15

chapters: we did not seek, and do not claim, that they all agree with one another. Nevertheless, their critiques have many elements in common. Each challenges an important aspect of orthodox economic theory and policy prescription.

By 'orthodox' we mean the view that dominates public debate about economic policy. Within the academic discipline of economics there are lively arguments about many aspects of theory and policy. But mainstream economic discourse rests to a powerful extent on a very simple underlying conception of how capitalism works. This is that capitalism is an economic system characterised by competitive markets. In these markets privately owned companies, seeking to make profits for their shareholders, compete with one another to supply goods and services to other businesses and freely choosing consumers. In individual markets, neoclassical theory (on which the orthodox view is based) holds that such competition drives economic efficiency, which in turn maximises welfare. Markets are assumed to tend towards equilibrium, while businesses are assumed to be fundamentally alike, analysed as 'representative agents' constrained to act in the same ways by the external pressures of the market. At the level of the economy as a whole, it is competition between firms which is believed to generate innovation, and therefore leads to long-run economic growth.

The orthodox model understands that markets do not always work well. It therefore uses the concept of 'market failure' to explain why suboptimal outcomes occur and how they can be improved. Markets fail under various circumstances: when firms have monopolistic power which restricts competition; when there are information asymmetries between producers and consumers; when there are 'externalities' or impacts on third parties which are not properly reflected in market prices; and where public and common goods exist whose benefits cannot be captured by individual producers or consumers.[36] The propensity of real-world markets to fail in these various ways means that 'free' markets do not maximise welfare. So the theory of market failure provides a rationale for government intervention. Public policy should seek to 'correct' market failures—for example by promoting competition; by requiring information about goods and services to be more widely available; by forcing economic actors to pay for externalities through means such as pollution taxes; and by providing or subsidising public goods.

At the same time, the orthodox view emphasises that it is not only markets which fail; governments do too. Even well-meaning ones can intervene badly, creating outcomes worse than if they had left markets alone—not least because private actors often adjust their behaviour to compensate. And public institutions are never disinterested—they develop goals and incentives of their own which may not reflect the general welfare of society as a whole. So public policy interventions always have to balance the goal of correcting market failures with the risk of generating government failures which outweigh them.[37]

Broadly speaking, it is this general model of capitalism which underpins most public economic commentary and policy-making today. And it leads to some familiar policy conclusions. Chief among these is that markets generally produce positive outcomes which increase welfare, and should therefore be allowed to operate without much interference wherever possible. A basic regulatory framework of employment, consumer and environmental protection is required to correct for clear externalities and information asymmetries; but governments should not seek to direct markets or shape the businesses which operate in them. The 'invisible hand' of the market knows best, generating the highest welfare-producing activities where firms seek to maximise value for their shareholders. Even where the market might seem to get it wrong, governments cannot presume to know better. So governments should be extremely wary of seeking to 'pick winners' through industrial and innovation policy; of seeking to push banks and other financial institutions to make specific forms of investments; or of investing in the private economy them-selves. Public investment—particularly if funded by borrowing—will simply 'crowd out' private investment. Governments should seek to use competitive private enterprise to deliver public utilities and services wherever possible. Getting the public finances into balance should be the overwhelming priority of fiscal policy. Taxation is necessary; but because it tends to disincentivise wealth creation and work, it should be kept as low as possible. Within each of these propositions lurks many a disagreement among academic economists, often informed by subtly complex theory and detailed empirical evidence. But it is not hard to find these views expressed in public debate; and they have dominated the practice of policy-making over recent years.

The orthodox model provides an attractively simple framework for think-ing about economics and policy. It combines the mathematical elegance of neoclassical microeconomics with plausible claims about the macroeconomy. The fact that many of the policy prescriptions which follow from it favour those in positions of incumbent economic power has given it a powerful grip on public discourse.

But it's not an adequate model for understanding how capitalism works. For markets are not simple structures which behave in the ways set out in economics textbooks; and 'market failure' is not a helpful concept for analys-ing capitalism's major problems or how to address them. These idealised theories assume away many of capitalism's key features, or treat them as 'imperfections' rather than structural, systemic characteristics. They ignore much of the evidence on how different economies actually function, and when and why they have performed well or badly. None of the key problems which Western capitalism has experienced over recent decades— weak growth and financial instability, declining investment and financialisa-tion, the stagnation of living standards and rising inequality, dangerous environmental risk—are explained by them.

Capitalist economies are not theoretical abstractions but complex and dynamic systems, embedded in specific societies, as well as in natural

17

environments governed by biophysical laws. They are formed of multiple relationships between real and heterogeneous economic actors whose behaviour is not that of idealised 'representative agents', but arises from their particular characteristics and choices in different circumstances. These relationships give rise not to equilibrium, but to dynamic patterns of growth and change. The macroeconomic outcomes they generate are more than simply the sum of their microeconomic parts. Their problems are not failures of markets which 'normally' succeed, but arise from fundamental characteristics and structures. So to understand how they work, and to explain how policy can help them work better, we need a much richer approach.

Fortunately, there are plenty of resources within economics with which to do this. For these characteristics of capitalist economies are hardly revelatory. They have been analysed in theory and documented in practice for more than a hundred years of economic scholarship. They underlie the work of some of the greatest economists of the past century—such as Karl Polanyi, Joseph Schumpeter and John Maynard Keynes—and of the more recent schools of evolutionary, institutional and post-Keynesian economics. As the separate chapters in this book show, analysis based on these foundations can generate searching critiques of current policy, and powerful alternative perspectives.

Three key insights underpin a rethinking of capitalism in these ways.

First, we need a richer characterisation of markets and the businesses within them. It is not helpful to think of markets as pre-existing, abstract institutions which economic actors (firms, investors and households) 'enter' to do business, and which require them, once there, to behave in particular ways. Markets are better understood as the *outcomes* of interactions between economic actors and institutions, both private and public. These outcomes will depend on the nature of the actors (for example, the different corporate governance structures of firms), their endowments and motivations, the body of law and regulation and cultural contexts which constrain them and the specific nature of the transactions which take place. Markets are 'embedded' in these wider institutional structures and social, legal and cultural conditions.[38] In the modern world, as Polanyi pointed out, the concept of a 'free' market is a construct of economic theory, not an empirical observation.[39] Indeed, he observed that the national capitalist market was effectively forced into existence through public policy—there was nothing 'natural' or universal about it.[40]

The orthodox notion of competition between firms is equally misleading. Many of the most important markets in modern capitalism are oligopolistic in form, characterised by economies of scale and 'network effects' that lead to concentration and benefit incumbents. But even where there is greater competition, capitalist businesses are not all the same, forced to behave in similar ways by the external forces of 'the market'. On the contrary, as Lazonick shows, what we actually observe is persistent heterogeneity, both in businesses' internal characteristics and in their reactions to different

18

market circumstances. Given that they must compete through innovation, this is hardly surprising. As evolutionary economics has emphasised, this heterogeneity is not a short-run transition towards a world of similar actors, but a long-run feature of the system.[41] Different norms and routines combine to generate different behaviours and outcomes.

In fact, the evidence shows the particular importance of ownership and governance structures. Over the past thirty years the orthodox view that the maximisation of shareholder value would lead to the strongest economic performance has come to dominate business theory and practice, in the US and UK in particular.[42] But for most of capitalism's history, and in many other countries, firms have not been organised primarily as vehicles for the short-term profit maximisation of footloose shareholders and the remuneration of their senior executives. Companies in Germany, Scandinavia and Japan, for example, are structured both in company law and corporate culture as institutions accountable to a wider set of stakeholders, including their employees, with long-term production and profitability their primary mission. They are equally capitalist, but their behaviour is different. Firms with this kind of model typically invest more in innovation than their counterparts focused on short-term shareholder value maximisation; their executives are paid smaller multiples of their average employees' salaries; they tend to retain for investment a greater share of earnings relative to the payment of dividends; and their shares are held on average for longer by their owners. And the evidence suggests that while their short-term profitability may (in some cases) be lower, over the long term they tend to generate stronger growth.[43] For public policy, this makes attention to corporate ownership, governance and managerial incentive structures a crucial field for the improvement of economic performance.

In short, markets are not idealised abstractions, but concrete and differentiated outcomes arising from different circumstances. Contrary to the claims of orthodox economists that 'the laws of economics are like the laws of engineering: one set of laws works everywhere',[44] there are in fact many different kinds of market behaviour, and several varieties of capitalism.[45]

The second key insight is that it is investments in technological and organisational innovation, both public and private, which are the driving force behind economic growth and development. The diffusion of such innovations across the economy affects not just patterns of production, but of distribution and consumption. It has been the primary source of improvements in productivity, and consequent rises in living standards, for the past 200 years.[46] Thus a theory of how capitalist economies work must include at its centre the dynamics of innovation, understanding both the specific nature of the investments needed and the turbulent, non-equilibrium outcomes that result.

But this requires a much more dynamic and accurate understanding of how innovation occurs than is provided by the orthodox economic theories of imperfect competition. Drawing on Schumpeter's original analysis of the

19

processes of 'creative destruction',[47] modern evolutionary economics has done much to explain how firms operate with bounded rationality in circumstances of uncertainty, where markets tend towards disequilibrium and change is path-dependent. Growth results from the co-evolution of technologies, firms and industry structures and the social and public institutions which support them, connected by complex feedback processes.[48]

Promoting innovation therefore requires attention to be paid to each of these elements. The economy needs firms with risk-taking management cultures and incentives which reward long-run perspectives, rather than those, as Haldane notes, focused largely on short-term financial returns. Innovation requires very specific forms of finance: patient, long-term and committed. As Griffith-Jones and Cozzi argue, this creates a particular role for public banks, able to steer finance towards long-run projects, leverage private capital and stimulate multiplier effects. Taxation policies need to incentivise long-term investment.

Critically, as Mazzucato shows, innovation also needs well-funded public research and development institutions and strong industrial policies. These need to be directed across the entire innovation chain, not only in the classic 'public good' area of basic science. A crucial recognition is that innovation has not only a rate, but also a *direction*.[49] Historically, that direction has often been determined by 'mission-oriented' public policies, which have steered both public and private investments into new fields. During the mass production era, as Perez notes, it was policies around suburbanisation that allowed the new technologies of mass production to be fully diffused and deployed. Mazzucato observes that public funding drove both the IT revolution and other fields such as bio- and nano-technologies and today's green technologies.[50] Each of these has involved both supply-side and demand-side policies, in which new markets as well as new products have been created and public investment has 'crowded in' private.

By setting societal missions, and using their own resources to co-invest with long-term capital, governments can do far more than 'level the playing field', as the orthodox view would allow. They can help *tilt* the playing field towards the achievement of publicly chosen goals. Just as the creation of the welfare state in the postwar period, and the information technology revolution in the decades around the turn of the century, unleashed new waves of economic growth and widened prosperity, so new missions today have the potential to catalyse new innovation and investment. Foremost among them must be the transformative challenge of reducing and eventually eliminating greenhouse gas emissions to limit dangerous climate change, and of constraining the economy's wider environmental impacts within biophysical boundaries. As Perez argues, there is particular potential for such a 'green' direction, allied to the continuing development of information and communications technologies, to drive a new wave of structural transformation and growth.

Recognition of the role of the public sector in the innovation process informs the third key insight. This is that the creation of economic value is a collective process. Businesses do not create wealth on their own. No business today can operate without the fundamental services provided by the state: schools and higher education institutions, health and social care services, housing provision, social security, policing and defence, the core infrastructures of transport, energy, water and waste systems. These services, the level of resources allocated to them and the type of investments made in them, are crucial to the productivity of private enterprises. The private sector does not 'create wealth' while taxpayer-funded public services 'consume' it. The state does not simply 'regulate' private economic activity. Rather, economic output is *co-produced* by the interaction of public and private actors—and both are shaped by, and in turn help to shape, wider social and environmental conditions.

Keynes' analysis of the business cycle was crucial in this regard.[51] His key insight was that private investment was both too volatile and too pro-cyclical. It reinforces its own tendencies both to boom and slump. Government investment is thus needed not just to stabilise aggregate demand when spending is too low, but also to stimulate the 'animal spirits' of the business sector, which invests only when it is confident of future areas of growth. This point is about much more than the herd and bandwagon behaviour of the financial markets, as some have interpreted it.[52] It makes the fundamental case for public investment as a means of creating economic opportunities and thereby increasing the willingness of firms to invest. As Zenghelis argues, the creation of expectations about future growth is a crucial role for government, and not just during downturns. It is why mission-oriented innovation policy—bringing Keynes and Schumpeter together—has such an important role to play in driving stronger economic performance. Indeed, Keynes argued that the 'socialisation of investment'—which, as Mazzucato suggests, could include the public sector acting as investor and equity-holder—would provide more stability to the investment function and hence to growth.[53]

It is because public expenditure is critical to the co-production of the conditions for growth, as Kelton highlights, that the austerity policies which have reduced it in the period since the financial crash have proved so futile, increasing rather than diminishing the ratio of debt to GDP. And as Wray and Nersisyan emphasise, the endogenous nature of money created by 'keystrokes' in the banking system gives governments far greater scope to use fiscal policy in support of economic growth than the orthodox approach allows.

So the size and functions of the state matter profoundly to the performance of capitalist economies. In orthodox economic commentary it is frequently asserted that the role of the public sector should be minimised in order to free private enterprise from the 'dead hand' of regulation and the perverse impact of 'crowding out'. In fact, successful economies have almost

21

all had states actively committed to their development.[54] This is not just about the role of the state in providing or co-investing in infrastructure (as is sometimes conceded even by those otherwise sceptical of public investment), though this is indeed important. Its role in innovation is also key, as we have seen. At the same time, the development of a skilled and adaptive labour force requires deep investment in education, training, health, child-care and social care. These functions cannot simply be outsourced or privatised—as Crouch shows, when this is done the goal of greater competition almost always degenerates into private oligopoly, where public purpose is lost, and corporate political influence increases. We need to acknowledge, rather, the interdependence of private enterprise and the public sector; of market and non-market activities.

This has an important implication for the role of taxation. The orthodox economic view characterises taxation as an essentially negative activity in which the value generated by private firms is confiscated by the state. But understanding the role of the public sector in the co-production of economic output allows a more profound perspective. Taxation is the means by which economic actors pay the public sector for its contribution to the productive process. The orthodox model claims that reducing the share of taxation in overall economic output will tend to strengthen growth. If taxation is used productively by an active public sector, the opposite can be the case.

The collective nature of capitalist production makes the distribution of income and wealth an important variable for growth. In the orthodox model the rewards to labour and capital are believed to reflect their (marginal) productivity. But as Stiglitz argues, this theory cannot explain the dramatic growth in inequality over recent decades. It is evident, rather, that share-holders and senior executives—particularly in the financial sector—are extracting unearned rent from the value firms produce. And as Thomas Piketty has shown, the inheritance of capital (particularly land and property), whose increase in value outpaces that of the economy as a whole, skews the overall distribution of wealth far away from any notion of earned productivity.[55] This has a profound effect on the fairness and inclusivity of today's economies. But it also negatively impacts on growth itself. There is striking evidence—now gathered and acknowledged by the OECD and IMF —that economies with more equal distributions of income and wealth have stronger and more stable economic growth than those with greater inequality.[56] Redistributive policies which reduce inequality are found to have in general a positive impact on growth.[57]

This creates a powerful case for the rebalancing of the distribution of earnings between capital and labour. Employees have in effect become too weak, as trade unions have lost powers and membership, and deregulated, 'flexible' labour markets have allowed employers to bargain wages and working conditions down. Crucially, as experience of legal minimum wages has shown, raising wages tends to force firms to invest in improving productivity, which strengthens economic performance.[58] Public policy therefore has an important role in regulating labour markets, promoting both trade union membership and employee ownership of capital, and managing markets in housing and land. It should also ensure progressive tax systems: of wealth as well as income, and of corporate as well as individual taxation.

One further aspect of co-production, with important distributional implications, is also critical. All economies operate within biophysical systems. From an ecological point of view, economic activity generates value by using material resources and energy which are subsequently returned to the environment as waste, in a thermodynamically more disordered (entropic) state.[59] Economic growth can derive from expanding the use of biophysical resources, or from an increase in the economic value generated per unit of throughput. Today, with many of the natural environment's biophysical functions at or close to their safe limits, it powerfully matters—not least to the distribution of wealth between present and future generations—which of these predominates. In the context of dangerous climate change, as Zenghelis argues, the centrality of carbon to industrial economies makes an understanding of structural change—not just corrections to marginal market failures—particularly vital to economic analysis.

These three insights therefore have profound implications for how we think about economic policy-making. Public policies are not 'interventions' in the economy, as if markets existed independently of the public institutions and social and environmental conditions in which they are embedded. The role of policy is not one simply of 'correcting' the failures of otherwise free markets. It is rather to help create and shape markets to achieve the co-production, and the fair distribution, of economic value. Economic performance cannot be measured simply by the short-term growth of GDP, but requires better indicators of long-term value creation, social well-being, inequality and environment sustainability.[60]

Western capitalism has not been functioning well in recent years. Mainstream economic policies, reflecting an outdated economic orthodoxy, have proved themselves unable to set it on a new course. We hope the ideas set out in this book show that there is nothing inevitable about this failure. A more innovative, sustainable and inclusive economic system is possible. But it will require fundamental changes in our understanding of how capitalism works, and how public policy can help create and shape a different economic future.

Notes

1 http://www.telegraph.co.uk/news/uknews/theroyalfamily/3386353/The-Queen-asks-why-no-one-saw-the-credit-crunch-coming.html (accessed 12 April 2016).
2 Following the Queen's question, the British Academy held a seminar to enquire into how it should be answered, and subsequently wrote to the sovereign to explain their conclusions. See http://www.britac.ac.uk/news/newsrelease-econo my.cfm (accessed 12 April 2016).

3 S. Verick and I. Iyanatul, *The Great Recession of 2008–2009: Causes, Consequences and Policy Responses*, Discussion Paper No 4934, Bonn, Institute for the Study of Labor, 2010.

4 IMF, *World Economic Outlook: Uneven Growth—Short- and Long-Term Factors*, Washington, DC, International Monetary Fund, April 2015, p. 171. The three advanced economies that saw real GDP growth in 2009 were Australia, Korea and Israel.

5 International Monetary Fund, International Labour Organization, *The Challenges of Growth, Employment and Social Cohesion*, 2010, http://www.osloconference2010.org/discussionpaper.pdf (accessed 12 April 2016).

6 *Wall Street Aristocracy Got $1.2 Trillion in Secret Loans*, Bloomberg, 11 August 2011, http://www.bloomberg.com/news/articles/2011-08-21/wall-street-aristocracy-got-1-2-trillion-in-fed-s-secret-loans (accessed 12 April 2016); National Audit Office, *Taxpayer Support for UK Banks, FAQs*, https://www.nao.org.uk/highlights/taxpayer-support-for-uk-banks-faqs/ (accessed 12 April 2016). These figures relate to peak exposure on a single day. In the US, the cumulative amount committed by the Federal Reserve to shoring up the financial system has been calculated at between $7.77 trillion by Bloomberg—*Secret Fed Loans Gave Banks $13 Billion Undisclosed to Congress*, Bloomberg Markets, 28 November 2011, http://www.bloomberg.com/news/articles/2011-11-28/secret-fed-loans-undisclosed-to-congress-gave-banks-13-billion-in-income (accessed 12 April 2016)—and $29 trillion by James Felkerson, *$29,000,000,000,000: A Detailed Look at the Fed's Bailout by Funding Facility and Recipient*, Working Paper No. 698, Levy Economics Institute of Bard College, 2011, http://www.levyinstitute.org/pubs/wp_698.pdf (accessed 12 April 2016).

7 OECD, General government deficit (indicator), 2016, doi: 10.1787/77079edb-en (accessed 12 April 2016).

8 Testimony to the Congressional Committee on Oversight and Government Reform, 23 October 2008, https://www.gpo.gov/fdsys/pkg/CHRG-110hhrg55764/html/CHRG-110hhrg55764.htm (accessed 12 April 2016).

9 R. J. Shiller, *Irrational Exuberance*, Princeton, NJ, Princeton University Press, 2000.

10 C. Reinhart and K. Rogoff, 'Growth in a time of debt', *American Economic Review*, vol. 100, no. 2, 2010, pp. 573–8.

11 L. Laeven and F. Valencia, *Systemic Banking Crises: A New Database*, IMF Working Paper No. 224, November 2008.

12 J. A. Turner, *Between Debt and the Devil: Money, Credit, and Fixing Global Finance*, Princeton and Oxford, Princeton University Press, 2016.

13 Unemployment was lower in 2014 than in 2007 in five OECD countries: Chile, Germany, Israel, Japan and Poland. Averaged across OECD countries, unemployment was at 5.6 per cent in 2007, peaked at 8.3 per cent in 2010 and was at 7.3 per cent in 2014. For EU28 countries, unemployment was lowest in 2008 at 7 per cent, and continued rising to a peak of 10.8 per cent in 2013. OECD, Unemployment rate (indicator), 2016, doi: 10.1787/997c8750-en (accessed 12 April 2016).

14 Low Pay Commission, *National Minimum Wage*, Low Pay Commission Report 2013, Cm 8816, London, The Stationery Office, 2014.

15 W. Lazonick, 'Profits without prosperity', *Harvard Business Review*, vol. 92, no. 9, 2014, pp. 46–55.

16 OECD, *OECD Compendium of Productivity Indicators 2015*, Paris, OECD Publishing, 2015, doi:10.1787/pdtvy-2015-en (accessed 12 April 2016).

17 R. J. Gordon, *Is US Economic Growth Over? Faltering Innovation Confronts the Six Headwinds*, Centre for Economic Policy Research, Policy Insight No. 63, September 2012, http://www.cepr.org/sites/default/files/policy_insights/PolicyInsight63.pdf (accessed 12 April 2016).

18 See for example L. H. Summers, 'U.S. economic prospects: secular stagnation, hysteresis, and the zero lower bound', *Business Economics*, vol. 49, no. 2, 2014, pp. 65–73, http://larrysummers.com/wp-content/uploads/2014/06/NABE-speech-Lawrence-H.-Summers1.pdf (accessed 12 April 2016); C. Teulings and R. Baldwin (eds), *Secular Stagnation: Facts, Causes and Cures*, London, CEPR Press, 2014, http://voxeu.org/sites/default/files/Vox_secular_stagnation.pdf (accessed 12 April 2016).

19 Real median US household income in 2014 was $53,657 compared with $52,623 in 1990 (using 2014 CPI-U-RS Adjusted Dollars). Source: US Bureau of the Census, made available by the Federal Bank of St Louis, https://research.stlouis-fed.org/fred2/series/MEHOINUSA672N (accessed 12 April 2016).

20 E. Stockhammer, *Why Have Wage Shares Fallen? A Panel Analysis of the Determinants of Functional Income Distribution*, Geneva, International Labour Office, 2013. The wage share is adjusted to take account of self-employment. 'Advanced economies' includes all high-income OECD countries, with the exception of South Korea.

21 ILO, *Global Wage Report 2012/13*, Geneva, International Labour Organisation, 2013.

22 OECD, *World Economic Outlook: Spillovers and Cycles in the Global Economy*, Paris, OECD Publishing, 2007, Figure 5.15.

23 OECD, *Income Inequality: The Gap between Rich and Poor*, Paris, OECD Publishing, 2015.

24 T. Piketty and E. Saez, 'Income inequality in the United States, 1913–1998', *Quarterly Journal of Economics*, vol. 118, no. 1, 2003, pp. 1–39, Tables A3 and A6—Updated version downloaded from http://eml.berkeley.edu/~saez/. Figures are in real 2013 dollars and include capital gains (accessed 12 April 2016).

25 OECD, *OECD Employment Outlook 2012*, Paris, OECD Publishing, 2012, http://dx.doi.org/10.1787/empl_outlook-2012-en (accessed 12 April 2016). Figures relate to countries for which data is available.

26 ILO, *Global Wage Report 2010/11*, Geneva, International Labour Organisation, 2010, Figure 20.

27 OECD, Youth unemployment rate (indicator), 2016, doi: 10.1787/c3634df7-en (accessed 12 April 2016).

28 OECD, *In It Together: Why Less Inequality Benefits Us All*, Paris, OECD Publishing, 2015, Figure 4.1.B, http://dx.doi.org/10.1787/888933208028 (accessed 12 April 2016).

29 Ibid, http://dx.doi.org/10.1787/888933207711 (accessed 12 April 2016).

30 Data from http://piketty.pse.ens.fr/files/capital21c/en/xls/, Figures 10.3 and 10.5, and Table S10.1 (accessed 12 April 2016).

31 J. Rockström et al., 'A safe operating space for humanity', *Nature*, no. 461, 24 September 2009, pp. 472–5, http://www.nature.com/nature/journal/v461/n7263/full/461472a.html (accessed 12 April 2016); W. Steffen et al., 'Planetary boundaries: guiding human development on a changing planet', *Science*, vol. 347, no. 6223, 13 February 2015, http://science.sciencemag.org/content/347/6223/1259855 (accessed 12 April 2016).

32 Intergovernmental Panel on Climate Change, *Climate Change 2014: Impacts, Adaptation, and Vulnerability: Summary for Policymakers*, Cambridge and New York,

Cambridge University Press, 2014, https://www.ipcc.ch/report/ar5/wg2/ (accessed 12 April 2016).

33 The first assessment report of the Intergovernmental Panel on Climate Change was published in 1990. See https://www.ipcc.ch/publications_and_data/publications_ipcc_first_assessment_1990_wg1.shtml (accessed 12 April 2016).

34 T. O. Wiedmann et al., 'The material footprint of nations', *Proceedings of the National Academy of Sciences of America*, vol. 112, no. 20, 2015, pp. 6271–6, http://doi:10.1073/pnas.1220362110 (accessed 12 April 2016).

35 There is a lively debate among monetary theorists over whether governments, as opposed to central banks, do in practice create new money through government spending, or whether they have to acquire bank-credit money through taxation or borrowing prior to government spending. In practice, in the UK and European Union, legal and institutional arrangements are designed to prevent the expansion of the money supply through government spending. But many economists would accept the fundamental argument that monetary expansion is key to achieving sufficient nominal demand growth, and that state money creation may be preferable to private bank credit creation. For a good discussion, see J. A. Turner, *Between Debt and the Devil: Money, Credit, and Fixing Global Finance*, Princeton, NJ, Princeton University Press, 2015.

36 The original account of market failure is in K. Arrow, *An Extension of the Basic Theorems of Classical Welfare Economics*, paper presented at the Second Berkeley Symposium on Mathematical Statistics and Probability, Berkeley, 1951.

37 G. Tullock, A. Seldon and G. L. Brady, *Government Failure: A Primer in Public Choice*, Washington, DC, Cato Institute, 2002.

38 P. B. Evans, *Embedded Autonomy: States and Industrial Transformation*, Princeton, NJ, Princeton University Press, 1995.

39 K. Polanyi, *The Great Transformation: The Political and Economic Origins of Our Time*, Boston, MA, Beacon Press, 2001 [1944].

40 As Polanyi put it: 'The road to free markets was opened and kept open by an enormous increase in continuous, centrally organized and controlled interventionism … Administrators had to be constantly on the watch to ensure the free working of the system.' Ibid, p. 144.

41 R. R. Nelson and S. G. Winter, *An Evolutionary Theory of Economic Change*, Cambridge, MA, Harvard University Press, 2009.

42 W. Lazonick and M. O'Sullivan, 'Maximizing shareholder value: a new ideology for corporate governance', *Economy and Society*, vol. 29, no. 1, 2000, pp. 13–35.

43 W. Hutton, *How Good We Can Be: Ending the Mercenary Society and Building a Great Country*, London, Abacus, 2015.

44 Lawrence Summers, October 1991, when Chief Economist at the World Bank; cited by M. Ellman, 'Transition economies', in H.-J. Chang, ed., *Rethinking Development Economics*, London and New York, Anthem Press, 2003, pp. 179–98 (p. 197).

45 P. A. Hall and D. Soskice, eds., *Varieties of Capitalism. The Institutional Foundations of Comparative Advantage*, Oxford, Oxford University Press, 2001.

46 C. Perez, *Technological Revolutions and Financial Capital: The Dynamics of Bubbles and Golden Ages*, London, Edward Elgar, 2002.

47 J. A. Schumpeter, *Capitalism, Socialism, and Democracy*, 3rd edn, New York, Harper, 1962 [1942].

48 Nelson and Winter, *An Evolutionary Theory of Economic Change*; see also R. Nelson, *Economic Development from the Perspective of Evolutionary Economic Theory*,

GLOBELICS Working Paper No. 2007-02, 2007, http://dcsh.xoc.uam.mx/eii/globelicswp/wpg0702.pdf (accessed 12 April 2016).

49 A. Stirling, '"Opening up" and "closing down" power, participation, and pluralism in the social appraisal of technology', *Science, Technology and Human Values*, vol. 33, no. 2, 2008, pp. 262–94 (accessed 12 April 2016).

50 D. Foray, D. C. Mowery and R. R. Nelson, 'Public R&D and social challenges: what lessons from mission R&D programs?' *Research Policy*, vol. 41, no. 10, 2012, pp. 1697–702; M. Mazzucato, 'From market fixing to market-creating: a new framework for innovation policy', forthcoming in special issue of *Industry and Innovation*: 'Innovation Policy – can it make a difference?', 2016, available at http://doi:10.1080/13662716.1146124 (accessed 12 April 2016).

51 J. M. Keynes, *The General Theory of Employment, Interest and Money*, London, Macmillan, 2007 [1936].

52 Shiller, *Irrational Exuberance*.

53 'I expect to see the State … taking an ever greater responsibility for directly organising investment … I conceive, therefore, that a somewhat comprehensive socialisation of investment will prove the only means of securing an approximation to full employment.' J. M. Keynes, *The Collected Writings of John Maynard Keynes*, vol. 7, Cambridge, Cambridge University Press, 1973, pp. 164, 378.

54 H.-J. Chang, *Globalization, Economic Development and the Role of the State*, London, Zed Books, 2002.

55 T. Piketty, *Capital in the 21st Century*, Cambridge, MA, Harvard University Press, 2014.

56 A. Berg and J. D. Ostry, *Inequality and Unsustainable Growth: Two Sides of the Same Coin?*, International Monetary Fund Staff Discussion Note No. 11/08, April 2011, https://www.imf.org/external/pubs/ft/sdn/2011/sdn1108.pdf (accessed 12 April 2016); F. Cingano, *Trends in Income Inequality and Its Impact on Economic Growth*, OECD Social, Employment and Migration Working Papers, No. 163, December 2014, http://www.oecd.org/els/soc/trends-in-income-inequality-and-its-impact-on-economic-growth-SEM-WP163.pdf (accessed 12 April 2016).

57 J. D. Ostry, A. Berg and C. G. Tsangarides, *Redistribution, Inequality and Growth*, IMF Staff Discussion Note, SDN 14/02, 2014, https://www.imf.org/external/pubs/ft/sdn/2014/sdn1402.pdf (accessed 12 April 2016). For a wider discussion on the relationship between economic performance, well-being and inequality, see R. G. Wilkinson and K. Pickett, *The Spirit Level: Why More Equal Societies Almost Always Do Better*, London, Allen Lane, 2009.

58 R. Riley and C. Rosazza Bondibene, *Raising the Standard: Minimum Wages and Firm Productivity*, NIESR Discussion Paper 449, National Institute for Economic and Social Research, 2015, http://www.niesr.ac.uk/sites/default/files/publications/Minimum%20wages%20and%20firm%20productivity%20NIESR%20DP%20449.pdf (accessed 12 April 2016).

59 N. Georgescu-Roegen, *The Entropy Law and the Economic Process*, Cambridge, MA, Harvard University Press, 1971; M. Jacobs, *The Green Economy*, London, Pluto Press, 1991; H. E. Daly and J. Farley, *Ecological Economics: Principles and Applications*, Washington, Island Press, 2011.

60 J. E. Stiglitz, A. Sen and J. P. Fitoussi, *Report by the Commission on the Measurement of Economic Performance and Social Progress*, Paris, Commission on the Measurement of Economic Performance and Social Progress, 2010.

2. The Failure of Austerity: Rethinking Fiscal Policy

STEPHANIE KELTON

Introduction

WHEN GLOBAL financial meltdown hit the world economy in 2007–2008, triggering the worst economic contraction in decades, great attention was understandably directed to assessing how, where and why systemic financial distress had been originated. Nearly a decade after the crash, industrialised countries are still coping with the aftermath of the crisis. Yet the full-blown catastrophe that the financial crash could have triggered has been averted; an economic depression like the one experienced after the 1929 crash did not materialise. It is thus crucial to ask what brought the failed system that produced the 2007–2008 crash back on its feet. As I will argue in this chapter, the answer can only be found in the prompt reaction—partly intentional but partly automatic—of fiscal and monetary policy variables. This is what really differentiated the present crisis from that of 1929: the combination of aggressive liquidity provision, actively enforced by central banks, plus large public deficits, mainly due to a mechanical reaction of government budgets to the economic downturn, prevented a new Great Depression.

Nevertheless, a few years after the implosion, policy-makers in advanced capitalist countries have turned to the old doctrine of balanced budgets and fiscal austerity. The core purpose of this chapter is to show that austerity—or, as it is often called, 'fiscal consolidation'—is the wrong strategy to deal with the aftermath of the crisis. Behind it, there is a flawed theory of the role of budget deficits, which neglects their relation with private sector debt. We need to radically rethink this strategy and embrace a new and more ambitious approach to the use of government budgets, in order to replace a system characterised by unequally shared sacrifice with one capable of generating broadly based prosperity. To make these points and highlight the actual nature of fiscal budgets in a modern economy, this chapter employs a narrative structure, analysing the events of the 'post-Lehman' years through the lens of the sectoral financial balances approach.

'Deficits saved the world'

The global financial crisis (GFC) began in 2007 as a liquidity crisis,[1] triggered when credit markets seized up and 'shadow banks' like Lehman Brothers

Published by John Wiley & Sons Ltd, 9600 Garsington Road, Oxford OX4 2DQ, UK and 350 Main Street, Malden, MA 02148, USA

and Bear Stearns[2] found it impossible to refinance their positions in assets. Next came the wave of insolvencies that led to the failing or shoring up of a large number of home mortgage specialists such as AIG and Merrill Lynch. The world watched as the Federal Reserve sprung into action—first with interest rates cuts and liquidity provision and later with more unorthodox measures such as quantitative easing (QE)[3]—to contain the unfolding crisis in the financial system. And contain it it did.

The Federal Reserve did what it was designed to do—function as a lender of last resort during times of crisis. It did this domestically as well as internationally. Funding was provided to US banks via the Term Auction Facility (TAF)[4] and to financial institutions in other jurisdictions via reciprocal currency arrangements ('swap lines') with other central banks.[5] This is not to suggest that all of this went off without a hitch. On the contrary, the Fed had to aggressively expand liquidity provision following the bankruptcy of Lehman on 15 September 2008 and then again as financial market conditions continued to deteriorate. At its peak, the Fed's outstanding swap lines topped $580 billion.[6] This is what it took to effectively deal with the GFC: open-ended liquidity provision carried out by a Big Central Bank. But this is only half of the story.

The rest of the tale centres on the ways in which Big Government responded, via fiscal policy, to the Great Recession. By mid-2008, it had become clear that the financial crisis, which had its roots in the mortgage industry, was bleeding over into the US economy on a massive scale (see Figure 1). Job growth had turned sharply negative and by winter the labour market was haemorrhaging, losing nearly 800,000 jobs per month. Within a few months, Congress had cobbled together a plan, and on 17 February 2009 President Obama signed the American Recovery and Reinvestment Act (ARRA) into law.[7]

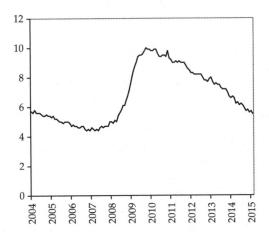

Figure 1: Unemployment rate in the US
Source: US Bureau of Labor Statistics

Commonly referred to as the 'stimulus bill', this package, worth some $787 billion, was aimed at stopping the downward slide, with $275 billion in tax cuts and more than $500 billion in increased spending. Over the next three years, the stimulus made its way into the US economy, providing a much-needed boost to infrastructure investment, direct aid to cash-strapped state and local governments and tax breaks to help struggling students, homeowners and companies. The White House hailed it an unequivocal triumph, insisting that these proactive measures succeeded in staving off another Great Depression by saving or creating an estimated 1.6 million jobs per year between 2009 and 2012.[8]

But did the ARRA really do the heavy lifting on this front, or were other, potentially more potent, forces at work? It's an important question, and one that Nobel prize-winning economist Paul Krugman has answered in the opinion pages of the *New York Times*. In one piece, aptly titled 'Deficits Saved the World', Krugman credits the automatic stabilisers,[9] not the deliberate actions of Congress and the White House, with cushioning, and ultimately reversing, the decline in output and employment.[10] The arguments are so important that they merit developing in greater detail here.

The reasoning is informed by the 'sectoral financial balances' approach, conceived by the Cambridge economist Wynne Godley.[11] The basic intuition is that at the level of the whole economy, income equals expenditures. This is an accounting identity: it is necessarily true. Thus, if we consider different sectors of the economy—typically the public, private and foreign sectors— the financial imbalance of any sector must necessarily be compensated by an opposite and equal imbalance in the other sectors, so that income equals expenditures at the aggregate level. In other words, in order for one sector to spend less than its income, there must be another sector (or more than one) which spends more than its income; and the first sector will accumulate net claims on the second.

Now, it's worth remembering that the crisis unfolded at a time when the *private* sector (in the US and elsewhere) had amassed record levels of debt, accumulated after years of spending in excess of its income. The black line in Figure 2 shows the private sector's financial balance, defined as the difference between private income and private spending, or equivalently between saving and investment (S-I). As the data show, the private sector's financial balance deteriorated over much of the 1990s, and by 1997 it had forsaken its habitual state of surplus as it began spending in excess of its income (i.e. running deficits) for the first time in generations.

The pattern that led to the crisis was strikingly similar to that theorised by Minsky's 'financial instability hypothesis'.[12] During the boom, private actors —especially households and banks, in this case—started piling up debt at an increasing rate. Then, suddenly, after a fall in house prices, the speculative fever was reversed, generating systemic financial distress and pushing most private actors to try to reduce their indebtedness simultaneously. In other

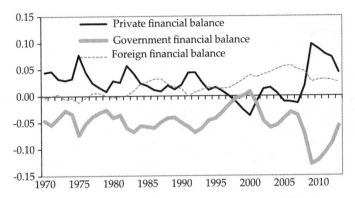

Figure 2: Sectoral financial balances in the US (% of GDP; 1970–2013)
Source: US Department of Commerce

words, when the housing bubble burst, the private sector looked to delever-age by spending less, saving more and paying down debt. There was a strong desire to return to a surplus position.[13]

The problem, as Keynes explained in his 1936 masterwork *The General Theory*, is that the spending multiplier also works in reverse.[14] That is, a diminution in aggregate spending tends to have an amplified effect on GDP as the initial decline in spending lowers income, which then leads to further decreases in spending, and so on. When the desire to cut spending is strong enough, as it surely was following the collapse of the housing bubble, the blow to output and employment can be devastating. Left unchecked, the contraction in GDP might well have escalated to Great Depression levels. But that didn't occur, and the overriding reason it didn't is because the modern capitalist system has a 'big government', equipped with powerful stabilisers that *automatically* work to accommodate shifts in the private sector's desire to net save. As Krugman explained:

In the 1930s the public sector was very small. As a result, GDP basically had to shrink enough to keep the private-sector surplus equal to zero; hence the fall in GDP labeled 'Great Depression'. . . . This time around, the fall in GDP didn't have to be as large, because falling GDP led to rising deficits, which absorbed some of the rise in the private surplus. Hence the smaller fall in GDP labeled 'Great Recession'. . . . [T]he initial shock—the surge in desired private surplus—was if anything larger this time than it was in the 1930s. This says that absent the absorbing role of budget deficits, we would have had a full Great Depression experience. What we're actually having is awful, but not that awful—and it's all because of the rise in deficits. Deficits, in other words, saved the world.[15]

The deficits that carried out this rescue were not small. As Figure 2 shows, government deficits exploded, topping roughly 11 per cent of US GDP in 2009.[16] And while policy-makers and pundits across the US reacted to these mushrooming deficits with moral outrage, a handful of analysts, including

STEPHANIE KELTON

the chief economists at both Goldman Sachs and PIMCO, could see what
was really happening.[17]

First, the deficit hadn't exploded because of anything anyone in Washington, DC had done. The automatic stabilisers were built to operate with or
without Congressional blessings. In practice, this meant that as hundreds of
thousands of people lost their jobs, tax receipts (T) fell sharply and government spending (G) to support the jobless (e.g. unemployment compensation,
food stamps, etc.) rose rapidly. The result was a non-discretionary (i.e.
endogenous) spike in the deficit (G-T) that reflected the severity of the crisis,
something Martin Wolf noted[18] in his regular column at the *Financial Times*.
'I look at this through the lens of sectoral financial balances', Wolf said,
continuing:

The idea that the huge fiscal deficits of recent years have been the result of decisions
taken by the current administration is nonsense. No fiscal policy changes explain the
collapse into massive deficit between 2007 and 2009, because there was none of any
importance. The collapse is explained by the massive shift of the private sector from
financial deficit into surplus ... The government responds in a largely passive way.

But the government's deficit did more than just *passively reflect* the private
sector's attempt to deleverage; it *actively restored* private sector balance sheets
by providing the very (financial) assets the private sector was seeking. To
appreciate this, look back at Figure 2 and compare the private sector's financial balance (black line) at the start of the crisis (2007) with what took place
post-2007.

The upsurge in the private sector's financial position, the largest in postwar history, was mirrored by an equally stunning downturn in the public
sector's balance. What happened is of critical importance. It is also something that too many economists and virtually all policy-makers still fail to
acknowledge, at least in polite company. Simply put, there is an 'upside' to
government deficits. As PIMCO's Paul McCulley put it, 'Fiscal deficits are
facilitating the private sector's desire to save more, delevering their balance
sheets. Remember, the government sector's liability is the private sector's
asset!'[19]

Further evidence that fiscal deficits have been the *result* of the financial
crash—and of the deleveraging process in the private sector—comes from
the experience of the UK. Britain was similarly affected by the financial
crash, with highly indebted households, financial institutions full of toxic
assets and a huge housing bubble. Correspondingly, its sectoral financial
balances reveal a dynamic that is strikingly similar to that of the US.

Sectoral financial balances in the UK are depicted in Figure 3. The left
panel displays the net balances of the private, public and foreign sectors,
while the right panel further divides the private sector between households
and firms. Like the US, the UK has had a persistently negative external
balance, which resulted in the foreign sector being constantly in surplus in the
past fifteen years. This had of course to be offset by deficits in the domestic

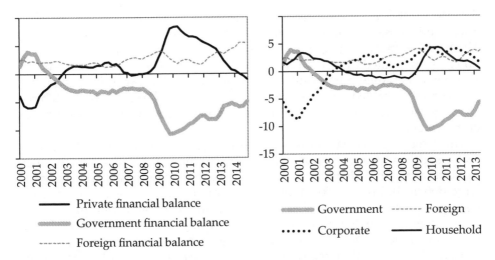

Figure 3: Sectoral financial balances in the UK (% of GDP; 2000–2014)
Source: UK Office for Budget Responsibility

sectors. Other salient features that stand out are (a) the shift in the private business sector's net balance position (from net borrower to net lender) in the period 2001–2005 and (b) the deterioration of households' balance sheets in the 2002–2007 period (right panel). But the most violent dynamic is that displayed by the whole private sector at the onset of the financial crash: private units suddenly rushed to deleverage; and this movement was of course matched—and allowed—by a sharp increase in the public deficit (Figure 3, left panel). It appears that, in the UK, as in the US, huge government deficits 'saved the world' by providing net assets to the private sector.

As economists, we are trained to think of the government deficit as containing inputs, G (government spending) and T (tax revenues), which are primarily a matter of discretionary policy choice (i.e. exogenous in nature). Moreover, we are accustomed to thinking of deficits as something that requires borrowing, which we presume takes financial resources *away* from savers, thereby 'crowding out' other forms of economic activity. But, as anyone who understands monetary operations knows, this gets things completely backwards.[20] To see this, one can run through the balance sheet entries, tracing the debits and credits that arise as the government spends, taxes and issues bonds.[21] Or, perhaps more straightforwardly, one can rely on the internal logic of double-entry bookkeeping and simply interpret the sector balance model. Either way, careful analysts will discover that deficits add to (rather than subtract from) the financial balances of other economic agents.

Simply put, government deficits are a *flow* of funds that increases the *stock* of net financial assets to the non-government sector.[22] The government's deficits (flow) accumulate to financial debt (stock). But those

33

deficits are the accounting record of surpluses in another part of the economy, and those surpluses (flow) accumulate to financial assets (stock). Thus, government deficits *provision* some other part of the economy with dollar-denominated assets (Treasuries, in the US) that increase the recipients' net financial wealth. In the wake of the Great Recession, this provisioning enabled the private sector to quickly[23] return to its habitual state of surplus, thereby halting the downward slide in output and employment.

This process is crucial, so it is worth discussing it in detail. If the private sector suddenly wants to run a huge surplus (in order to deleverage), there must be a public sector that is able to accommodate this shift by running a large deficit. If, instead, the public sector is not willing to increase its deficit enough, another variable has to adjust, and this variable is output: as Krugman recognises, in the absence of a large public deficit, GDP would have decreased much more. Given that savings are an increasing function of income, the great fall in output would have offset the rise in the willingness to save, preventing the private sector from increasing its net surplus and thus bringing the system at balance, but at a dramatically lower level of income.

So deficits saved the world. But instead of celebrating their healing powers and being grateful that it didn't take an act of (an increasingly dysfunctional) Congress to fend off a second Great Depression, pundits, politicians and many economists blamed the slow recovery on the appearance of big government deficits (in the US and elsewhere), obsessively pointing to unfolding events in the euro zone as evidence that 'markets' would surely punish any country that failed to restore balance to the government budget.[24] With that, deficits became public enemy no. 1, fiscal policy shifted in favour of austerity and the Fed was compelled to do more.

The fiscal retreat and the monetary plunge

The rationale for fiscal tightening went something like this: government deficits weigh on the psyche of private sector agents, who respond to government 'profligacy' by saving more (spending less) in anticipation of an inevitable rise in future tax burdens. This, of course, is the well-known theory of Ricardian equivalence. According to that theory, fiscal policy can never influence aggregate demand, because any increase in the public deficit will cause a corresponding decrease in private spending, in particular in private consumption. Every time the government deficit rises, individuals will predict higher taxes in the future and set aside money to pay them, thus reducing their spending by an amount equal to the increase in the public deficit. While Ricardo himself rejected[25] the notion that people actually behave this way, the theory remains a mainstay in neoclassical economics. As McCulley mused, the fiscal austerians are really reverse-Ricardians, preaching:

[T]hat if only governments would reduce their deficits, the private sector, freed from the fear of future tax increases, will spontaneously reduce their surpluses. Put differently, it is argued, if only governments would put their fiscal houses in order, the private sector would immaculately regain confidence in their own fiscal affairs, pull down their savings and borrow more, boosting aggregate demand. Really, that is the argument, made with a straight face.[26]

While new classical economists like Robert Barro[27] made the argument with a straight face, Keynesians like Paul Krugman[28] derided reverse-Ricardianism, likening it to summoning the 'confidence fairy' to restore prosperity. But politics frequently trump sound theory and, besides, policy-makers insisted that real-world events were validating their economic intuition.

It was late 2009, and much of Europe was in turmoil. The euro zone was in recession and, as a consequence, the hardest-hit nations blew through the 3 per cent and 60 per cent upper limits on their deficit- and debt-to-GDP ratios, respectively.[29] The limits themselves implicitly (and erroneously) suggest that governments have ultimate discretion over their budget outcomes; that they were not, in fact, overwhelmingly endogenous. This represents a serious weakness in the design of the fiscal rules that were meant to constrain budget deficits within the euro zone, but it is what happened next that emboldened the fiscal austerians and helped to fuel the balanced budget obsession in the US and beyond.

Markets reacted. After roughly a decade of indifference, capital markets developed a strong aversion to the bonds of highly indebted members of the economic and monetary union (EMU). Default risk premiums soared as lenders rightly concluded that they were lending euros to governments that might not be able to pay them back. Unable to finance themselves at affordable rates, many countries had no choice but to go, hat in hand, to their euro zone partners and the International Monetary Fund (IMF). The poster child for fiscal imprudence was, of course, Greece, which had to negotiate not one but two bailout packages. The first came in May 2010, when the government agreed to the terms of a €100 billion bailout, followed by a €130 billion package in February of 2012. (A third was negotiated in August 2015.) Ireland, too, sought assistance, taking a €67.5 billion bailout in November 2011, after an ill-advised bank rescue put the government on the hook for billions in unsecured debt. Soon it was Portugal's turn, agreeing to €78 billion in rescue loans in May 2011. The world watched as governments were toppled, technocrats rose to power and millions took to the streets in protest at the harsh austerity imposed as a condition for the bailouts. A powerful narrative took shape: Deal with your debt problems, or they will deal with you.[30]

Meanwhile, in 2010, President Obama wanted a plan. He ordered the creation of a bipartisan commission—the National Commission on Fiscal Responsibility and Reform—and charged it with developing a strategy to put the government's fiscal house in order. No one wanted to end up like Greece. The Commission's final report detailed a plan to reduce government deficits by some $4 trillion, but it failed to garner enough support from its own members to mandate Congressional action. For the next two years, law-makers debated the best way to reduce deficits. Republicans favoured spending cuts, insisting that the nation owed its fiscal woes to a persistent 'spending problem', while Democrats fought to raise taxes in order to deal with what they perceived as primarily a 'revenue problem'.

Remarkably, the debate between fiscal 'hawks' and 'doves' completely failed to recognise the fundamental difference between economies like the US, the UK, Canada and Australia on the one hand and the euro zone on the other. The former all have monetary systems that are 'wedded' to their fiscal systems. Their governments can finance deficit spending just by crediting bank accounts with money issued by their central bank. In other words, these governments are *issuers* of their own currency. They do not need to 'get' money from financial markets or taxpayers in order to finance their spending. They just issue the money that they spend. In these countries taxes are collected and bonds issued because the government *wants* to do so for several reasons (like stabilising bank reserves, avoiding inflation, providing assets to the private sector), not because it needs them to finance government spending.[31]

To the contrary, in the euro zone there has been a 'divorce' of fiscal and monetary institutions under EMU. Fiscal policy remained at the national level, while monetary authority has been transferred to a single European Central Bank (the ECB). By abandoning control over the issuance of their sovereign currency, the governments of the euro zone have become *users*— and no longer issuers—of a non-sovereign (stateless) money. In short, they can no longer 'print' money to pay their bills, and thus they are forced to borrow at the terms dictated by private financial markets. Their debts can thus become unsustainable the moment markets are no longer willing to finance them at feasible interest rates. But as Nersisyan and Wray argue in their chapter in this volume, this cannot happen to governments that control their own currency, like the US and the UK. The latter can coordinate their fiscal and monetary operations and prevent financial markets from dictating the terms of finance.

Because of the flawed institutional design of the EMU, Southern euro zone countries have practically handed their fiscal policy-making authority over to bond markets. As a result of this—and of the misguided economic doctrines followed by European policy-makers—they have been forced to embark on austerity programmes. The consequences have been disastrous, to say the least. Rather than enhancing the confidence of private investors, austerity led to sharp recessions in the countries that were administered the treatment and to acceleration—rather than reversal—in the growth of their public debts.[32] Austerity failed to reverse the escalation of financial tension in the markets of southern European government bonds. Interest rates fell from their peak and returned to safer levels only when, in summer 2012, the ECB eventually declared its willingness to act as a lender of last resort.[33]

But let us go back to the US and its panic-driven debate on deficit reduction. As the debate raged on, the deficit quietly fell. And fell. By 2012, the Congressional Budget Office (CBO) reported that the US budget deficit had been shrinking at its fastest rate since the demobilisation from World War II. Once again a sizable adjustment in the government's fiscal stance had occurred without any deliberate effort to engineer it. It happened endogenously, and it happened with little fanfare. Indeed, Congress was too busy scrambling to come up with a way to cut the deficit to notice that the deficit was quietly retreating on its own.[34]

Meanwhile, Chairman Bernanke watched with frustration as Congress continued to work toward a 'Grand Bargain' to reduce the deficit, even as the CBO warned that fiscal tightening risked slowing the pace of recovery. In testimony on Capitol Hill, Bernanke defended against boisterous criticisms that the Fed's policies, which by this point included two rounds of quantitative easing (Q1 and Q2) plus so-called 'Operation Twist',[35] hadn't done enough to jumpstart the economy. Tensions ran high and Bernanke was feeling the pressure. The Fed was already relying on extraordinary measures to stimulate the economy, and now it appeared that Congress was going to increase the burden on the Fed by imposing austerity in a weak recovery. Bernanke understood that he needed markets to remain confident in the Fed's ability to act, but he also needed Congress to understand that he could use the help of fiscal policy. In a moment of extreme candor, an exasperated Bernanke leveled with law-makers, confessing, 'Monetary policy is not a panacea. It's not even the ideal tool. I'd like to see other parts of the government play their roles.'[36]

It may not have been the ideal tool, but it had become the only option. Fiscal headwinds were on the horizon, and there was growing pressure on the Fed to do more. Columbia University's Michael Woodford led the charge with his presentation at Jackson Hole in August 2012.[37] Woodford gained notoriety for insisting that 'forward guidance', rather than a renewed round of quantitative easing, was the way to gain traction at the zero lower bound (ZLB). On 13 September 2012, the Fed went all-in, announcing the open-ended bond-buying programme known as QE3, along with 'forward guidance' to reassure market participants that the Fed was likely to keep the federal funds interest rate near zero at least through 2015.[38] The Fed continued its elevated bond-buying programme for more than a year before it began tapering its purchases by $10 billion per month in December 2013.

What happened in the US in 2013 will be the subject of debate for years to come. Fiscal policy tightened as the government raised taxes and initiated more than $1 trillion in spending cuts. The tax increases went into effect on 1 January 2013 when President Obama signed the American Taxpayer Relief Act of 2012. The legislation kept some of the 'Bush tax cuts' in place, but it raised the top marginal tax rate on individuals making more than $400,000 per year (and $450,000 for married couples filing jointly), and it allowed the payroll tax cut to expire, effectively raising taxes by 2 per cent on more than

150 million working Americans. In addition to higher taxes, the 'sequester' triggered the start of more than $1 trillion in automatic, across-the-board spending cuts (split equally between defence and non-defence spending) on 1 March 2013.[39] Austerity had come to America.

The CBO sounded the alarm, predicting that sequestration would shave 0.6 per cent off GDP growth in 2013. The IMF followed suit, projecting a sequester-induced slowdown from 2.0 to 1.5 per cent. Before long, there was a chorus of voices, including Alan Krueger, the head of the White House Council of Economic Advisors, warning of fiscal headwinds that would slow the pace of recovery in US labour markets. Bernanke hoped it wouldn't happen; testifying[40] in February 2013, he advised:

Congress and the Administration should consider replacing the sharp, front-loaded spending cuts required by the sequestration with policies that reduce the federal deficit more gradually in the near term but more substantially in the longer run. Such an approach could lessen the near-term fiscal headwinds facing the economy.

Despite the warnings, an intransigent Congress allowed sequestration to take effect the following month. Yet growth picked up, accelerating from an annual rate of 2 per cent in 2012 to 2.6 per cent in 2013. How could that be? Were the fiscal headwinds exaggerated? Was this proof that austerity worked? Had Bernanke been too pessimistic about the relative efficacy of monetary policy? Did doubling down with QE3 and forward guidance at the end of 2012 not only prevent a slowdown but also so juice the economy that growth actually accelerated in 2013?

Scholars will undoubtedly debate these questions for a while yet. At present, economic opinion appears to be coalescing around the following narrative. First, experience demonstrates that monetary policy can counteract fiscal tightening, even at the ZLB, provided it is carried out by a sufficiently credible and committed central bank. Second, the Fed's aggressive easing worked primarily through a wealth effect, as investors 'reached for yield', driving up prices across a range of asset classes, especially equities, housing and corporate bonds. Third, the rise in asset prices disproportionately benefited those at the top of the income ladder, widening the gap between rich and poor. Finally, there is some risk that the Central Bank's policies encouraged too much risk-taking, overinflating asset prices and laying the groundwork for the next financial crisis—a scenario Janet Yellen described soon after taking the helm as Fed Chair:[41]

[M]onetary policy has powerful effects on risk taking. Indeed, the accommodative policy stance of recent years has supported the recovery, in part, by providing increased incentives for households and businesses to take on the risk of potentially productive investments. But such risk-taking can go too far, thereby contributing to fragility in the financial system.

Thus, it appears that the Fed's aggressive plunge into uncharted monetary waters 'worked' in the sense that it provoked enough risky activity to offset the fiscal pullback of 2013. But, as Bernanke cautioned, it wasn't the ideal tool. It heightened risks in financial markets, exacerbated wealth and income inequality and did little to improve labour market conditions for the long-term unemployed. It was a decision, arrived at under substantial duress, by a central bank with a mandate[42] to achieve macroeconomic objectives that could have been more effectively carried out by fiscal policy.[43]

It is worth noting that, also in this respect, events in the UK have borne some resemblance to those observed in the US. The increase in the fiscal deficit during the financial crisis has been attributed to 'profligate' government spending. The more serious argument that the public deficit was, in fact, related to deleveraging in the private sector has been totally absent from the mainstream debate. Also in Britain, the government has embraced austerity (though to a much lesser extent than in southern euro zone countries), while the Central Bank has aggressively expanded its balance sheet through quantitative easing, boosting stock market valuations and house prices. And of course the government deficit has only come down, endogenously, when the private sector has increased its propensity to risk. As can be seen from Figure 3, the UK private sector's balance sheets progressively deteriorated during the recovery, returning to deficit (i.e. to increasing indebtedness) in 2014. The recovery of the UK economy—like that of the US—has been robust in terms of aggregate growth rates, but characterised by widening inequality, stagnating real wages and a return to household indebtedness and potential financial fragility.

A balanced budget or a balanced economy?

In the opening sentence to the final chapter of *The General Theory*, John Maynard Keynes described what he considered to be the two most striking flaws in the capitalist order: 'The outstanding faults of the economic society in which we live are its failure to provide for full employment and its arbitrary and inequitable distribution of wealth and incomes.'[44]

After more than two decades of steady improvement on these fronts, both problems resurfaced in the 1970s, and, with brief exceptions, both have intensified with the rise of the neoliberal economic agenda—supply-side tax cuts, sweeping deregulation and renewed focus on balancing government budgets.

Along with aggressively deregulating financial (and other) markets, nearly every OECD country has substantially cut taxes over the past thirty years. The average marginal income tax rate on top earners dropped from 66 per cent in 1981 to 43 per cent by 2013. Average corporate income tax rates were also cut sharply, plunging from 47 per cent to 25 per cent, and taxes on dividend income declined from 75 per cent to 42 per cent over the same period.[45] Instead of unleashing the job creators and extending prosperity to all, these supply-side manoeuvres were closely associated with widening inequality[46] and greater financial instability.[47] In other words, these experiments have failed. Capitalism has become more unstable, the distribution of wealth and income has become more unequal and it takes the system longer and longer to claw back the jobs that are lost each time we suffer a recession.[48]

What can be done? Contributions to this volume offer a wide range of specific policies to address these and other challenges facing capitalist economies in the twenty-first century. My contribution is more general in nature, but it provides an essential framework within which to contemplate various proposals to transform the capitalist order. Policies to improve the human condition should be evaluated on the basis of their anticipated social and economic outcomes rather than on narrow budget considerations. This means eschewing the current obsession with balancing the budget and embracing a more ambitious use of fiscal policy to transform the system into one that replaces shared sacrifice with broadly based prosperity.

To get there, we must liberate ourselves from the flawed theories and destructive policies that govern current thinking. This requires, first and foremost, dispensing with the convenient, but mistaken, idea that governments, like households, must balance their budgets. As the experience of the US and UK has shown, budget outcomes are mostly endogenous, oscillating along with changing conditions in the real economy. In the US, for example, the automatic stabilisers move the budget in near perfect tandem with changing conditions in the job market (see Figure 4).

Rising unemployment drags the government budget down just as improvements in the labour market drag it up. On rare occasions, conditions get so tight that the budget may even move into surplus. This happened in 2000, when the unemployment rate fell to just 4 per cent, and there was one job vacancy for every job seeker in America.[49] Unfortunately, policy-makers have been conditioned to think of things the wrong way around, viewing widening budget deficits as the cause rather than the result of weakness in the real economy. Instead of allowing the budget to come to rest at a place where conditions in the economy are stabilised, governments have tried to

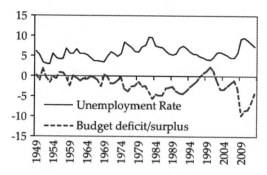

Figure 4: Unemployment rate vs. Federal Budget (as a % of GDP), US
Source: US Bureau of Labor Statistics

force the economy to balance the budget. It is a violation of the intuition shared by Keynes in 1933:

You will never balance the Budget through measures which reduce the national income ... It is the burden of unemployment and the decline in the national income which are upsetting the Budget. Look after the unemployment, and the budget will look after itself.[50]

And while that may sound like little more than a clever quip, there is now ample evidence to support it. Witness Europe, for example, where governments have tried to cut deficits with spending cuts and tax increases (i.e. austerity), only to suffer the self-defeating effects of fiscal tightening, as slower growth pushed debt-to-GDP ratios higher.[51] Elsewhere, in the US, the post-World War II era gives us sixty-four years of data against which to judge Keynes' intuition. If the budget really does look after itself when the economy does well, then one should expect deficits to check themselves in good times. And this is exactly what history confirms. Indeed, as Table 1 reveals, budget deficits have touched 3 per cent of GDP or higher only twenty times in the past sixty-four years, and only when the burden of unemployment was 5.5 per cent or higher.[52]

This is important evidence for policy-makers obsessed with balancing the budget. But there are even more critical lessons that must be learned.

It is not enough simply to relieve anxiety about occasional budget deficits. What we need, instead, is a fundamental change in the way we define 'fiscal responsibility'. Policy goals, such as full employment, can occur with the budget in deficit, surplus or balance. Thus, policy-makers should never *target* a particular budget outcome, for the budget is not an end in itself. Instead, the budget should be used as an ongoing means of achieving societal goals aimed at raising living standards and promoting a more equitable distribution

Table 1: Unemployment when the federal budget deficit is 3% or higher, 1949–2013

Year	Unemployment (% of working pop.)	Federal Budget Deficit (% of GDP)	Year	Unemployment (% of working pop.)	Federal Budget Deficit (% of GDP)
1975	8.5%	3.2%	1992	7.5%	4.4%
1976	7.7%	3.9%	1993	6.9%	3.7%
1982	9.7%	3.8%	2003	6.0%	3.3%
1983	9.6%	5.7%	2004	5.5%	3.4%
1984	7.5%	4.6%	2008	5.8%	3.1%
1985	7.2%	4.9%	2009	9.3%	9.8%
1986	7.0%	4.8%	2010	9.6%	8.7%
1987	6.2%	3.0%	2011	8.9%	8.4%
1990	5.6%	3.7%	2012	8.1%	6.7%
1991	6.9%	4.4%	2013	7.4%	4.0%

of income. Without a more ambitious use of the government budget, the system will never deliver the public investments in education, technology and infrastructure that are critical for long-term prosperity.

For some countries, this is easier said than done.[53] But for nations that spend, tax and borrow in their own non-convertible fiat currencies, there is the potential for a radical break from the prevailing economic wisdom that promotes shared sacrifice over prosperity-enhancing investments in our people and planet. The case for such a break was laid out most cogently by Abba Lerner,[54] who urged policy-makers to abandon the paralysing philosophy of so-called 'sound finance' in favour of a mission-oriented approach he dubbed 'functional finance'. For all of their power and importance, the automatic stabilisers will never move the budget into the mission-critical investments that will reshape our future. Only we can do that. Rediscovering the lessons of 'functional finance' is a necessary first step in the journey toward rethinking capitalism.

Notes

1 In general, a financial institution faces a liquidity crisis when more money is being withdrawn than the liquid funds it has available in the short run. To meet its liabilities, the institution will have to borrow (often at a higher interest rate). If it does not find a lender, it could face bankruptcy, and what started as a liquidity crisis could end up as an insolvency crisis.
2 The shadow banking system comprises a network of institutions, such as investment banks, hedge funds, structured investment vehicles, and so on. They do not receive traditional deposits as retail banks do, and as such they are essentially unregulated. Their activity takes place, so to speak, in the shadows of regulatory oversight.
3 QE is an operation that can be executed by a Central Bank and which consists in buying government bonds with newly created money. These bonds can be bought directly from the fiscal authority in bonds' auctions, or they can be purchased in secondary markets, i.e. from banks or other financial institutions.
4 See the Federal Reserve website for an explanation of TAF: http://www.federal reserve.gov/newsevents/reform_taf.htm (accessed 4 May 2016).
5 More details on central bank liquidity swaps can be found at http://www.feder alreserve.gov/monetarypolicy/bst_liquidityswaps.htm (accessed 4 May 2016).
6 See M. J. Flemming and N. J. Klagge, 'The Federal Reserve's foreign exchange swap lines', *Current Issues in Economics and Finance*, vol. 16, no. 4, April 2010, https://www.newyorkfed.org/research/current_issues/ci16-4.html (accessed 28 April 2016).
7 More detail on the 'stimulus bill' can be found at https://www.treasury.gov/ initiatives/recovery/Pages/recovery-act.aspx (accessed 4 May 2016).
8 See C. Romer and J. Bernstein, 'The job impact of the American Recovery and Reinvestment Plan', 10 January 2009, http://www.ampo.org/assets/library/ 184_obama.pdf (accessed 4 May 2016).
9 Automatic stabilisers are those parts of the government budget which tend to automatically increase deficits when the economy slows down (and, symmetrically,

to reduce them when the economy accelerates). In this way they reduce the amplitude of economic fluctuations. During a slump, for instance, tax revenues decrease while unemployment benefits rise, thus increasing the deficit and counter-balancing (at least partially) the slump. During a boom, tax revenues automatically rise, while unemployment benefits decrease, thus decreasing the government deficit and moderating the boom.

10 P. Krugman, 'Deficits saved the world', *New York Times*, 15 July 2009, http://krugman.blogs.nytimes.com/2009/07/15/deficits-saved-the-world/ (accessed 4 May 2016).

11 See W. Godley, *Money, Finance and National Income Determination: An Integrated Approach*, Levy Economic Institute Working Paper No. 167, June 1996.

12 See for example H. Minsky, *The Financial Instability Hypothesis*, Levy Economics Institute Working Paper No. 74.

13 Richard Koo of Nomura Research has popularised this dynamic as a 'balance sheet recession'. See R. Koo, 'The world in balance sheet recession: causes, cure, and politics', *Economic Review*, issue 58, http://www.paecon.net/PAEReview/issue58/Koo58.pdf (accessed 4 May 2016).

14 J. M. Keynes, *The General Theory of Employment, Interest and Money*, London, Macmillan, 1965 [1936].

15 Krugman, 'Deficits saved the world'.

16 State and local government budgets also moved sharply into deficit, accounting for the additional rise seen in Figure 2. Historical data on the federal budget is available at http://www.whitehouse.gov/omb/budget/historicals (accessed 4 May 2016).

17 Jan Hatzius of Goldman Sachs and Paul McCulley of PIMCO, the world's largest bond fund, both relied on Wynne Godley's sector financial balances framework to help them see the positive role of government deficits in facilitating the deleveraging process. See for example Hatzius' 2012 interview with the Business Insider: http://www.businessinsider.com/goldmans-jan-hatzius-on-sectoral-balances-2012-12?IR=T (accessed 4 May 2016).

18 M. Wolf, 'The balance sheet recession in the US', *Financial Times*, 19 July 2012, http://blogs.ft.com/martin-wolf-exchange/2012/07/19/the-balance-sheet-recession-in-the-us/ (accessed 4 May 2016).

19 P. McCulley, *Global Central Bank Focus: Facts on the Ground*, Policy Note 2010/2, Levy Economics Institute of Bard College, 2010, p. 3, http://www.levyinstitute.org/pubs/pn_10_02.pdf (accessed 4 May 2016).

20 L. R. Wray, *Understanding Modern Money: The Key to Full Employment and Price Stability*, London, Edward Elgar Publishing, 1998.

21 S. Kelton, 'Yes, deficit spending adds to private sector assets even with bond sales', *New Economic Perspectives*, 2010, http://neweconomicperspectives.org/2010/11/yes-deficit-spending-adds-to-private.html (accessed 4 May 2016).

22 Figures 2 and 3 also depict the foreign sector (grey dashed line), which is part of the non-government sector. The foreign sector may also accumulate net financial assets (NFAs) as a consequence of government deficit spending; however, the point here is to focus on private sector balance sheets. For a full treatment, see W. Mitchell and L. R. Wray, 'Introduction to monetary and fiscal policy operations', Chapter 9.

23 As Wolf ('The balance sheet recession in the US') notes, 'the financial balance of the private sector shifted towards surplus by the almost unbelievable cumulative

total of 11.2 percent of gross domestic product between the third quarter of 2007 and the second quarter of 2009'.

24 Even those who took a more dove-ish position often emphasised the need to adopt policies aimed at balancing the budget in the medium or longer term, prompting opposition from post-Keynesians. See P. Davidson, J. K. Galbraith and R. Skidelsky, 'Open Letter', published at New Deal 2.0, 19 July 2010, http://roo seveltinstitute.org/statement-evanss-stimulus-letter-davidson-galbraith-skidelsky/ (accessed 4 May 2016).

25 In his 1820 'Essay on the Funding System', Ricardo wrote: 'But the people who paid the taxes never so estimate them, and therefore do not manage their private affairs accordingly. We are too apt to think that the war is burdensome only in proportion to what we are at the moment called to pay for it in taxes, without reflecting on the probable duration of such taxes. It would be difficult to convince a man possessed of £20,000, or any other sum, that a perpetual payment of £50 per annum was equally burdensome with a single tax of £1000.' (The essay is available at http://oll.libertyfund.org/titles/ricardo-the-works-of-david-ricardo-mcculloch-ed-1846-1888. Accessed 4 May 2016.)

26 McCulley, *Global Central Bank Focus*.

27 R. Barro, 'How to really save the economy', *New York Times*, 10 September 2011, http://www.nytimes.com/2011/09/11/opinion/sunday/how-to-really-save-the-economy.html (accessed 4 May 2016).

28 P. Krugman, 'Myths of austerity', *New York Times*, 1 July 2010, http://www.ny times.com/2010/07/02/opinion/02krugman.html (accessed 4 May 2016).

29 The hardest hit were the so-called PIIGS—Portugal, Ireland, Italy, Greece and Spain—whose deficits most exceeded the limits established under the Maastricht Treaty and reinforced in the Stability and Growth Pact.

30 Debt hysteria hit a fever pitch in the US, where politicians from *both* sides of the political divide penned op-eds and crowded onto the cable news shows to throw their weight behind the call for deficit reduction. Former president Bill Clinton delivered one of the most urgent warnings, telling an American audience, 'We've got to deal with this long-term debt problem, or it will deal with us'.

31 I have shown this in detail in S. Bell, 'Do taxes and bonds finance government spending?', *Journal of Economic Issues*, vol. XXXIV, no. 3, September 2000, pp. 603–20.

32 The broader social costs imposed by austerity were even more dramatic. See for example J. Henley, 'Recessions can hurt, but austerity kills', *The Guardian*, 15 May 2013, http://www.theguardian.com/society/2013/may/15/recessions-hurt-but-austerity-kills (accessed 4 May 2016).

33 See for example *The Economist*, 'Time to celebrate?', 19 January 2013, http:// www.economist.com/news/finance-and-economics/21569727-government-bond-markets-peripheral-countries-are-soaring-time-celebrate (accessed 4 May 2016).

34 Law-makers were trying to avoid going over the 'fiscal cliff' by working on a compromise piece of legislation to replace to the hastily concocted mix of across-the-board spending cuts and tax increases that was set to automatically take effect at midnight on 31 December 2012.

35 The Federal Reserve's maturity extensions programme, better known as 'Operation Twist', consisted in selling short-term bonds and using the proceeds to buy long-term bonds. In this way the average maturity of the securities held by the Federal Reserve would be extended, decreasing long-term interest rates. See https://www.federalreserve.gov/faqs/money_15070.htm (accessed 4 May 2016).

36 B. Bernanke, 'Testimony before the Joint Economic Committee, U.S. Congress', Washington, DC, 7 June 2012, http://www.federalreserve.gov/newsevents/testimony/bernanke20120607a.htm (accessed 4 May 2016).

37 M. Woodford's paper, 'Methods of policy accommodation at the interest-rate lower bound', was presented at the annual symposium sponsored by the Federal Reserve Bank of Kansas City, 2012.

38 QE3 started as a $40 billion per month commitment, but two months later, the Federal Open Market Committee (FOMC) announced that it was bumping its purchases to $85 billion per month.

39 The CBO has estimated that the sequester will reduce spending by $1.1 trillion versus pre-sequester levels over the period 2013–2021.

40 B. Bernanke, 'FRB testimony on the semiannual Monetary Policy Report to Congress', Federal Reserve, 26 February 2013, http://www.federalreserve.gov/newsevents/testimony/bernanke20130226a.htm (accessed 4 May 2016).

41 J. L. Yellen, 'Monetary policy and financial stability', presented at the 2014 Michel Camdessus Central Banking Lecture, International Monetary Fund, Washington, DC, http://www.federalreserve.gov/newsevents/speech/yellen20140702a.htm (accessed 4 May 2016).

42 The Federal Reserve is charged with carrying out a dual mandate that includes maximum employment and price stability. This stands in contrast to the ECB, which has a sole mandate to deliver price stability.

43 As Michael Woodford recently put it, 'I worry that ... [we] let Congress off the hook a little too easily': http://www.stlouisfed.org/publications/Connecting-Policy-with-Frontier-Research/Michael-Woodford.cfm (accessed 4 May 2016).

44 Keynes, *The General Theory*, p. 372.

45 OECD, 'Focus on top incomes and taxation in OECD countries: was the crisis a game changer?', May 2014, http://www.oecd.org/els/soc/OECD2014-FocusOnTopIncomes.pdf (accessed 4 May 2016).

46 See Stiglitz's chapter in this book for a detailed account of the increase in inequality in OECD countries and its relation with neoliberal policies.

47 See for example L. R. Wray, *Financial Keynesianism and Market Instability*, Levi Economics Institute Working Paper No. 653, March 2011; J. Kregel, *The Natural Instability of Financial Markets*, 2009, IDEAs Working Paper no.04/2009, 2009; J. Crotty, 'Structural causes of the global financial crisis: a critical assessment of the "new financial architecture"', *Cambridge Journal of Economics*, vol. 33, no. 4, 2009, pp. 563–80.

48 In the US, it took twenty-eight months to recover all of the jobs that were lost in the 1981 recession, thirty-two months to recover after 1990, forty-seven months to replace the jobs lost due to the 2001 recession and a staggering seventy-five months to recover from the Great Recession that began in 2007.

49 Improving labour market conditions alone did not push the budget into surplus. The dot-com bubble, which led to a huge spike in capital gains taxes, also played an important role.

50 Cited in W. R. Garside, *British Unemployment 1919–1939: A Study in Public Policy*, Cambridge, Cambridge University Press, 1990, p. 347.

51 See e.g. P. De Grauwe and J. Yuemei, 'Panic-driven austerity in the eurozone and its implications', Vox, 2013, http://www.voxeu.org/article/panic-driven-austerity-eurozone-and-its-implications (accessed 4 May 2016).

52 There is no special reason for delineating at 3 per cent in this example, apart from the fact that there is a sort of natural break in the data at this rate. It is also close to the average (3.1 per cent) level of deficits the US has run from 1974 to 2013.

53 Countries that borrow in a foreign currency (including the eighteen countries that now use the euro) and those that operate a convertible currency (i.e. fixed exchange rate) face an entirely different set of constraints that limit their policy options. Frank Newman, former Deputy Secretary of the US Treasury, provides a more detailed explanation in his recent book *Six Myths That Hold America Back: And What America Can Learn From the Growth of China's Economy*, Kansas City, MO, Diversion Publishing.

54 A. P. Lerner, 'The economic steering wheel', *University of Kansas Review*, June 1941; 'Functional finance and the federal debt', *Social Research*, vol. 10, no. 1, 1943, pp. 38–51; *The Economics of Control*, New York, Macmillan, 1944; *The Economics of Employment*, New York, McGraw Hill, 1951.

3. Understanding Money and Macroeconomic Policy

L. RANDALL WRAY AND YEVA NERSISYAN

Introduction

MACROECONOMIC POLICY is not working. The best part of a decade after the financial crisis, developed economies have still not returned to anything like normal conditions. Unprecedentedly low interest rates, continuing high deficits, weak growth in most countries and anxieties over the risks of deflation indicate painfully that policy-makers have not been successful in restoring their economies to health.

Yet it is not for want of trying. Though initially governments reacted to the crisis by introducing fiscal stimulus packages, these were short-lived. As growth rates plunged, initial fiscal stimulus measures, combined with falling tax revenues and other automatic stabilisers, served to raise government deficits and debt. These in turn fuelled calls for fiscal austerity. As sovereign debt in the euro zone rose, further support was lent to the claim that governments had to balance their budget or else face the catastrophic consequences of higher borrowing costs and unsustainable debt repayments. The successive crises in which Greece found itself were said to be a warning to all.[1]

With the emphasis turning toward fiscal austerity, governments looked toward respective monetary authorities and monetary policy to help lift their economies out of a slump. The US Federal Reserve and the Bank of England started by using conventional policy tools, lowering interest rates. But in the face of continuing recession they then found themselves compelled to try more unconventional approaches, first providing liquidity facilities to financial institutions and then engaging in large-scale asset purchase programmes, known as quantitative easing (QE). The European Central Bank (ECB) gradually followed suit, despite anxieties that this would violate its constitutional powers. The scale of these operations was staggering: between 2008 and 2014 the cumulative total of the bail-out, liquidity support and credit guarantees the Federal Reserve provided to the financial sector amounted to $27.8 trillion.[2] The Fed also purchased over around $4.5 trillion of assets under QE mechanisms. The Bank of England started its asset purchase programme in 2009, buying £375 billion worth of assets, largely gilts, by autumn 2012.[3] Yet both banking systems and economies as a whole remain worryingly fragile.

The justifications for austerity policies are rooted in orthodox monetary theory. In this view, government spending should be constrained by the

Published by John Wiley & Sons Ltd, 9600 Garsington Road, Oxford OX4 2DQ, UK and 350 Main Street, Malden, MA 02148, USA

amount of revenue it raises through taxation and borrowing. The government should try to balance its budget, if not every year, then at least over the medium term, so as to avoid an unsustainable increase in its debt. Government finances should be subjected to close market scrutiny and discipline. To reduce market uncertainty and allay lenders' concerns about any potential risk of government insolvency and default, sovereign debt levels should be limited to what governments can readily service out of tax revenues. More importantly, governments should not be allowed to 'print money' to finance their spending. To do so would be inflationary.

While in most countries these principles are a matter of policy, in the euro zone they are built in to the design. Individual governments effectively gave up their power to 'print money' when they adopted the euro issued by the supranational ECB; any flexibility they might have is only with the acquiescence of the ECB. They also agreed to fiscal rules that set ceilings on government deficits and debt as a proportion of gross domestic product (GDP). As these limits risked being exceeded during any downturn as a result of the operation of automatic stabilisers, the aim was for governments to balance budgets over the course of the business cycle—surpluses in good times would provide the policy space to run small deficits in recessions. In sum, orthodox theory places the government on the same footing as private firms and households, whose ability to spend is constrained by their income and borrowing and by financial markets' view of their creditworthiness.

While the orthodox view underpinning current macroeconomic policy is widely acknowledged, it is less often observed that this in turn rests on a very particular theory of money. Rarely questioned in ordinary life, the creation and regulation of money in modern economies is in fact a highly complex—and contested—subject. In this chapter we shall show how different theories of money give rise to very different views on macroeconomic policy.

In particular we explore how the approach known as 'modern money theory' offers a much richer understanding of how money works than the orthodox view; and in turn how this casts new light on why current macroeconomic policy has not succeeded—and what would do better.[4] We will seek to show how this understanding of contemporary financial systems can demonstrate why fiscal policy is a much more powerful and effective tool than monetary policy for combating recessionary forces and stimulating growth. For a nation with its own currency, government spending is not constrained by available funding from taxation or borrowing. Government budgets are not like household budgets and thus the current emphasis on fiscal austerity is misplaced. We shall argue that low interest rates and unconventional monetary policy measures, such as QE, are at best weak in stimulating aggregate spending in the economy and do little to address concerns about the indebtedness of households and companies.

The deeper problems today's economies face are complex, related to the longer-term processes of increased financialisation. This is discussed by William Lazonick, Andrew Haldane and Mariana Mazzucato in their chapters in this volume.[5] In this chapter we confine the analysis to arguing that only with a proper understanding of the nature of money can the role of national fiscal policy be properly understood.

The orthodox view: exogenous money

Many economics textbooks offer brief accounts of the origins and evolution of money.[6] Some typically note how money reduced the inefficiencies of barter, thereby facilitating the exchange of goods and services, and then go on to describe the evolution of paper money as a promise 'to pay the bearer' a specified amount of a valuable commodity such as gold or silver in exchange. The available supply of the precious metal set limits on the amount of paper IOUs ('I-owe-yous') that could be issued. In turn, there was always a risk of default—failure to pay the valuable commodity if there was a sudden rush to redeem paper for gold. Eventually, according to this basic account, governments issued 'fiat money', that is, national currencies no longer backed by any commodity.

But from an orthodox perspective, the problem with fiat money is that there are no natural limits to its supply once it is freed from a commodity backing such as gold. The growth of fiat money can outstrip the growth in the volume of output produced each year in the economy. This creates the danger that excess growth in the supply of fiat money would lead to inflation, with 'too much money chasing too few goods'. This 'quantity theory of money', subsequently developed by Milton Friedman, argued that if governments were allowed simply to 'print money' to finance spending, this would inevitably lead to higher inflation.[7]

Consequently, orthodox economists believe that government spending should largely be constrained by tax revenue. Governments can also borrow, but this must necessarily be limited. First, if governments borrow to finance spending they will compete with the private sector for loanable funds and will thus push up interest rates, which in turn will 'crowd out' private borrowing and spending. Second, forward-looking households will take the view that deficit spending today will have to be paid for by taxes in the future; accordingly, they will curb spending today and save more. In the extreme case, proponents of the orthodox view believe that government spending has no positive impact on the economy, since private spending decreases sufficiently to offset the increase in government spending, effectively making for a zero multiplier effect. Lastly, if government debt as a proportion of GDP gets too high, and financial markets believe there is a high risk of default, governments may be charged such high interest rates that they are effectively shut out from financial markets and left unable to borrow at all.

From an orthodox perspective, the quantity of fiat money in existence appears to be 'exogenous' to the real economy. That is, the supply of money is determined by the central authorities independently and separately from the production of goods and services. This idea lies at the heart of the 'classical dichotomy' in macroeconomics, where monetary variables are seen as independent of real variables. In the orthodox view an excess growth of this exogenously determined money supply relative to the growth in real output causes a rise in the general price level; for this reason, controlling the money supply is central to the control of inflation.

Endogenous money and modern money theory

But this view of money does not actually accord with the facts. As Hyman Minsky pointed out, money is not created simply by the central authorities.[8] It is effectively created whenever commercial banks lend money, since such lending increases the purchasing power of those who borrow. It is therefore the demand for loans by businesses and households in the economy which determines the money supply. Money, in other words, is *endogenous* to the real economy, and is not independent of the production of goods and services at all. It is this insight which lies at the heart of 'modern money theory'.[9]

But though most money is not created by government, the state nevertheless has a crucial role in its supply of the currency, which in modern economies is a 'fiat' IOU issued by the treasury or central bank. The question arises as to why anyone would accept fiat money at all. On a British £5 note is written 'I promise to pay the bearer on demand the sum of five pounds'. But the Bank of England would not give the holder of this note anything other than another government IOU—that is, another £5 note (or the equivalent sum in coins). It is frequently assumed that the acceptance of government IOUs is due to the simple fact that they are 'legal tender' within a particular national jurisdiction. But in fact this is neither a sufficient nor a necessary condition; after all, in several countries the US dollar is used interchangeably with the local currency despite it having no official legal tender in these jurisdictions. In reality, the reason why, for example, British households and business accept pounds, and US ones dollars, is because they have to make payments—including, importantly, taxes—to their respective governments. It is the tax obligations that are required and enforced by the sovereign state that ensure wider use of their currency. While the government cannot readily force others to use its currency in private payments, it can force use of its own currency to meet the tax obligations it imposes.

The ability of the state to impose and enforce taxes creates an important advantage for a sovereign government. If the state's currency is not pegged to another currency or metal, then it is *the* means of final settlement in an economy. This allows the government to spend by issuing its own IOUs.[10] The imposition of taxes grants the government credit against the entities who owe taxes. The ability to spend by issuing tokens of indebtedness therefore allows the government to move resources from the private to the public sector—the basis of its capacity to achieve public purposes.

In the past, states directly spent their metallic coins and paper notes into existence and then collected them as payment. In contemporary English the word revenue can be traced from the Latin *revenire*, meaning return, through the old French *revenue*, meaning returned. What was returned? The state's own debts. We still use the term 'tax return' from which most of the state's revenue derives. But today, states no longer spend coins and notes into existence, nor accept tax payments in those forms. Rather, state spending and taxing is handled through electronic book-keeping, a computerised system of debits and credits on the balance sheets of the central bank and private banks. This adds a layer of operations that obscures, but does not fundamentally change, the nature of sovereign spending.

The modern financial system is an elaborate system of electronic record-keeping. Instead of money being created 'at the stroke of a pen' it is now created through a series of keystrokes on the computer. Credits and debits are entered electronically. Understanding the central bank's balance sheet provides a critical insight into the nature of government spending and finances.[11] Commercial banks hold their own accounts at the central bank and the latter also acts as banker to the government (e.g. the Federal Reserve acts as banker to the US Treasury). Government spending and taxation occur through electronic entries. When the US government spends, the Fed credits the reserves of private banks who have accounts with the central bank. When taxes are paid, the central bank debits the private bank's reserves.

Some may find that somewhat bewildering. Yet the relationship between the treasury and the central bank and that between the central bank and commercial banks is not as complex as it first appears.[12] When governments pay civil servants this occurs via electronic transmission to the commercial bank accounts of the employees. The central bank credits the receiving bank's reserves, while the commercial bank credits the employee's deposit account. For this reason, any spending by the national government results in a rise in bank reserves held at the central bank. The key point is that the government did not have to wait for any tax revenue to be made available in order to pay the civil servants in the first place. It happened at a keystroke.

It follows from this that the claim that a sovereign government is financially constrained is simply wrong. A sovereign government cannot become insolvent in its own currency and it clearly does not need tax revenue before it can spend. On the contrary: if taxpayers need to use the national currency (i.e. government fiat money IOUs) to pay taxes, then the government must spend before taxes can be paid. In practice, tax payments reverse the procedures outlined above: the deposit account of the taxpayer is debited by the commercial bank, and the central bank debits the reserves of the commercial bank. If the state is the only source of government IOUs, then, as a matter of logic, it must issue them first and receive them later. Once government IOUs are 'returned' in the form of tax or other payments to the state, they simply cancel the government's 'debt' as the outstanding stock of IOUs is reduced. It is this 'cancelling out' that occurs electronically on central bank balance sheets.

This process is perhaps easier to see in relation to government bonds (such as US Treasury bonds), since bonds are normally what make up most of 'government debt' (the rest takes the form of cash plus bank reserves). When a bond matures, the government pays the bondholder by crediting the bond-holder bank's reserve account at the central bank; the commercial bank then credits the bondholder's account at their private bank. While it may seem that this operation reduces government debt, in reality it simply substitutes one type of debt for another, as the outstanding stock of bonds (government liabilities or IOUs) goes down, but the level of reserves (also government liabilities or IOUs) goes up. By contrast, when tax payments are made to the government, the level of reserves goes down without an offsetting increase in any other government liability, thus lowering the outstanding level of government IOUs and debt.

This may seem as if we are suggesting that governments *sometimes* 'print money' to finance their spending. It is often thought that governments have a choice on how to finance their spending, through taxation, borrowing or printing money. But 'printing money'—or, more accurately, crediting bank accounts through electronic keystrokes, as it is currently done—is not something government can either choose to do or to avoid. Rather, it is the *only* way that a sovereign government spends. Through the system of electronic credits and debits, government spending *always* leads to an increase in bank reserves. Arguing that governments have a choice between debt financing (which is regarded as unsustainable) and money financing (which is seen to be inflationary) is based on a misunderstanding of how modern governments spend. In fact, both tax payments and bond sales logically come *after* the government has spent.

One may wonder, then, why sovereign governments sell bonds if they do not need to raise revenue by 'borrowing'. After all, policy-makers typically think that when governments sell treasury bonds they are engaging in a borrowing operation to finance their spending, whereas when the central bank sells bonds this is regarded simply as an 'open market operation' for purposes of monetary policy. From the point of view of the respective sellers this is a valid way of looking at the operations. However, from the point of view of the buyers of bonds, the impact is exactly the same: the private banks will end up holding fewer reserves and more bonds. In either case, reserves must exist before government bonds can be purchased, since the purchase can be completed only by debiting bank reserves.

Another simple example serves to illustrate this point. The only avenue for private entities to purchase government bonds is through their commercial bank account. So when a government sells its bonds, the buyer's bank facilitates the purchase for them by offering reserves they hold at the central bank. The central bank will then debit that bank's reserves and credit the balance of the government treasury. The net result is that the central bank has reduced its IOUs to the commercial bank but increased its IOU to the treasury; the treasury's IOU to the bond purchaser is balanced by its claim on the central bank; the commercial bank's claim on the central bank as well as its deposit IOU to the bond purchaser are eliminated; and the bond purchaser's deposit claim on the commercial bank is exchanged for a bond claim on the treasury. The key point here is that banks must already have reserves before they buy treasury bonds. The reserves must have been created by the central bank to allow the purchase of treasury bonds to go forward.

So for the sale of government bonds to proceed, the central bank and private banks will need to have put in place operating procedures to ensure banks can obtain reserves that can be used to purchase the bonds when they are sold. There are a number of ways that reserves to purchase bonds can be provided, either in advance or simultaneously: (a) the central bank can stand ready to lend them; (b) treasury spending will lead to credits to banking system reserves; (c) the central bank can buy bonds (open market purchase) at the same time that the treasury sells bonds; and (d) the central bank could also allow the banks more 'float', that is, let them buy bonds while postponing debiting their reserves (which amounts to the same thing as lending reserves).

We do not need to go more deeply into the technical details. All that is important to understand is that banks *must have* reserves (a debt at the central bank branch of government) in order to buy treasury bonds (a debt at the treasury branch of government). These reserves must have been created either through the central bank or by government spending to allow the purchase to go forward. The effect of bond sales is to substitute higher-earning bonds for low-earning reserves in the portfolio of the private sector.

So seen from the perspective of modern money theory, sovereign governments do not need to 'borrow' their own currency in order to spend. They offer bonds on which banks, households, businesses and foreigners can earn interest. They do this out of choice rather than necessity. Governments do not need to sell bonds *before* they spend; indeed, they cannot sell them without reserves being in place. Reserves are provided either through government spending (i.e. fiscal policy) or through central bank operations (i.e. lending or open market purchases).

In sum, modern money theory observes, a sovereign government with its own currency (and central bank) is *not* financially constrained. Its spending is not 'financed' by tax and bond revenue. As a matter of logic, government spending or central bank lending must precede tax collections and bond sales. Moreover, all government spending is already 'money financed' and can remain so simply by leaving the reserves in the system and foregoing bond sales.

We should be clear that this *does not* mean that government should spend without limits. Although modern money theory recognises that a sovereign government with its own currency can always afford to spend (via a few keystrokes on computerised accounting systems), it does not suggest that it should. While governments do not face financial constraints, they do have to deal with real resource constraints. For example, spending in excess of the output gap can lead to inflation. Spending on particular resources that are already being fully utilised in the private sector can lead to higher prices for those resources (though not necessarily a general price increase). Inflation results from too much spending, not too much money per se, although the two are usually conflated. How this spending is 'financed' does not determine its inflationary impact.

The recognition that the government is not financially constrained does not necessarily lead to a particular view on how much a government *should* spend. There may be good reasons why the government should spend less, but claims that the government is 'running out of money' or 'is becoming insolvent' should not be one of them. Austerity efforts in the US and UK are now rarely done in the name of 'controlling inflation'. Rather, the case for fiscal consolidation is based on claims that these countries are 'running out of money' or spending in excess of 'hard-working taxpayers' money' such that governments need to 'tighten their belts', as if the government budget were the same as a household budget. By contrast, a fiscal policy based on a correct understanding of the nature of money would only call for austerity measures if the economy were facing inflationary pressures.

Money and monetary policy

We observed earlier that the orthodox view of money is particularly concerned that an exogenously determined excess amount of money in the economy will lead to inflation. As Marvin Goodfriend has put it in relation to the ending of the gold-dollar standard underpinning international monetary relations in the early 1970s: 'With the collapse of Bretton Woods, for the first time in modern history, all the world's currencies were de-linked from gold or any other commodity. The lack of any formal constraint on money creation contributed to nervousness about inflation.'[13] Orthodox economists, informed by the quantity theory of money, felt that monetary policy-makers should ensure that the quantity of money available in the economy did not contribute to inflation.

The push to mandate central banks to target inflation can be understood as a way to establish some anchor for the value of 'fiat money'. As Paul Volcker, the former chair of the Federal Reserve Board (1979–87), observed in the midst of the subprime crisis: 'We all live in a world of fiat money. Nothing lies behind the dollar, the euro, or any national currency other than trust—trust that, at the end of the day, central banks and governments will resist the temptation to inflate. Maintaining that trust is particularly crucial in the case of a nation and a currency that has been, and still is, at the heart of the international financial system.'[14] Since the dollar is not backed by any 'real' commodity, the entity that controls its quantity must be committed to price stability to ensure that citizens and businesses continue to accept their paper money. Today, having been given greater independence in the overall conduct of monetary policy, most central banks are explicitly committed to the pursuit of price stability as part of their constitutional mandates.

Despite what many commentators may believe, central banks do not independently and directly inject money into the economy. Almost all of the money we use today has been created by private banks through their lending. Central bank money in the form of reserves is held only by commercial banks and cannot get into the economy; central bank money in the form of paper notes does get into the economy, but only to satisfy the public's demand for cash (as bank deposits are converted at ATM machines—changing the form of the money but not the quantity in the hands of the public). Nevertheless, orthodox monetary theory has long argued that the central bank can control the amount of money available in the economy.

In the orthodox view, private banks are merely financial intermediaries who receive deposits from customers and then lend these funds to borrowers. They keep a proportion of the deposited funds back in the form of reserves, so as to meet day-to-day withdrawals and clearing. Banks may voluntarily set their own reserve ratio that they deem prudent, or it may be a legal requirement (as in the US). The person who borrowed the money will spend it and the recipient will deposit money received at their own bank, allowing further bank loans to be made. As this process of further bank lending continues, the total amount of deposits (bank money) created is a simple multiple of the initial increase in the first bank's reserves created by the initial deposit. Alternatively, the central bank can lend reserves to commercial banks, which then allows them to create a multiplied quantity of bank money through loans through a similar process. This is the so-called 'money or deposit multiplier' familiar to economic students taught the orthodox view.

Since central banks are the ultimate source of reserves in the economy, this view holds that a central bank can control the amount of bank lending by constraining private banks' access to reserves. It can do so directly through open market sales—if the central bank sells securities to the private sector, banks will have to pay for these with reserves, thereby reducing them. Alternatively the central bank can use indirect means to curb bank lending. If, for example, it decides to increase the interest rates at which it lends to banks, it makes borrowing more costly for banks and thereby discourages further lending. Finally, the central bank can tighten up on its own lending of reserves.

For proponents of modern money theory, however, this view of the process of bank credit creation, and the accompanying belief that the central bank can control the quantity of money available in the economy, is a fiction. Banks do not in fact lend from the deposits made by households and businesses. When a household goes to a bank for a loan, the bank does not wait for others to deposit funds of equal value in order to be able to approve the borrowing request and make the loan. Assuming they judge the household to be creditworthy, the bank will simply credit the household's account with the deposit money requested. In other words, new money has been created on demand. Banks do not need to have deposits or reserves before they issue loans—they create the deposits as they make the loans.

In contrast to the orthodox view in which deposits create loans, modern money theory sees bank loans as creating deposits, thus creating the need for reserves either to meet reserve requirements or for clearing purposes. If necessary, banks will turn to the central bank to borrow reserves. In other words, the supply of bank money is not independent of the demand for bank money; it results from it, as banks create deposits when they make loans to creditworthy borrowers who want them. This is what is meant by money being endogenously determined. Bank money is created to meet the demand, regardless of the quantity of reserves in the system. While the orthodox money multiplier view of monetary policy is still taught in most textbooks, it is not how money is created in practice. Today even central bank economists acknowledge that banks do not wait for deposits, that bank money is created on demand and that lending is not reserve-constrained.[15]

One may argue that the central bank can limit banks' access to reserves, thus discouraging them from granting loans. But this would ignore the reality of central bank policy-making today. If a central bank pursues an interest rate target, then it cannot, in practice, refuse to supply reserves. If a commercial bank does not have enough reserves for clearing or to maintain a required amount, then it will try to borrow them from other banks in the money market at the overnight interest rate. If the banking system as a whole is short of reserves, the competition between banks for a limited amount of reserves will bid up the overnight rate—possibly above the central bank's target interest rate. So if the central bank wants to secure its target rate, it will *have to* supply reserves. This is usually done through an open market purchase, where the central bank buys a security, paying for it with reserves. In the opposite situation, when banks have more reserves than they desire, the central bank needs to drain reserves through an open market sale to prevent the interest rate from dropping below its target. In this sense open market operations are defensive operations, where the central bank supplies or drains reserves to private banks to 'defend' its interest rate target from pressures that push the actual overnight interest rate away from its target. But more importantly, the central bank has to provide reserves when banks need them, or else risk jeopardising clearing between banks. This is indeed arguably the most important reason why the central bank cannot choose not to supply the reserves.[16]

In sum, while the orthodox view sees central banks as choosing between controlling reserves and controlling interest rates, endogenous money theory argues that interest rate control is in fact the only tool at the central bank's disposal. The quantity of money in the economy in practice depends on many variables, with interest rates being only one of them. In any case, once one disposes of the quantity theory of money, the stock of money in the economy becomes a relatively unimportant variable. What is important for the economy is the total level of aggregate demand, and the quantity of money does not determine its level, but rather is mostly a consequence of the decision to lend to finance desired spending.

Quantitative easing

Since the onset of the financial crisis in the US and Europe, and with inflation below central bank targets, increasing attention has been paid to the risk of economies descending into a deflationary spiral similar to that experienced during the so-called 'lost decade' in Japan in the 1990s (now approaching three lost decades).[17] Monetary policy-makers were confronted with the limits of the conventional tools of monetary policy: how could they attempt to stimulate private spending with further cuts to interest rates when their key short-term rates were already near zero? The situation was exacerbated by the fact that private banks were displaying greater caution in lending to households and businesses, as they tightened up assessments of creditworthiness and sought to meet domestic prudential banking reforms and international guidelines in relation to leverage ratios and capital requirements.

The result was the use of unconventional monetary policy tools such as QE designed to increase liquidity in credit markets and to encourage banks to lend to households and businesses. The US Federal Reserve embarked on three QE programmes (2008–2014) amounting to a cumulative total of $4.2 trillion. The Bank of England undertook £375 billion of asset purchases under QE over the period between March 2009 and July 2012. The European Central Bank was slower to embark on QE. Nevertheless, a minimum of €1 trillion was allocated for QE and the ECB committed €60 billion per month from January 2015 through to March 2017.[18]

These central banks differed slightly in their rationales for QE and their views regarding the precise nature and duration of the 'transmission mechanism', that is, the process whereby the provision of extra liquidity would translate into higher spending and output. But in general policy-makers hoped that QE would promote the necessary spending to sustain hesitant economic recoveries. The policy of QE was based on the view that the banking system following the financial crisis was somehow 'starved of cash' and that the purchase of bonds and other securities by the central bank would therefore provide the reserves required for recalcitrant banks to lend to credit-constrained private businesses and households. In this way growth in the economy would be rekindled. Some opponents of QE, from a more orthodox perspective of money, warned that this electronic 'printing of money' by the central bank to purchase securities held privately would eventually prove to be inflationary. From the perspective of modern money theory, however, both these views are misguided. Both misunderstand how money is created in the modern banking system.

As we saw in the previous section, bank lending is not constrained by reserves. Banks do not need additional reserves to push them to lend, nor can banks lend reserves except to one another (the reserves created through QE remain in the banks and cannot get out into the economy to finance spending). Therefore having more reserves will not induce banks to lend more. What banks need are willing and creditworthy borrowers, and these have been relatively lacking in recent years as both households and firms have focused on paying down their accumulated debts and governments have reduced public spending. The problem, in other words, lies in the demand for finance, not its supply. If borrowers do emerge, then banks will increase lending, which in turn will boost spending in the economy. And so long as the economy experiences only weak recovery, with continuing spare capacity and high unemployment in the economy, QE is also unlikely to prove inflationary. Banks could have made additional loans even without the additional reserves they acquired through QE. Therefore, QE is no more inflationary than any central bank open market operation designed to increase reserves in the banking system.

When the central bank buys bonds and other securities, at a keystroke it electronically credits the reserves of the banks equivalent to the value of securities it has purchased. So QE is essentially an electronic accounting adjustment reflecting the exchange of securities for reserves. In other words, what QE really does is exchange one type of asset (long-term government securities) for another (bank reserves) held on bank balance sheets. This change in the composition of commercial bank portfolios does not raise the incomes of private businesses and households, and should not therefore be expected to generate more spending.

The manner in which QE 'works' is in fact not unlike the way conventional monetary policy uses interest rates to shape business and household borrowing and spending. QE affects longer-term interest rates through the central bank's purchases of longer-term bonds and securities, raising their price and lowering their return. It may also affect other interest rates in the economy by reducing the 'term spread' (the difference between short-term and long-term interest rates) and 'risk spread' (the difference on yields between different debt instruments according to market perceptions of credit risk).[19] Lowering long-term rates, in turn, will boost any interest-sensitive spending. The housing sector, for example, is generally considered to be more sensitive to interest rate movements, although this varies across countries.

In sum, the impact of QE on aggregate demand, and thus on the real economy, largely depends on the ability of interest rate reductions to stimulate more spending. In practice, since overnight rates were already near to zero and longer-term rates were very low, QE was not able to lower rates much. However, were QE to work, it would do so almost entirely through private sector leverage, not through additional income or net wealth for the sector.[20] And increasing private sector indebtedness is arguably not a desirable course of action in economies that continue to suffer from debt overhang.

There is a way in which QE can create additional private sector income. If its scale is significant enough to push up the prices of the financial assets being purchased by the central bank, this would represent an increase in the private sector's equity via a capital gain. When realised, this would generate income. In this sense, QE would effectively be an act of fiscal policy.[21] But this is not the professed goal of quantitative easing, in the United States or elsewhere. As Ben Bernanke—chair of the Federal Reserve Board throughout the financial crisis—argued, asset purchases 'with a fiscal component, even if legal, would be correctly viewed as an end run around the authority of the legislature, and so are better left in the realm of theoretical curiosities'.[22]

Yet we should also note that, if the goal of QE is to boost aggregate demand, its impact may not be entirely positive. While lower rates *may* boost interest-sensitive spending, they also lower private sector interest income (in particular, interest received from government bonds) and thus consumption.[23] And concerns have been raised about the distributional effects. The Bank of England has concluded that QE in the UK disproportionately benefited higher income groups: by pushing up a range of asset prices, asset purchases have boosted the value of households' financial wealth held outside pension funds. Such holdings are heavily skewed, with the top 5 per cent of households holding 40 per cent of these assets.[24]

Overall, QE suffers from the same problem that plagues conventional monetary policy: it is a blunt tool for stimulating aggregate demand. If policy-makers were finally to recognise that the core problem of the developed economies today is insufficient aggregate demand, then there is a better tool for tackling that, namely fiscal policy. With a proper understanding of the nature of money, we could use this powerful tool to boost income and employment without having to engage in roundabout QE gymnastics.

Implications for the euro zone: the re-integration of money and fiscal policy

The region of the world which has experienced perhaps the most damaging outcomes from the application of the orthodox theory of money to macroeconomic policy-making is the euro zone. In many ways the design of the European single currency was based on the orthodox theory, and it has severely limited the ability of euro-zone countries to deal with the aftermath of the financial crisis.

It is crucial to recognise here that the emergence of sovereign debt problems within the euro zone after the crisis broke in 2008 cannot be simply put down to 'profligate spending' by irresponsible governments. Notwithstanding legitimate concerns about Greek accounting practices and tax collection, most economies on Europe's periphery (Greece, Italy, Spain, Portugal and Ireland) only experienced debt problems once their economies had entered into recession after the crash. But from that point on, they were severely hampered in their attempts to respond.

As Stephanie Kelton's chapter in this volume explains, the financial positions of the private sector, the public sector and the foreign sector are interlinked. If one sector is in deficit, then it follows that at least one of the other sectors must be in surplus. This is a matter of basic national macro-economic accounting identities: together, all sectoral balances must add up to zero. This simple insight offers the key to understanding the nature of the economic problems afflicting the euro zone.

From the perspective of sectoral financial balances, what happened in euro-zone economies after the crisis was that the domestic private sector moved toward surplus, as indebted households cut back on spending, businesses shelved their investment plans and fragile financial institutions reduced their lending. At the same time most of these economies were experiencing persistent deficits on their trade balances, partly a reflection of the strength of Germany's exports with a competitive euro replacing its strong mark, and its resulting current account surplus. So it was simply a matter of macroeconomic accounting that the domestic private sector surplus in most countries (saving in excess of investment) had to be mirrored in national public sector deficits (government spending in excess of revenues).

While each country's circumstances were different (in Ireland and Spain, for example, the bursting of property bubbles had a big impact), the rise in government deficits and debt in the economies of Europe's periphery was mainly due to the operation of the 'automatic stabilisers' in the downturn resulting from lower tax and other revenues and higher social security payments, along with some discretionary spending measures aimed at rescuing ailing banks. Falling incomes, rising unemployment and deleveraging all contributed to falling private sector spending. The crisis triggered increased saving by households and a reduction in investment by businesses, which was then mirrored in rising public sector deficits. The latter were not the result of policy-makers purposefully and irresponsibly spending more than they could 'afford'.

Yet EU institutions responded to the financial crisis not by allowing public sector deficits to rise, but by strengthening their commitment to fiscal consolidation. The so-called 'fiscal compact' (Treaty on Stability, Coordination and Governance) embedded a commitment to balanced budgets while subjecting governments to greater EU-level surveillance. But domestic public sector balances can only move toward surplus if this is offset by rising budget deficits (except in those few countries that could achieve trade surpluses). If all governments are obliged to cut back on spending/or raise taxes simultane-ously, irrespective of the state of their economies, then this effectively imparts a deflationary bias to the euro-zone economy. Implementing austerity in weakened economies when the private sector is unwilling or unable to reduce net savings inevitably hit economic growth. As most euro-zone governments found, efforts to reduce government deficits were not only difficult but self-defeating, with deficits rising instead of declining.

Crucially, individual euro-zone governments could not rely on obtaining revenue from other EU countries or from the centre. Unlike the US, for example, where federal government revenues are automatically transferred to states experiencing slower growth and higher unemployment, the EU has no federal-level budget that automatically redistributes income from richer regions to poorer ones. (There is no 'Uncle Fritz' equivalent of 'Uncle Sam'.) The lack of an automatic fiscal transfer mechanism at EU level was reflected in the political tensions surrounding the negotiation of successive Greek rescue packages, where images were conjured up of hard-working German taxpayers having to bail out irresponsible and profligate governments in Athens. Such complaints—that New Yorkers have their hard-earned money transferred to poorer Mississippi—are rarely heard in the US. The EU budget is limited to around 1 per cent of EU GDP—smaller than Belgium's—and always has to be in balance.

Moreover, since euro-zone countries do not issue their own national currencies, the peripheral European governments could not indefinitely issue bonds to finance large and/or continuous budget deficits. At some point market discipline was going to catch up, forcing them into austerity. As countries accumulated debt, financial markets raised the risk premiums attached to their bonds. These higher interest rates only added to their deficits, risking accumulating sovereign debt turning into a wider solvency crisis and raising market fear of default. As Mathew Forstater noted in 1999, in euro-zone countries 'market forces can demand pro-cyclical fiscal policy during a recession, compounding recessionary influences'.[25] Most euro nations had no option but to turn to fiscal austerity at a moment when the opposite course was necessary.

The problem here arose directly from the orthodox view of money, which underpinned the euro zone. For any sovereign state that issues its own currency, in the quite unlikely event that financial markets refuse to buy government debt, there is always the option of its central bank acting as 'buyer of last resort'. That is, the central bank can purchase government bonds through an 'electronic keystroke.' But, unique among the major central banks, the ECB was set up without this function: it was explicitly prohibited from buying sovereign bonds in the new issue market. The orthodox view of money holds that if central banks can finance government deficits, this will erode fiscal discipline and lead to inflation. By not allowing the ECB to finance government deficits through electronic keystrokes, the EU therefore ensured that governments would be obliged to seek funding in financial

61

markets at market interest rates. If they borrowed too much, they would face the rising costs of servicing their debt and be forced to cut back on spending and/or to raise taxes. Limiting fiscal policy through market discipline was purposefully built into the design of the euro zone from the outset.

Had the ECB started buying the bonds of the deficit countries in the secondary markets early on, it would have mitigated market fears regarding the risk of sovereign default. It would also have lowered the interest rate these nations paid on their bonds, allowing them to stimulate their economies. While almost all major central banks intervened heavily during the financial crisis, the ECB did relatively little and then only gradually. In 2012, the ECB President, Mario Draghi, announced that it would do 'whatever it takes' to save the euro, establishing the Outright Monetary Transactions (OMT) programme through which the ECB would purchase an unlimited amount of sovereign bonds, but only in secondary markets and under certain conditions. This was a landmark decision, a de facto step toward 'buyer of last resort'; but it was later challenged in the German constitutional court, which declared that the ECB had violated its legal mandate.[26] Furthermore, in contrast to the Fed and the Bank of England, the ECB was also much slower to adopt quantitative easing (indeed, it did so at a time when the Fed had already begun the process of tapering its QE programme). With its own key interest rates at the zero bound, concerned about a prolonged period of inflation below its 2 per cent target, the ECB introduced its 'expanded asset purchase programme' in January 2015.[27]

The difficulty euro-zone governments have had in stabilising their economies and promoting growth results directly from the orthodox view of money under which the euro zone was created.[28] The euro zone was designed to prevent governments both from running large deficits and from creating money through central bank lending of last resort. Without the ability to keystroke their own currencies, and without fiscal transfers from richer regions, weaker euro-zone economies have been left largely unable to deal with accumulating sovereign debt and weak growth following the financial crisis and recession. The ECB's decision to 'bend the rules' and purchase unlimited quantities of sovereign bonds if needed—an explicit rejection of the orthodox view—gave the euro zone temporary respite. But if the prospect of long-term growth is to be restored, a much more fundamental recognition of the proper role of fiscal policy in boosting demand will be needed.

Conclusion

Prior to the financial crisis, policy-makers congratulated themselves for achieving low inflation, improving growth performance and financial stability. In the US, Fed Chairman Ben Bernanke described the apparent decline in macroeconomic volatility as the 'Great Moderation'. In Bernanke's view, it was largely due to the introduction of a successful monetary policy framework focused on ensuring price stability.[29] In Britain, Chancellor of the

Exchequer, and later Prime Minister, Gordon Brown declared that the Labour government (1997–2010) had aimed to avoid returning to the 'boom and bust' of previous eras. His confidence stemmed from his early decision to grant operational independence to the Bank of England in the conduct of a monetary policy. In his initial letter to the Bank of England, Brown wrote: 'price stability is a precondition for high and stable levels of growth and employment, which in turn will create the conditions for price stability on a sustainable basis.'[30]

But the Great Moderation thesis was blown away by the global financial crisis. And in the past decade the failure of macroeconomic policy based on the orthodox theory of money has been laid bare.

Resting on the belief that governments, like households, are financially constrained by their income, policy-makers have forced fiscal austerity onto their already weak economies and instead put their faith in the ability of monetary policy—both conventional and unconventional—to secure sustainable economic growth. Central banks in Japan, the US, the UK and the euro zone have all engaged in QE in hopes of boosting borrowing through lower interest rates. In the periphery of Europe, financial markets and the euro-zone authorities have pressurised countries to reduce their debt burdens even at the expense of mass unemployment and rising economic hardship. Even countries that did not face similar market pressures, such as the UK, have engaged in programmes of fiscal consolidation.

While central bank intervention as a lender of last resort is a critical component in the early stages of a financial crisis, once any run to liquidity is halted, there is not much more monetary policy can do once interest rates have fallen to the zero bound. Yet as we have seen, for countries whose fundamental problem is a lack of total spending in the economy, QE is a very blunt policy tool for increasing aggregate demand, to say the least. If it succeeds in doing so, it will only be by increasing already high levels of indebtedness in the private sector. Fiscal policy, on the other hand, can directly stimulate aggregate demand, with governments having a large degree of control as to where—and for whom—to boost spending. Further, such fiscal expansion can raise demand without worsening private sector balance sheets; indeed, government deficit spending actually improves private sector finances by providing income and safe government liabilities to accumulate in portfolios. As we have argued in this chapter, governments with monetary sovereignty are not financially constrained: they spend as they issue their own IOUs. They can use this capacity to buy real resources, and in doing so to promote full employment.

The priority of fiscal policy as a tool for economic stabilisation and management of growth is of course not a revelation: it was well understood in the postwar period. But the understanding at that time was incomplete. While it was commonplace to recognise that budget deficits were needed in downturns, the connection between fiscal policy and the *nature* of money was not well understood by most economists. So-called 'Keynesian' fiscal activism rested on weak monetary foundations. Similarly, the 'money' or 'deposit multiplier' view of private money creates a weak foundation for monetary policy. Modern money theory provides an alternative view of the endogenous nature of money in modern financial systems which leads to a much richer understanding of both fiscal and monetary policy. Applied intelligently, it would do much to make modern macroeconomic policy-making effective.

Notes

1 Several insightful publications on the Greek economy can be found at the Levy Economics Institute. See http://www.levyinstitute.org/topics/greek-economic-crisis (accessed 19 April 2016).

2 J. A. Felkerson, *$29,000,000,000,000: A Detailed Look at the Fed's Bailout by Funding Facility and Recipient*, Working Paper No. 698, Levy Economics Institute, December 2011.

3 Federal Reserve, http://www.federalreserve.gov/monetarypolicy/bst_crisisresponse.htm (accessed 19 April 2016); Bank of England, http://www.bankofengland.co.uk/monetarypolicy/Pages/qe/qe_faqs.aspx (accessed 19 April 2016); and M. Joyce and M. Spaltro, *Quantitative Easing and Bank Lending: A Panel Data Approach*, Bank of England Working Paper No. 504, 2014, http://www.bankofengland.co.uk/research/Documents/workingpapers/2014/wp504.pdf (accessed 19 April 2016).

4 L. R. Wray, *Modern Money Theory: A Primer on Macroeconomics for Sovereign Monetary Systems*, 2nd ed., Basingstoke, Palgrave Macmillan, 2015.

5 Other aspects of financialisation can be found in L. R. Wray, *Financial Markets Meltdown: What Can We Learn from Minsky?* Public Policy Brief Highlights No. 94A, Levy Economics Institute, 2008, http://www.levyinstitute.org/publications/financial-markets-meltdown-what-can-we-learn-from-minsky (accessed 19 April 2016). Alternative perspectives can be found in G. Epstein, ed., *Financialization and the World Economy*, Cheltenham, Edward Elgar, 2005.

6 See for example N. G. Mankiw, *Macroeconomics*, 9th ed., New York, Worth Publishers, 2016, and A. Abel, B. Bernanke and D. Croushore, *Macroeconomics*, 9th ed., Oxford, OUP, 2016.

7 M. Friedman, 'The role of monetary policy', *American Economic Review*, vol. LVIII, no. 1, 1968, pp 1–17. See also M. Friedman, 'An interview with Milton Friedman', Library of Economics and Liberty, September 2006, http://www.econlib.org/library/Columns/y2006/Friedmantranscript.html (accessed 19 April 2016).

8 H. P. Minsky, *Stabilizing an Unstable Economy*, New York, McGraw Hill, 2008. See also L. R. Wray, *Why Minsky Matters: An Introduction to the Work of a Maverick Economist*, Princeton, NJ, Princeton University Press, 2015.

9 Wray, *Modern Money Theory*.

10 It should be noted that within the European Union the Maastricht Treaty places legal limits on the ability of governments to increase public spending through money creation; but in principle those countries within the EU which have retained their own currencies could do so.

11 Wray, *Modern Money Theory*. See also L. R. Wray, *Understanding Modern Money: The Key to Full Employment and Price Stability*, Cheltenham, Edward Elgar, 1998; E. Tymoigne and L. R. Wray. *Modern Money Theory 101*, Working Paper No. 778, Levy Economics Institute, November 2013.

12 G. Rule, *CCBS Handbook No. 32 – Understanding the Central Bank Balance Sheet*, Bank of England, 2012, http://www.bankofengland.co.uk/education/Pages/ccbs/handbooks/ccbshb32.aspx (accessed 19 April 2016).

13 M. Goodfriend, *How the World achieved Consensus on Monetary Policy* (No. w13580), Cambridge, MA, National Bureau of Economic Research, 2007, p. 5.

14 P. A. Volcker, 'Rethinking a bright new world of global finance', *International Finance*, vol. 11, no. 1, 2008, pp. 101–7.

15 M. McLeay, A. Radia and R. Thomas, 'Money creation in the modern economy', *Bank of England Quarterly Bulletin*, vol. 54, no. 1, Q1, 2014, pp. 14–27.

16 S. T. Fullwiler, 'Timeliness and the Fed's daily tactics', *Journal of Economic Issues*, vol. 37, no. 4 (December 2003), 851–80.

17 'Europe's deflation risk', *OECD Observer No 300*, Q3 2014, October, http://www.oecdobserver.org/news/fullstory.php/aid/4485/Europe_92s_deflation_risk.html (accessed 19 April 2016). See also OECD Deflation Watch, http://www.oecdobserver.org/news/fullstory.php/aid/4807/Deflation_watch.html (accessed 19 April 2016).

18 Federal Reserve, http://www.federalreserve.gov/monetarypolicy/bst_crisisresponse.htm (accessed 19 April 2016); Bank of England, http://www.bankofengland.co.uk/monetarypolicy/Pages/qe/qe_faqs.aspx (accessed 19 April 2016); Joyce and Spaltro, *Quantitative Easing and Bank Lending*; ECB, https://www.ecb.europa.eu/mopo/implement/omt/html/index.en.html (accessed 19 April 2016).

19 A. Blinder, 'Quantitative easing: entrance and exit strategies', *Federal Reserve Bank of St. Louis Review*, vol. 92, no. 6, November/December, 2010, pp. 465–79.

20 S. T. Fullwiler, 'An endogenous money perspective on the post-crisis monetary policy debate', *Review of Keynesian Economics*, vol. 1, no. 2, summer 2013, pp. 171–94.

21 Ibid.

22 B. S. Bernanke, 'Japanese monetary policy: a case of self-induced paralysis?', paper presented at the ASSA meetings, Boston, MA, 9 January 2000, p. 24.

23. W. B. Mosler, 'The Fed is starving economy of interest income', *CNBC*, 24 January 2012, http://www.cnbc.com/id/46115110 (accessed 19 April 2016).

24 Bank of England, *The Distributional Effects of Asset Purchases*, 2012, http://www.bankofengland.co.uk/publications/Documents/news/2012/nr073.pdf (accessed 19 April 2016).

25 M. Forstater, 'The European Economic and Monetary Union: introduction', *Eastern Economic Journal*, vol. 25, no. 1, winter 1999, pp. 31–4.

26 P. De Grauwe, 'Economic theories that influenced the judges of Karlsruhe', *Vox*, 13 March 2014, http://www.voxeu.org/article/economic-flaws-german-court-decision (accessed 19 April 2016).

27 ECB, *Asset Purchase Programmes*, https://www.ecb.europa.eu/mopo/implement/omt/html/index.en.html (accessed 19 April 2016).

28 D. Papadimitriou and L. Randall Wray, *Euroland's Original Sin*, Levy Economics Institute Policy Note 2012/8, 2012.

29 B. S. Bernanke, *The Great Moderation*, Federal Reserve Board, 2004, http://www.federalreserve.gov/boarddocs/speeches/2004/20040220/ (accessed 19 April 2016).

30 G. Brown, *The New Monetary Policy Framework*, 1997, http://www.bankofengland.co.uk/monetarypolicy/Documents/pdf/chancellorletter970506.pdf (accessed 19 April 2016).

4. The Costs of Short-termism[1]

ANDREW G. HALDANE

Introduction

IS THE world becoming short-sighted? As individuals, it sometimes feels that way. Information is streamed in ever greater volumes and at ever rising velocities. Timelines for decision-making appear to have been compressed. Pressures to deliver immediate results seem to have intensified. Tenure patterns for some of our most important life choices (marriage, jobs, money) are in secular decline.[2] Some have called this the era of 'quarterly capitalism'.[3]

These forces may be altering not just the way we act, but also the way we think. Neurologically, our brains are adapting to increasing volumes and velocities of information by shortening attention spans. Technological innovation, such as the internet, may have caused a permanent neurological rewiring, as did previous technological revolutions such as the printing press and typewriter.[4] Like a transistor radio, our brains may be permanently retuning to a shorter wavelength.

If these forces are real, they might be expected to be particularly important in capital markets. These are a key conduit for choice over time. An efficient capital market transfers savings today into investment tomorrow and growth the day after. In that way, it boosts welfare. But modern capital markets are also well known to come with costs. As recent events have shown, the most visible and violent of those costs are experienced at times of financial crisis. These costs, for example in foregone output, have been extensively studied.[5]

But there is a second potential cost of modern capital markets—the cost of short-termism. Although it has no off-the-shelf definition, short-termism is generally taken to refer to the tendency of agents in the financial intermediation chain to weight too heavily near-term outcomes at the expense of longer-term opportunities.[6] This has opportunity costs, for example in foregone investment projects and hence future output.

Unlike crises, these opportunity costs are neither violent nor visible. Rather, they are silent and invisible. Perhaps for that reason, there have been very few attempts to capture the potential costs of short-termism in quantitative terms. Nevertheless, existing survey evidence is strongly suggestive of short-termist tendencies in modern capital markets. For example, a 2004 MORI survey of members of the Investment Managers Association (IMA) and the National Association of Pension Funds (NAPF) found one-third and two-thirds of members respectively believed their investment mandates encouraged short-termism.[7]

© 2016 Bank of England. The Political Quarterly © The Political Quarterly Publishing Co. Ltd. 2016
Published by John Wiley & Sons Ltd, 9600 Garsington Road, Oxford OX4 2DQ, UK and 350 Main Street, Malden, MA 02148, USA

A survey of Chief Executive Officers (CEOs) at Fortune 1000 firms indicated that the discount rates applied to future cash-flows were around 12 per cent, much higher than either equity holders' average rate of return or the return on debt.[8] Another survey of more than 400 executives found that more than 75 per cent would give up an NPV-positive project to smooth earnings.[9]

If investors discount future returns excessively, a manager seeking to maximise the value of the firm will prioritise near-term cash-flows over distant ones. In this chapter we provide evidence suggesting that investors do indeed apply an inefficiently high discount rate. We then show that ownership of the firm matters: private firms tend to invest more than equivalent publicly owned firms. Together, these findings suggest that short-termist distortions can affect materially the rates of investment by companies and the stock of capital. Finally, we draw out the implications, and policy choices, which flow from these costs of short-termism.

The literature on short-termism

The short-termism debate is not new. Excess discounting of future outcomes was a familiar theme among Classical economists. For Jevons, 'the untutored savage, like the child, is wholly occupied with the pleasures and troubles of the moment; the morrow is dimly felt; the limit of his horizon is but a few days off'.[10] For Marshall, people acted like 'children who pick the plums out of their pudding to eat them at once'.[11] For Pigou, it demonstrated a 'defective telescopic faculty' such that 'we see future pleasures on a diminished scale'.[12]

And nowhere were these problems more acute than in financial markets. Keynes, himself a part-time speculator, was well aware of the perils of short-termism in investment choice, both moral and financial: 'It is from time to time the duty of a serious investor to accept the depreciation of his holdings with equanimity without reproaching himself. Any other policy is anti-social, destructive of confidence and incompatible with the working of the economic system.'[13]

In the US, these sentiments were echoed in the immediate postwar era by Benjamin Graham, the original 'value investor' and yesteryear investment guru to today's investment guru, Warren Buffett: 'A serious investor is not likely to believe that the day-to-day or even month-to-month fluctuations of the stock market make him richer or poorer.'[14] And, famously, 'in the short run, the market is a voting machine but in the long run, it is a weighing machine'. Whether an untutored savage, defective telescope or anti-social voting machine, something sounded amiss.

Thus far, however, this evidence was largely anecdotal. It was not until the 1960s that the short-termism hypothesis was first tested empirically. This drew on survey evidence from investing firms. It was found that investors typically expected full payback on an investment within three to five years.

ANDREW G. HALDANE

At the time, the average life of plant and equipment was often ten times that.[15] Firms played short even when they desired long.

Fifty years on, formal, quantitative evidence on short-termism remains relatively thin on the ground. An exception is the work of Miles.[16] Using an augmented version of a basic asset pricing framework, he finds evidence of excessive discounting of future cash-flows using company-level equity price data from the UK. Similar approaches, applied to longer time-series across a range of countries, have reached broadly similar conclusions.[17]

There is also relatively little empirical evidence linking short-termism and investment. Asker, Farre-Mensa and Ljungqvist provide a test based on a panel of US companies.[18] They find that firms whose share prices (and, by implication, investors) are very sensitive to earnings announcements tend to forgo good investment opportunities. Firms that are held privately invest significantly more than similar public firms and are more responsive to investment opportunities.

Bernstein's work considers patents as a measure of innovation output.[19] The author compares US firms which went from private to public by listing on NASDAQ with similar ones which had started the process but did not complete it. The author finds that, after going public, firms do not reduce the number of patents registered, but they do tend to reduce innovation novelty (as measured by patent citations).

Some theoretical papers link short-termism and investment explicitly. This literature relies on informational problems which dividends can help solve, but at the expense of investment. In the model proposed by Miller and Rock, managers know the current state of earnings but investors do not.[20] Dividends provide a signal about earnings that investors can observe. This means the manager has the incentive to surprise the market with high dividends, even if this means cutting investment. Investors understand this and discount these inflated dividend signals accordingly.

A different type of information asymmetry is studied by Stein.[21] In his model, investors base their valuation of the firm on expected future earnings. Future earnings are known to be correlated with current earnings. The manager understands this and cuts investment to boost current earnings. This lifts expectations of future earnings, increasing the firm's share price.[22] In equilibrium, the manager's signal has no effect on share prices, but this behaviour continues to reduce investment.

Investors might also be uncertain about the quality of the manager, as in Narayanan's work.[23] In this model, shareholders cannot observe the manager's ability or the project that is selected. Profits are observable and boost the investor's perception of managerial ability, which translates into higher wages. Knowing this, the manager may select a project that yields short-term profits, even if there are better long-term projects available. Wagenhofer and Gigler, in two recent papers, explore how frequency of accounting disclosures may induce short-termism in firms, with adverse implications for investment.[24]

Empirical evidence of short-termism

A testable hypothesis from these models is that short-termism may have dented the willingness of firms to engage in investment spending. There are two related but distinct channels through which this might occur. The first is that short-termism raises to too-high levels the marginal cost of new capital to finance projects. This is the channel explored in the next section. The second channel is that short-termism induces firms to distribute an excessively high share of their revenues and profits to shareholders in the form of dividends. As William Lazonick argues in his chapter in this volume, this would come at the expense of ploughing back profits into the business to finance future investment growth opportunities. The section following provides illustrative estimates of the potential cost of short-termism in terms of forgone investment.

The impact of short-termism on investors' discount rates

In our first empirical assessment of short-termism we use a data set which comprises a panel of 624 firms listed on the UK FTSE and US S&P indices over the period 1980–2009.[25] Using an asset pricing formula, we can quantify the degree of short-termism that is implicit in firms' equity prices. Specifically, our model allows us to measure empirically the extent of excess discounting by investors. Our indicator of short-termism is the parameter x. If x equals one, investors apply the 'correct' discount rate (i.e. the one that reflects fundamentals). When x is lower than one, investors are applying an excessively high discount rate, meaning that market valuations are distorted by short-termism. We estimate the parameter x for each of the years 1985 to 2004.[26]

In the first decade (1985–1994) we find little evidence of excess discounting: on average x is approximately one. In the second decade (1995–2004), however, we find statistically significant evidence of short-termism: x is significantly lower than one in eight years out of ten. On average over this more recent period, the estimated x is 0.94, which implies a 6 per cent excess discounting.

The estimates of short-termism are economically as well as statistically significant. The estimates for x often lie between 0.90 and 0.95, suggesting excess discounting of between 5 per cent and 10 per cent per year. To illustrate the impact of this degree of myopia, let us consider a riskless investment project costing $60, which will pay a $10 dividend at the end of each of ten years. Figure 1 shows the present value of these income streams under three counter-factual assumptions: rational discounting; myopic discounting—lower bound (5%); and myopic discounting—upper bound (10%). The cumulative impact is fairly dramatic. Ten-year-ahead cash-flows under rational discounting (i.e. in the absence of short-termism) are valued similarly to between six-year (lower bound) and four-year (upper bound) ahead cash-flows under myopic discounting.

69

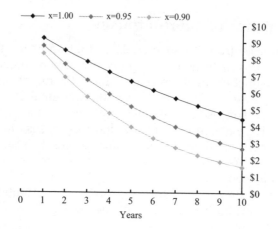

Figure 1: Present value of future cash-flows
Notes: The chart assumes $10 is paid at the end of each year. The risk-free discount rate used is 1.085.

This is illustrated even more clearly if we consider payback periods. Under rational discounting, payback occurs in nine years (Figure 2). Under upper-bound myopic discounting, the investor today would erroneously assume that payback would never be made. These differences have the potential to alter radically project choice. The net present value of this project evaluated over fifty years falls from $56 under rational discounting to a loss of $11 under extreme myopia. In other words, an NPV-positive project would be rejected.

The impact of short-termism on investment

Short-termism may induce firms to distribute an excessively high share of their revenues and profits to shareholders in the form of dividends, at the expense of retaining, or ploughing back, profits into the business to finance future growth opportunities. There is anecdotal evidence that firms may increasingly be seeking to actively manage the quantum and timing of their dividends. Haldane has presented evidence on firms seeking to maintain and smooth dividends.[27] Others have observed that firms engage in 'equity recycling'—issuing new equity at the same time as paying dividends, even though it would be less costly to simply cancel the dividend.[28] Over recent years, some firms continued to pay dividends, even though they were running at a loss. This is in stark contrast to dividend behaviour in the nineteenth and early twentieth centuries, when US and UK firms were as likely to reduce dividends as to raise them.[29]

As Mariana Mazzucato notes in her chapter in this volume, there is also evidence that investment in long-term research in the US and UK, two

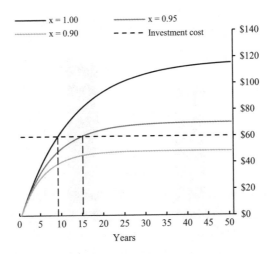

Figure 2: Cumulative present value of future cash-flows
Notes: The cumulative NPV of $10 cash-flows rises to $61 in year 9 under rational discounting. With mild myopia (x=0.95) it only passes $60 at year 15. With severe myopia (x=0.90) the investor calculates that payback is not achieved.

countries where capital market financing is most developed, is lagging behind other countries. Japan, South Korea and China have increased their R&D-to-GDP ratio since 1980. By comparison, the US has dropped back, maintaining its R&D intensity at a roughly stable level over the past thirty years. The UK R&D record is worse still, with the ratio of R&D to GDP having fallen secularly. These aggregate numbers are borne out in firm-level data. In 1993, ninety-four of the top 200 firms by R&D expenditure were American or British. By 2009, just seventy-seven were.[30] Could this be due to short-termism?

One way to answer this question is to look at whether investment patterns are different for quoted firms relative to private firms. To test this, we use a cross-section of around 140,000 UK firms in 2010, comprising both quoted and private firms.[31] We focus on measures of the capital stock, rather than the investment flow in a particular year, to pick up the long-term or accumulated influence of short-termism on investment choice.

Specifically, we look at corporates' stock of fixed assets. We define the variable of interest as the ratio of the stock of fixed assets to the flow of profits or turnover of a company. Profits and turnover are used as a normalising measure of the flow of resources available for investment in a given year, as well as helping to control for the different sizes of (public versus private) firms.[32]

On average, private firms tend to have materially larger stocks of fixed assets relative to their incoming resources (profits or sales turnover) than public firms (Figure 3). The average ratio of fixed assets to profits is over 100 for private firms but only 24 for quoted firms. Similarly, if we compare

71

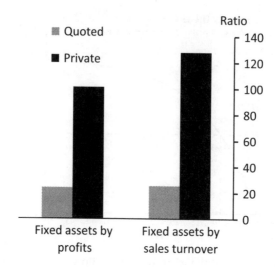

Figure 3: Stocks of fixed assets of private and quoted firms scaled by profits and sales
Source: Bureau van Dijk and authors' calculations.

stocks of fixed assets to sales turnover, private firms have stocks of fixed assets 127 times larger than their sales turnover, while for quoted firms they are 25 times larger. In other words, investment stocks are four or five times larger in our sample for private firms than for quoted firms. This is consistent with private firms re-investing a larger proportion of their profits or sales in fixed assets than quoted firms.

In order to quantify more precisely the difference in investment between private and publicly owned firms (which we call the 'investment multiplier'), we have estimated empirically a model of firms' investment behaviour on our dataset. This empirical exercise revealed that the investment multiplier from being a private firm is slightly higher than 4. Ceteris paribus, the accumulated capital stock of a private firm tends to be four times larger than that of a quoted one.

If we restrict our analysis to the five largest sectors (agriculture, manufacturing, wholesale/retail trade, financial intermediation and real estate), which comprise over 92,000 firms and cover more than 90 per cent of total corporate assets in the sample, the result is even more dramatic. Private firms in these five sectors appear to have built even larger stocks of fixed assets relative to their profits than quoted firms—the investment multiplier from being a private firm is 5.2.

When we have taken into account additional factors in our analysis, such as the age of companies and the sector in which they operate, the estimated investment multiplier of private firms remained very relevant and statistically significant. Relative to the median sector,[33] private firms in the sectors of manufacturing; transport, storage and communication; financial intermediation; real estate; health and social work; and community services exhibit positive multipliers on their investment relative to quoted firms, with multipliers ranging from 4 to 15. These results suggest, overall, that UK private firms tend to plough back between four and eight times more of their profits into their business over time than publicly held firms.

Policy implications

On the basis of the evidence presented here, short-termism in capital markets appears to come with a potentially significant price tag, albeit one which is often hidden from view. The evidence is drawn from asset prices in capital markets and from investment decisions by companies. Both point to a quantitatively significant degree of short-termism in capital markets, whether measured by the cost of capital or investment intentions.

To assess the broader implications of these estimates for the economy, consider a simple ready-reckoner. Assume the short-termism problem can be approximated by the difference in the investment performance of public and private firms. Given the public/private split of firms, the stock of capital at quoted firms would then be several times larger in the absence of short-termism—and so would be the corresponding level of output in the economy. But how much larger?

Assume a standard type of production function (a tool used in economics to approximate the relation between available production factors and output).[34] Assume also that, in the absence of short-termism, the capital-starved public companies would like to match that of private companies. Given the share of quoted companies in the capital stock, then a simple back-of-the-envelope exercise suggests that the elimination of short-termism would result in a level of output around 20 per cent higher than would otherwise be the case. Even if this is an upper bound, it suggests the gains are potentially very substantial.

Given the scale of the gains, what would be an appropriate public policy response to correct this capital market failure? A number of proposals have been suggested by various authors. These include:

(a) Transparency: The lightest touch approach would be to require greater disclosures by financial and non-financial firms of their long-term intentions—for example, their long-term performance, strategy and compensation practices.[35] For financial firms, this might include metrics of portfolio churn and compensation practices for senior executives. For senior executives, the UK Parliamentary Commission on Banking Standards has called for more forward-looking details of compensation plans to be disclosed.[36]
(b) Contract design: There have been various attempts over the past few years to make compensation contracts more sensitive to long-term performance and risk. Among the key initiatives have been new rules requiring the deferral of pay-outs and the possibility of forfeiture in

73

certain circumstances. In 2014, the Bank of England issued a consultation document proposing that even compensation that had been fully paid out should be capable of being clawed back. Changes in the compensation instrument can also help—for example, remunerating in equity is better than in cash and remunerating in junior or convertible debt might be better than either.[37] EU rules now require at least half of the individual's bonus to be paid in equity or debt.

(c) Governance: A more intensive approach would involve acting directly on shareholder incentives. For example, the Kay Review has proposed an investor forum to coordinate the views and actions of long-term institutional investors.[38] A more interventionist approach would be to act on investor voting rights. For example, fiduciary duties on managers could be expanded to recognise explicitly long-term or broader objectives.[39] Some authors have proposed that shareholder rights could be enhanced for long-term investors, perhaps with a duration-dependent sliding scale of voting rights—as is the case for some French companies, for example.[40]

(d) Taxation/Subsidies: Some authors have suggested a variety of ways in which government could penalise short-duration holdings of securities, or incentivise long-duration holdings, using tax and/or subsidy measures. These measures differ in detail, but the underlying principle is to link them to the duration of an investor's holdings or the length or nature of a company's investment.[41] Among the more obvious are alterations to the tax code to provide companies with stronger incentives to retain (rather than distribute) profits and to provide investors with stronger incentives to hold (rather than churn) investment assets—for example, by issuing 'loyalty bonuses'.[42]

From a research perspective, further work could usefully be done to better calibrate these gains. Using alternative methodologies to gauge the potential impact of short-termism on investment choice is one potential avenue—for example, the effects of firms switching from private to public or vice versa. Comparing the experience of different countries, with different sets of company law and different patterns of capital market financing, may also be revealing. This would help reinforce what is already a strong and mounting case for public policy interventions to lean against short-termism, whose costs seem likely to be both high and rising.

Notes

1 This is a significantly amended version of a paper by Richard Davies, Andrew G Haldane, Mette Nielsen and Silvia Pezzini on 'Measuring the Cost of Short-Termism', published in the *Journal of Financial Stability* (2013).

2 A. Haldane, 'Patience and finance', speech given at the Oxford China Business Forum, Beijing, 2010, http://www.bankofengland.co.uk/publications/speeches/2010/speech445.pdf (accessed 2010).

3 D. Barton, 'Capitalism for the long term', *Harvard Business Review*, March 2011.

4 N. Carr, 'Is Google making us stupid? What the Internet is doing to our brains', *Atlantic Magazine*, July–August 2008.

5 See for example G. Hoggarth, R. Reis and V. Saporta, 'Costs of banking system instability: some empirical evidence', *Journal of Banking & Finance*, vol. 26, no. 5, 2002, pp. 825–55.

6 See A. Haldane, 'Capital discipline', remarks based on a speech given at the American Economic Association, Denver, 2011, http://www.bankofengland.co.uk/archive/Documents/historicpubs/speeches/2011/speech484.pdf (accessed 2010).

7 MORI, *NAPF/IMA Short-termism Study Report*, 2004, http://www.theinvestmentassociation.org/assets/components/ima_filesecurity/secure.php?f=press/2004/20040913-01.pdf (accessed 2010).

8 J. Poterba and L. H. Summers, 'A CEO survey of U.S. companies' time horizons and hurdle rates', *Sloan Management Review*, vol. 37, no. 1, Fall 1995.

9 J. R. Graham, C. R. Harvey and S. Rajgopal, 'The economic implications of corporate financial reporting', *Journal of Accounting and Economics*, vol. 40, no. 1–3, 2005, pp. 3–73.

10 W. S. Jevons, *The Theory of Political Economy*, Macmillan and Company, 1871.

11 A. Marshall, *Principles of Economics*, London, Macmillan and Company, 1890.

12 A. C. Pigou, *The Economics of Welfare*, London, Macmillan and Company, 1920.

13 J. M. Keynes, 'JMK letter to Francis Curzon, 18th March 1938', in R. Skidelsky, *John Maynard Keynes: Vol. 3 Fighting for Britain 1937–1946*, Macmillan, 2000.

14 B. Graham, *The Intelligent Investor*, HarperCollins, 1949.

15 P. R. Neild ('Replacement policy', *National Institute Economic Review*, 1964) and National Economic Development Office (*Investment in Machines Tools*, HMSO, 1965) used questionnaire-based evidence. A large proportion of firms in the sample claimed to use a pay-back criterion and of these the modal pay-back period was three to five years. Census evidence from this period indicated that the average useful lifespan of machines was more than fifteen years. The distribution of plant and equipment lives in G. Dean and J. Irwin ('The stock of fixed capital in the UK in 1961', *Journal of the Royal Statistical Society*, vol. 3, 1964, pp. 327–58) implied a mean economic life of thirty-four years.

16 D. Miles, 'Testing for short termism in the UK stock market', *The Economic Journal*, vol. 103, no. 421, 1993, pp. 1379–96.

17 K. Cuthbertson, S. Hayes and D. Nitzsche, 'The behaviour of UK stock prices and returns: is the market efficient?', *The Economic Journal*, vol. 107, no. 443, 1997, pp. 986–1008; A. Black and P. Fraser, 'Stock market short-termism—an international perspective', *Journal of Multinational Financial Management*, vol. 12, 2002, pp. 135–58.

18 J. Asker, J. Farre-Mensa and A. Ljungqvist, *Comparing the Investment Behavior of Public and Private Firms*, NBER Working Paper 17394, 2011; J. Asker, J. Farre-Mensa and A. Ljungqvist, *Corporate Investment and Stock Market Listing: A Puzzle?*, Working Paper, 2013, http://papers.ssrn.com/sol3/papers.cfm?abstract_id=1603484 (accessed 2010).

19 S. Bernstein, *Does Going Public Affect Innovation?* Working Paper, Stanford Graduate School of Business, 2012.

20 M. H. Miller and K. Rock, 'Dividend policy under asymmetric information', *The Journal of Finance*, vol. 40, no. 4, September 1985, pp. 1031–51.

21 J. C. Stein, 'Efficient capital markets, inefficient firms: a model of myopic corporate behavior', *Quarterly Journal of Economics*, vol. 104, no. 4, November 1989, pp. 655–69.

22 The model used is one of 'signal-jamming'—i.e. firms engage in costly behaviour to *prevent* information from appearing, rather than investing in a costly signal that conveys information.

23 M. P. Narayanan, 'Managerial incentives for short-term results', *Journal of Finance*, vol. 40, no. 5, December 1985, pp. 1469–84.

24 A. Wagenhofer, 'Trading off costs and benefits of frequent financial reporting', *Journal of Accounting Research*, vol. 52, no. 2, May 2014, pp. 389–401; F. Gigler, C. Kanodia, H. Sapra

and R. Venugopalan, 'How frequent financial reporting can cause managerial short-termism: an analysis of the costs and benefits of increasing reporting frequency', *Journal of Accounting Research*, vol. 52, no. 2, May 2014, pp. 357–87.

25 Data are from Thomson Reuters Datastream.

26 We use a non-linear least squares regression to estimate our model. Because the estimation uses expected values up to five periods ahead, the estimates only run to 2004. Complete results, together with the regression equations and the underlying theoretical model, can be found in the already cited article 'Measuring the costs of short-termism'.

27 Haldane, 'Capital discipline'.

28 Weld (*Recycled Equity*, Working Paper, Cornell University, 2008) finds that 40 per cent of common equity issuance is by firms that are making regular positive dividend payments, and that 20 per cent of this raised equity could be avoided if firms eliminated dividends.

29 See A. Haldane, 'Capital discipline', for a fuller discussion. See W. N. Goetzmann, R. G. Ibbotson and L. Peng, 'A new historical database for the NYSE 1815 to 1925: performance and predictability', *Journal of Financial Markets*, vol. 4, no. 1, 2001, pp. 1–32, and F. Braggion and L. Moore, *Dividend Policies in an Unregulated Market: The London Stock Exchange 1895–1905*, Discussion Paper 2008-83, Tilburg University, Centre for Economic Research, for the US and UK history.

30 Source: Department for Business Innovation and Skills *R&D Scoreboard*. In the 1993 survey, eighty-one of the top 200 firms were US firms and thirteen were UK firms; the numbers in 2009 were sixty-eight and nine respectively.

31 Data are from Bureau van Dijk. Quoted firms are 1.1 per cent of all UK firms in this sample.

32 Other works (for example Bernstein, *Does Going Public Affect Innovation?*) use the number of patents as the dependent variable. We consider this as an *outcome* of investment, while in this chapter we focus on the choice of investment *expenditure*. Also, not all corporate investment results in patents, so such a study investigates only a particular subsample of firms.

33 The benchmark category is the wholesale and retail trade sector, with the median ratio of fixed assets to profits in the sample.

34 Specifically, we assume a standard Cobb–Douglas production function with constant returns to scale and an elasticity of output with respect to capital of 0.3.

35 Aspen Institute, *Overcoming Short-termism: A Call for a More Responsible Approach to Investment and Business Management*, The Aspen Institute Business and Society Program, 9 September 2009; Chartered Financial Analyst Institute, *Breaking the Short Term Cycle. Discussion and Recommendations on how Corporate Leaders, Asset Managers, Investors and Analysts can Refocus on Long-term Value*, CFA Centre for Financial Market Integrity/Business Roundtable Institute for Corporate Ethics, 2006.

36 House of Lords and House of Commons, 'Changing banking for good', Report of the Parliamentary Commission on Banking Standards, http://www.parliament.uk/documents/banking-commission/Banking-final-report-volume-i.pdf (accessed 2010).

37 See Haldane, 'Capital discipline'.

38 J. Kay, *The Kay Review of UK Equity Markets and Long-Term Decision Making*, Department for Investment, Business and Skills, July 2012.

39 E. Duruigbo, 'Tackling shareholder short-termism and managerial myopia', *Kentucky Law Journal*, vol. 100, 2012, p. 531.

40 Securities and Exchange Commission, *Facilitating Shareholder Director Nominations*, 15 November 2010; Aspen Institute, *Overcoming Short-termism*.

41 Aspen Institute, *Short-Termism and US Capital Markets, A Compelling Case for Change*, 2010; see also Poterba and Summers, 'A CEO survey'.

42 P. Bolton and F. Samama, *L-Shares: Rewarding Long-term Investors*, mimeo, 2010, Committee on Global Thought, Columbia University.

5. Innovative Enterprise and the Theory of the Firm

WILLIAM LAZONICK

Introduction: what makes capitalism productive?

ECONOMISTS STUDY the allocation of resources to the production of goods and services that people want or need at prices that they are willing or able to pay. The economist wants to know how this resource-allocation process can improve the well-being of the people who constitute members of society. To make society materially better off, productivity needs to grow over time. The extent which productivity growth contributes to economic well-being depends on how the productivity gains are distributed among a society's members.

We know that the system of production that we generally call 'capitalism' has been successful in raising productivity over the long run. In certain periods, this system has resulted in a reduction of income inequality. As a profession, however, economists are remarkably ill-equipped to understand the relationships among resource allocation, productivity growth and income distribution. The reason: economists are trained to think of the capitalist economy as a 'market economy', and look to markets to effect the allocation of resources that can result in superior economic performance, measured in terms of stable and equitable economic growth.[1] Indeed, I contend that the conventional economic perspective on how the capitalist economy functions and performs imbues the economist with a 'trained incapacity' (to borrow a phrase from Thorstein Veblen[2]) to comprehend the relation between resource allocation and economic performance in the actual economy.

The problem is that adherence to the theory of the market economy prevents the economist from understanding the microeconomic sources of productivity growth in the economy. It is organisations—including household families, business enterprises and government agencies—and not markets that invest in the productive capabilities embodied in physical and human capital that generate productivity. Markets can give organisations *access* to labour, land, finance and intermediate products, but, as recognised explicitly in the views of both Karl Marx and Joseph Schumpeter, market exchange *per se* does not enhance the productivity of these inputs.[3] Organisations enhance productivity by first developing and then utilising the productive resources that they have under their control. In any economy characterised by significant productivity growth, the investment strategies and organisational structures

Published by John Wiley & Sons Ltd, 9600 Garsington Road, Oxford OX4 2DQ, UK and 350 Main Street, Malden, MA 02148, USA

of business enterprises drive productivity growth. I call these business organisations 'innovative enterprises'.

The purposes of this chapter are (a) to show that the neoclassical theory
of the firm in perfect competition is a theory of the *unproductive firm*, and
hence, as Schumpeter put it, 'perfect competition is not only impossible
but inferior, and has no title to being set up as a model of ideal efficiency';[4] (b) to reveal the strengths and weaknesses of the Marxian theory
of the *productive firm*; (c) to lay out the central concepts of a theory of
innovative enterprise that overcomes the limits of the Marxian theory of the
firm for understanding productivity under capitalism; and (d) to draw out
the methodological implications of the theory of innovative enterprise as
an analytical approach for understanding the possibilities and problems of
capitalist development.[5]

The neoclassical theory of the unproductive firm

Every year, throughout the world, millions of students, often in their very
first semester of college, take courses in introductory microeconomics. Virtually all of them learn that an industrial structure known as 'perfect competition' constitutes the most efficient of all economic worlds. Their professor
might tell them that in fact we live in a world of 'imperfect competition',
and that perfect competition cannot actually be achieved. But that only
means that the unrealisable state of perfect competition is the ideal benchmark against which the efficiency of the actual state of imperfect competition
must be measured.

What then is 'perfect' about perfect competition? At the core of the theory
of perfect competition is the notion that the optimal output of each individual firm that competes in an industry is so small relative to the total output
of the industry that it can sell all of the output that maximises its profit
without having a discernible impact on the industry's product price.
Similarly, the demand of each of these firms for inputs of labour and capital
is so small relative to the size of the markets that supply them with these
inputs that each individual firm can purchase the factors of production
required by its optimal output without having a discernible impact on factor
prices.

The neoclassical economist's proof of the economic superiority of perfect
competition as a state of economic affairs is the theory of monopoly, a mode
of imperfect competition in which only one firm exists in the industry. As
explained in virtually every microeconomics textbook, in representing the
whole industry, the monopolist faces the industry's downward-sloping
demand curve rather than the perfectly elastic demand curve faced by each
firm in perfect competition. The textbooks then show graphically that the
monopolist maximises profit at a level of output that is lower and at a price
that is higher than the aggregate output and price decisions made by profit-
maximising firms under so-called perfect competition.

It therefore follows from this comparison with output and price under monopoly that perfect competition results in an 'optimal' level of economic performance, and hence perfect competition is the benchmark state of industry structure against which the economic performance of all other states should be compared. These other states are hence modes of 'imperfect competition'. Some economists see imperfect competition as an inevitable state of affairs, while others see it as a condition that can be overcome through appropriate government policy. In either case, whether attainable or not, perfect competition is held up as the model of economic efficiency. Moreover, those liberal economists who view the distribution of the costs and benefits from the operation of market competition, whether perfect or imperfect, as socially undesirable, can invoke 'market failure' as a rationale for the government to intervene with policies to improve social welfare. But all economists who accept the validity of the theory of the firm in perfect competition will agree that in a capitalist economy it is markets, not organisations, that allocate resources to their most economically efficient uses. And the perfection of markets occurs when no individual firm's output decisions can affect the market price.

There is, however, a fundamental flaw in the neoclassical economist's proof of the economic inferiority of monopoly that vitiates the entire intellectual exercise. The problem is not with the internal logic of the constrained-optimisation model that economists use to analyse the combination of output and price at which the firm maximises profits, whether in its perfectly competitive or monopoly form. Rather, *the problem is with the logic of comparing the competitive model with the monopoly model within the constrained-optimisation framework.*[6] If technological and market conditions make perfect competition a possibility, how can one firm (or even a small number of firms) come to dominate an industry?

One would have to assume that the monopolist somehow differentiated itself from other competitors in the industry. But the constrained-optimisation comparison that supposedly demonstrates the inferiority of monopoly argues that both the monopolist firm and perfectly competitive firms *optimise subject to the same cost structures* that derive from externally imposed technological and factor-market conditions. Indeed, except for the assumption that, in one case, the firm as a 'price-taker' can make its profit-maximising output decision as if it can sell all of its output at a constant price (according to a perfectly elastic demand curve), and that, in the other case, the firm as a 'price-maker' is so large that it can only sell more output at a lower price (according to a downward-sloping demand curve), there is absolutely nothing in terms of the structure or operation of the firm that distinguishes the perfect competitor from the monopolist! So how would monopoly ever emerge under such conditions?

In fact, as I argue later in this chapter, the logical comparison is between the firm of neoclassical theory, which takes as given its cost structure (the combination of exogenously determined factor prices and technological alternatives), and the firm of innovation theory, which shapes its own cost structure by making high fixed-cost investments with a view to transforming them into high-quality products at low unit costs. Under such a comparison, the theory of the firm in perfect competition becomes *a theory of the unproductive firm* as the industry standard for economic efficiency, with the market being divided among a very large number of firms that are, by assumption, *all equally unproductive*. To see why, let us look at the assumptions that, since the 1930s, neoclassical economists have made about the key characteristics of the firm that form the foundation for the theory of perfect competition.

The firm in perfect competition optimises at a level of output that is small relative to the industry's output because, as it expands its output, it experiences increasing average variable costs. These outweigh inevitably decreasing average fixed costs, so that its total average costs rise, resulting in the well-known U-shaped cost curve. This increase in average costs—that is, the onset of inefficiency—could, in principle, occur at any level of output. But *for the sake of perfect competition it must occur at a very low level of output* so that the firm is so small relative to the size of the industry that its output decisions have no discernible impact on the industry's product price. Moreover, perfect competition assumes that *all firms in the industry experience this rise in unit costs at the same low level of output*. Hence they all have identical cost structures that ensure that each firm in the industry has a level of output that is very small relative to the industry's total output. In perfect competition, all firms are equally unproductive.

Most current economics textbooks do not explain why, in the construction of the theory of the firm in perfect competition, average costs rise at a very low level of output. The authors of these textbooks just plot the U-shaped cost curve and then posit that the firm is so small relative to the size of its industry that it is a 'price-taker'. But earlier textbooks (for example, the 1948 version of Samuelson's classic, *Economics*) provided two reasons for the small size of the optimising firm that forms the foundation for perfect competition.[7]

The first reason is that the employer invests in a factory—the firm's fixed cost—that has an output capacity that is very small relative to the industry's output. As the firm hires more labour—its variable cost—to expand output, overcrowding occurs that lowers the average productivity of workers as they bump into each other, interfering with each other's ability to produce output. Hence the average productivity of labour falls, resulting in rising average variable costs that, if sustained over larger amounts of output, can outweigh the decline in average fixed costs, and yield the familiar U-shaped cost curve. And for all firms in the industry, this triumph of rising variable costs over declining fixed costs occurs at such a low level of output that 'perfect' competition is the result.

The second reason for this result is that, as more workers are hired, the employer loses supervisory control over the effort that workers expend.

Again, the average productivity of labour declines, causing average variable costs to rise, and if they rise sufficiently to outweigh falling fixed costs per unit of output, the firm faces an upward sloping marginal-cost curve. If this loss of productivity because of rising variable costs happens at such a low level of output for all firms in the industry that no one firm's output decisions can have a discernible impact on the industry product price, then the neoclassical economist states that 'perfect' competition prevails.

To sum up, for the sake of perfect competition, it is assumed that this diminished productivity of labour occurs at such a low level of output relative to industry output that it outweighs the decline in average fixed costs due to economies of scale. Moreover, also for the sake of perfect competition, it is assumed that *all firms in the industry experience to the same degree the same adverse effects of factory overcrowding and supervisory control loss.*

It does not take much pondering on these assumptions to recognise that the conditions for the existence of perfect competition entail rather bizarre notions of how firms in an industry do, or do not, compete with one another.[8] Why don't some entrepreneurs invest in a factory that is, say, two or three times the size of the very small industry norm and avoid the problem of overcrowding, even as, provided they can capture a sufficient extent of the market, they benefit from declining unit costs from economies of scale? Then they could use their supernormal profits to hire supervisory labour to overcome the problem of declining labour productivity, and rising average variable costs, because of control loss. Or they could share some of these supernormal profits with workers as incentives to maintain their levels of work effort as the firm expands its output. Under these conditions, output would increase and average costs would decline with the growth of the firm. This would render the firm in so-called perfect competition *the worst*, not the best, production unit of all possible conditions of industry structure.

To be sure, as the size of the fixed-cost investment in the factory increases, the employer assumes greater risk that the firm will have excess capacity. But isn't risk-taking an essential feature of a capitalist economy? It is also possible that the extra cost of close supervision or added wage incentives will outweigh the value of the extra work effort that these expenditures yield. But isn't the management of labour an essential feature of a capitalist economy? In effect, the theory of the firm in perfect competition assumes that the capitalist employer is allergic to taking any risk; that is, to the practice that we call entrepreneurship. The theory of the firm in perfect competition also has no notion that part of the employer's function is to figure out how to get productivity out of the workers whom he employs, a practice we know as management.

In sum, the theory of the firm in perfect competition is a firm in which entrepreneurship and management play no roles. Indeed, based as it is on the assumptions of productivity losses because of overcrowding of the factory and the presence of workers who are unwilling to work, the neoclassical firm in perfect competition has a striking resemblance to a sweatshop. It is no exaggeration to say that the sweatshop is the foundation of the theory of perfect competition. The economics of the sweatshop, rooted in the 'ideal' of 'perfect' competition, provides the intellectual rationale for both an unregulated free-market economy in the American conservative tradition of Milton Friedman and an interventionist policy to mitigate market imperfections and confront market failures in the American liberal tradition of Paul Samuelson. Both figuratively and literally, the theory of the firm in perfect competition manifests the poverty of neoclassical economics.

The Marxian theory of the productive firm

To construct an economic theory of the productive enterprise, it is useful—and I would argue essential—to go back to Karl Marx's explanation of the sources of surplus value laid out in his 1867 treatise, *Das Kapital*.[9] In arguing that the sources of productivity cannot be found in the process of market exchange but rather are found in the process of production, Marx originated a critique of the theory of the market economy that remains as relevant today as it was in the nineteenth century. And in focusing his theory of production on investments in productive capabilities and the management of the labour force, Marx provided a substantive theory of how the capitalist enterprise generates productivity—even though, as I explain below, key arguments about how capitalist employers extracted unremunerated labour effort from production workers in the British industrial revolution on which his theory of surplus value was based were empirically wrong.

Marx was no stranger to a general equilibrium theory of the market economy. In *Das Kapital*, Marx constructed the general equilibrium system of market exchange on the basis of *the labour theory of value*, in the tradition of what we now call the 'classical' economists, especially David Ricardo.[10] Marx argued that, in a general equilibrium of market exchange, capitalism presents itself as 'a very Eden of the innate rights of man' because all parties can exchange commodities, including the commodity 'labour power', at their own free will. A century after Marx wrote *Capital*, Milton Friedman would encapsulate this ideology of the market economy in his tract, *Capitalism and Freedom* (without, of course, invoking the labour theory of value), while subordinating production to the market through the theory of the firm in perfect competition (or what, as we have seen, should really be called the theory of the unproductive firm).[11]

In Parts 1 and 2 of *Capital*, Marx began the analysis of the capitalist system by laying out the logic of a general equilibrium system of exchange based on labour values, so that he could then demonstrate that capitalism does not in fact operate according to the ideology of 'Freedom, Equality, Property and Bentham' that market exchange appears to offer.[12] For Marx, the point of this exercise was not (as many Marxist and non-Marxist economists have wrongly believed) to explain relative market prices by the exchange value of labour inputs, but, to the contrary, to show that, as a theory of the market economy, the labour theory of value cannot explain the existence of capitalist profit (and hence market prices) in the economic system. If all commodities exchange for the value of the quantities of labour embodied in them, Marx asked, what is the source of capitalist profit, i.e. surplus value?

In asking how capitalists could extract profits from a supposed general equilibrium of market exchange, Marx argued that a theory of how capitalism generates productivity has to be rooted in *a theory of organised production*. It is only in a theory of production—i.e. in a theory of the firm—that one can discover the source of *surplus value*. Ignoring the warning 'no admittance except on business' by entering the realm of production, says Marx, 'we shall see, not only how capital produces, but how capital is produced. We shall at last force the secret of profit making.'[13]

Fundamental to Marx's theory of surplus value is the distinction between the commodity 'labour power', which the worker sells to the capitalist employer in exchange for a wage, and 'labour effort', which represents the actual amount of labour services that the worker performs in production. For a given wage, labour effort supplied in production will depend on the number of hours worked per day as well as the expenditure of labour effort per unit of time. Marx argued that the tendency of capitalist development was to generate a 'reserve army' of unemployed labour that would keep wages at a culturally determined minimum—the dark side of market forces —while giving capitalist employers the power to extract high levels of labour effort, and hence surplus value, from their employees in the production process.[14]

The key strength of Marx's theory of the firm is that it roots the analysis of the capitalist economy in the operation of the production process, with an emphasis on the dynamic interaction of technology and organisation, or what Marx called the forces and relations of production, in determining productivity.[15] Marx derived this theory from his understanding of the historical experience of the British industrial revolution, focusing especially on the factory system in the textile industries, which remained the leading sector of the British economy throughout the nineteenth century. It is therefore possible to re-examine Marx's argument in view of what we now know about that historical experience.[16] While the Marxian focus on investment in productive capabilities and management of the labour force remains essential to a theory of the firm, we can learn as much if not more from where Marx got the historical facts wrong as from where he got them right.

For Marx, the major factor in creating an industrial reserve army was labour-saving technological change. It not only displaced workers, adding to the reserve army, but also replaced their skills, thus undermining craft unions and increasing the power of the employer to extract unremunerated labour effort from the worker—now more easily replaceable—in the production process. Marx argued that, even with legislation that capped the length of the working day, capitalists could use technology to enhance their ability to extract labour effort, the value of which was in excess of the amount that had to be paid to labour as daily wages. The dependence of the worker on wage-labour for survival combined with the introduction of skill-displacing machinery was, according to Marx, the basis for the appropriation of labour effort that was the source of 'surplus value', or capitalist profit.

Marxian exploitation was and remains a source of profit in sweatshops, although these tend to be in workplaces in which advanced technology has *not* been introduced. In the case of the most technologically advanced work-places, Marx's case in point in *Capital* was the allegedly destructive impact of the introduction of the 'self-acting mule'—the central and most sophisti-cated technology of the nineteenth-century British cotton textile factory—on the employment and unionisation of skilled adult-male workers known as mule spinners. Marx argued that by the 1840s the adoption of the self-acting mule had made it possible to replace the adult males who had previously been employed with women and children who received lower wages and had less organised power than the men.

The case of the self-acting mule is a great story for proving the tendency of capitalism to subject even the most skilled workers to Marxian exploita-tion during the British industrial revolution. The problem is that, contrary to Marx, the introduction and diffusion of the more automated technology did not undermine the position of the adult-male mule spinners in the produc-tion process.[17] Well into the twentieth century, adult-male mule spinners, known as 'minders', remained the principal workers on the 'self-acting' machines, and indeed by the final decades of the nineteenth century had become one of the best-organised and best-financed craft unions in Britain.[18] More generally, even in the presence of factory automation, skilled shop-floor workers remained central to British manufacturing into the second half of the twentieth century.[19]

An understanding of where Marx went wrong is of substantial relevance for understanding the sources of productivity growth in the capitalist economy, not only in his time but also in ours. The mechanisation of certain motions on mule spinning machines that led them to be described as 'self-acting' still left a number of other functions that required the constant attention of experienced workers. In addition, in the British textile factories throughout the nineteenth and well into the twentieth century, the minders were directly responsible for hiring, training, supervising and paying junior workers known as piecers, some of whom might one day ascend to a minder position. The earnings of the minders were highly regulated by union-bargained wage lists that spelled out in great detail the relation between productivity and pay.

This effective cooperation between capitalists and workers raised produc-tivity in the cotton textile factories, while sharing productivity gains between them. As long as demand for cotton textile goods remained strong, workers' wages rose in tandem with productivity. Thus the minders emerged as members of an 'aristocracy of labour', part of the process that in the last half of the nineteenth century turned Britain into the 'workshop of the world'. In the twentieth century, competitive advantage in cotton textiles and other manufacturing industries would shift from Britain to the United States, Japan and Germany, among other nations. But in all these cases, the principle of capitalist development would remain the same: capitalist enterprise generates higher-quality, lower-cost products by sharing the value gains with its leading groups of workers, whose contributions of skill and effort are essential to the generation of productivity gains.[20]

Theoretically, Marx was looking in the right place—the production process—to explain the creation and distribution of value. Unlike neoclassical economists who use theory to ignore history, Marx sought to bring history into the service of theory. But he let his preconceived theory of labour exploitation take on a life of its own, imposing simplistic answers on a more complex process. We need to use theoretical precepts to explore history, and, as in the case of the self-acting mule, develop a more sophisticated analysis of the interaction of organisation, technology and markets in generating productivity and distribution outcomes.

Without this integration of theory and history, theory can become a barrier to comprehending reality—as the past two generations of neoclassical economists have amply demonstrated. And if we want to make use of Marx's insights into the dynamic interaction of technology and organisation—or forces and relations of production—in the process of capitalist development, we need to learn the fundamental lesson of the case of the self-acting mule: capitalism as a system that generates productivity requires the cooperation of labour. And as the products that the capitalist enterprise generates become more 'innovative', and hence as capitalism becomes more 'advanced', the need to motivate workers to generate productivity and to share the productivity gains with them becomes all the more important as a fundamental principle of the development of the economy. The rethinking of capitalism requires a theory of innovative enterprise.

The theory of innovative enterprise

Innovation is a *collective, cumulative* and *uncertain* process. It is collective because it takes the application of the skills and efforts of large numbers of people in hierarchical and functional divisions of labour to generate the organisational learning that results in competitive products. It is cumulative because the process of developing and utilising these value-creating capabilities must occur continuously over extended periods of time before competitive products emerge. And it is uncertain because a firm that seeks to be innovative may be incapable of transforming the technologies and accessing the markets that enable a product to be higher quality and/or lower cost than those of its competitors.

The collective, cumulative and uncertain characteristics of the innovation process have profound implications for understanding the relationship between value creation and value extraction. In the presence of innovation, it is organisations, not markets, that invest in the collective and cumulative learning processes that enable a firm to confront, and possibly overcome, the uncertainty inherent in innovation. Markets in labour, capital and products give the firm access to suppliers of inputs and buyers of outputs. But it is organisations that determine the *productivity* of these inputs, and hence the quality and cost of the outputs.

A major intellectual barrier to understanding the growth of the firm and its influence on economic performance is the neoclassical theory of the market economy. The development of a liquid stock market was the result, not the cause, of the rise and growth of the innovative enterprise. So too was the emergence of a highly mobile labour market for professional, technical and administrative personnel.[21] And it is innovative enterprise that generates the high-quality, low-cost goods and services that give households with employment incomes ample consumer choice on product markets. Developed markets in labour, capital and products are the result, not the cause, of the growth of innovative enterprise. Hence, if we want to understand the operation and performance of a modern economy, we need a theory of innovative enterprise.

The purpose of the business enterprise is to produce competitive goods and services: that is, products that buyers want or need at prices that they are willing or able to pay. Given market prices of labour and capital, a competitive good or service is higher quality and/or lower cost than one that does not succeed on the product market. A business that generates higher-quality, lower-cost products over a sustained period of time is an 'innovative enterprise'. When revenues generated through the sale of competitive products exceed the costs of producing and distributing those products, a business generates a profit. Costs, however, are not simply imposed on the business enterprise by exogenous technology and factor markets, as neoclassical economics textbooks tell us. Rather, these costs are the result of the innovative strategy of the business enterprise.

The innovative enterprise develops productive resources through collective and cumulative learning processes that, in and of themselves, burden the company with high fixed costs and expose it to the possibility of greater losses than competitors that eschew investments in collective and cumulative learning.[22] If, however, through organisational learning, these high fixed costs enable the business to generate products that are higher quality than its competitors, it can potentially gain a larger market share that, through economies of scale, transforms these high fixed costs into low unit costs. Through the generation of a good or service that is not only higher quality but also lower cost than those of competitors, potential losses can thus become actual profits. Through the development and utilisation of productive resources, the innovative enterprise transforms competitive disadvantage into competitive advantage.

As already emphasised, the essence of this innovation process is collective and cumulative—i.e. organisational—learning. Given that the innovation process is inherently uncertain, investments in organisational learning must be made without any guarantee of returns. The innovative enterprise faces three types of uncertainty: technological, market and competitive. Technological uncertainty exists because the firm may be incapable of developing the higher-quality processes and products envisaged in its innovative investment strategy. Market uncertainty exists because, even if the firm is successful in its development effort, it must access a large enough extent of the product market to transform the fixed costs of developing a new technology into low unit costs. Finally, even if a firm can overcome technological and market uncertainty, it still faces competitive uncertainty: the possibility that a competitor will have invested in a strategy that generates an even higher-quality, lower-cost product. Nevertheless, in the face of uncertainty, if a firm is to have the opportunity to profit and grow through innovation, it must invest in human capital that accumulates through organisational learning and complementary physical capital.

Many of the critical productive inputs related to physical infrastructure and human knowledge that the business enterprise utilises are made available through government spending, often in the form of public goods financed by tax revenues and public debt. Even the largest and most powerful business enterprises rely on government investments in physical and human resources to generate competitive products. In addition, as Mariana Mazzucato points out in this volume, business enterprises often receive government subsidies and procurement contracts that assist these enterprises in generating competitive products.[23]

The development and utilisation of the enterprise's own investments in productive capabilities render it a social organisation.[24] To contend with the uncertain, collective and cumulative characteristics of the innovation process, the generation of competitive products requires three social conditions of innovative enterprise: 'strategic control', 'organisational integration' and 'financial commitment', all of which are based in social relations.[25]

- *Strategic control* empowers executives who have the incentives and abilities to allocate a company's resources to invest in inherently uncertain innovation processes.
- *Organisational integration* mobilises the skills and efforts of people in a hierarchical and functional division of labour into the collective and cumulative learning processes that are the essence of innovation.
- *Financial commitment* ensures that financial resources are available to sustain the collective and cumulative innovation process from the time that investments in productive capabilities are made until the development and utilisation of those capabilities can generate competitive products that yield financial returns.

The most critical investments that a strategic manager makes are in integrated skill bases that can engage in organisational learning, and thereby generate the high-quality products that are essential for competitive advantage. For the profitable company, retained earnings represent the foundation of financial commitment that sustains investment in the productive capabilities until the firm can generate competitive products.[26] For the innovative enterprise, distributions to shareholders in the forms of cash dividends and stock repurchases must be constrained by the financial commitment required to invest in productive resources, including integrated skill bases, that can generate competitive products.[27]

When, through the generation of competitive products, a business becomes profitable, its stock price usually rises as, through earnings reports, public shareholders become aware of its success. These public shareholders may then begin to speculate on further increases in the corporation's stock price, even though the future earnings of the business are subject to uncertainty. The corporation in turn may seek to take advantage of the high price of its shares to augment its innovative capabilities by using its stock as a currency to combine with other companies, to compensate executives and other key employees or to raise cash that can fund investments in productive capabilities.[28]

There is a danger, however, that corporate executives who are incentivised by stock-based pay and who take advantage of stock market speculation for the purposes of combination, compensation and cash may use their positions of strategic control to manipulate earnings and stock prices for their own benefit, and in the process lose the incentive and ability to engage in innovation. Rather than invest in innovation, corporate executives might prefer to foment stock-price increases by distributing corporate cash to public shareholders. And they might legitimise this type of resource allocation by arguing that they are 'maximising shareholder value' (MSV). Indeed, this change in managerial incentives is precisely what has occurred in the United States since the 1980s as MSV has become the dominant managerial ideology of corporate resource allocation.[29] Andrew Haldane's chapter in this volume explores the evidence and some of the consequences of the 'short-termism'— a euphemism for excessive value extraction—that may be a result.

Given the very different political and cultural environments in which the managerial revolution occurred, the institutional characteristics of strategic control, organisational integration and financial commitment varied across nations. Take, for example, the US–Japanese comparison as it evolved in the post-World War II decades.[30] In the United States there was a much stronger conception than in Japan that public shareholders remained 'owners', not just of shares, but of the company itself. In the United States, shop-floor workers were largely excluded from the processes of organisational learning, whereas in Japan they were included even though, as was the case in the United States, managers and workers were two distinct sets of employees with different educational backgrounds and in-house career paths. In the

United States, companies funded investments in productive capabilities by leveraging retained earnings with long-term bond issues, whereas Japanese corporations secured this financial commitment through relations with 'main banks' that permitted much higher ratios of debt to equity than were generally tolerated in the United States.

The Japanese challenge to the United States in the last decades of the twentieth century came in industries such as automobiles, consumer electronics, machine tools, steel and microelectronics in which the US had been a world leader. The critical source of Japan's competitive advantage over the United States was 'organisational integration': through the hierarchical integration of shop-floor workers and the functional integration of technical specialists into processes of organisational learning, the Japanese perfected, and outcompeted, the US managerial corporation. Even though unionised blue-collar workers in the United States had a high degree of job security in the post-World War II decades, they had historically been excluded from the processes of organisational learning within the corporation, reflecting a distinctively American hierarchical segmentation between 'management' and 'labour'.

In sharp contrast, the hierarchical integration of shop-floor workers into the organisational learning processes that generated higher-quality, lower-cost products was the prime source of Japanese competitive advantage. Complementing this hierarchical integration, the collaboration of Japanese technical specialists in solving productivity problems in manufacturing encouraged the functional integration of their skills and efforts, again in contrast to the relatively high degree of functional segmentation of technical specialists in the United States. Supported by strategic control that favoured investment in innovation and financial commitment that sustained the process, it was a more powerful system of organisational learning that enabled the Japanese to outcompete the Americans.

The particular impacts of Japanese competition varied markedly across US industries. It virtually wiped out the US-based consumer electronics industry. During the 1980s US automobile manufacturers attempted to learn from the Japanese, but three decades later the US companies were still producing lower-quality, higher-cost cars, and, not surprisingly, had lost significant market share. In the machine-tool industry, the overwhelming success of the Japanese against the major US companies was followed in the 1990s by the emergence of export-oriented, small- and medium-sized enterprises producing for specialised niche markets. In the steel industry, the innovative response of the United States was the emergence of minimills, using electric arc furnaces and scrap metal, as distinct from the traditional vertically integrated mills that converted iron ore into crude steel before making finished products.

The most perilous, but ultimately successful, US response to Japanese competition was in the semiconductor industry. By the middle of the 1980s, the Japanese had used their integrated skill bases to lower defects and raise yields in the production of memory chips. This development forced major US semiconductor companies to retreat from this segment of the market, with Intel facing the possibility of bankruptcy in the process.[31] However, led by Intel with its microprocessor for the IBM PC and its clones, US companies became world leaders in chip design. Indeed, the IBM PC, with its open-systems architecture, was the basis for the rise of a 'New Economy business model' that has dramatically altered the conditions of innovative enterprise.

As I have detailed in a number of studies, the principles of strategic control, organisational integration and financial commitment remained central to the success of companies that pioneered or adopted the New Economic business model.[32] At the same time, however, innovative New Economy companies could eschew investment in integrated skill bases that were as deep and broad as those under the 'Old Economy' business model, because of the availability of accumulated knowledge from the research labs of the Old Economy corporations upon which these could draw. As Gordon Moore, founder of Intel, put it in a volume that sought to understand the precipitous decline in corporate research labs in the early 1990s:

Running with the ideas that big companies can only lope along with has come to be the acknowledged role of the spin-off, or start-up. Note, however, that it is important to distinguish here between exploitation and creation. It is often said that start-ups are better at creating new things. They are not; they are better at exploiting them. Successful start-ups almost always begin with an idea that has ripened in the research organisation of a large company. Lose the large companies, or research organisations of large companies, and start-ups disappear.[33]

While, some two decades after Moore made this statement, technology start-ups have yet to disappear, there is no doubt that the New Economy business model has been far better at commercialising existing technologies than developing new ones. Increasingly, moreover, US corporate executives look to the government to provide them with the new technologies that they need,[34] even as these executives have turned toward enriching themselves by boosting their companies' stock prices and with them their stock-based pay.[35]

Elsewhere I have analysed in detail the shift of US industrial corporations from a 'retain-and-reinvest' resource-allocation regime, under which corporate revenues and personnel are retained and re-invested in innovative capabilities, to a 'downsize-and-distribute' allocation regime in which these companies downsize their experienced labour forces and distribute corporate cash to shareholders in the name of 'maximising shareholder value'. Over the decade 2004–2013, 454 companies in the S&P 500 Index publicly listed over the decade expended $3.4 trillion on stock buybacks, equivalent to 51 per cent of net income, with another 35 percent of net income going to dividends.[36] Across this decade, about 9,000 US companies expended a total of $6.9 trillion on stock buybacks, equal to 43 percent of their combined net income, with dividends absorbing another 47 per cent.[37]

The theory of innovative enterprise provides an essential framework for understanding this dramatic change in the resource-allocation regime. The modes of stock-based pay that dominate the compensation of top executives in the United States give them incentives to use corporate cash to boost their company's stock price, even if temporarily. I would also hypothesise that top executives who are willing to spend hundreds of millions and often billions of dollars of corporate cash to boost their companies' stock prices also lose the ability to think about how those financial resources could have been used to invest in productive capabilities through an innovation process that is collective, cumulative and uncertain. Having accepted that the purpose of the corporation is to 'maximise shareholder value', these executives stop investing in the integrated skill bases that are essential to organisational learning, and that hence constitute the essence of the innovation process. And, given that corporate retentions provide the foundation for financial commitment, through distributions to shareholders the business enterprise ensures that investments in collective, cumulative and uncertain productive capabilities cannot and will not be made.

The integration of theory and history

The theory of innovative enterprise confronts the methodology of conventional economics by demonstrating the importance of an analysis that integrates theory and history so that theory functions as both a distillation of what we know and a guide to what we need to know. In my view, the greatest barrier to making the theory of innovative enterprise central to the study of the economy and the teaching of economics is, as stated at the outset, a trained incapacity of professional economists to integrate theory and history.

The theory of innovative enterprise posits that, under certain conditions, at certain times and in certain industries, a business enterprise can exert its power over the allocation of labour and capital to transform the technological and market conditions that it faces to generate higher-quality, lower-cost products. It follows that an 'optimising firm' that takes technological and markets as given in making its resource-allocation decisions cannot generate innovation. The relation between an innovating firm and an optimising firm can be modeled by asking how, by transforming technological and/or and market conditions, a small number of innovative enterprises might be able to differentiate themselves from other firms in an industry to gain sustained competitive advantage.

The innovative enterprise becomes dominant by transforming the industry cost structure and producing a larger volume of output that it can sell at lower prices than the industry's optimising firms. By confronting and transforming technological and market conditions rather than accepting them as given constraints on its activities, the innovative enterprise can outperform the optimising firm. By expanding output and lowering prices, the innovative enterprise grows to be larger than the optimising firm. Beyond that logical statement, however, the elaboration of the theory of innovative enterprise requires systematic comparative–historical research on the organisational and institutional determinants of the processes that transform technological and market conditions to generate goods and services that are higher quality and lower cost than those that previously existed.

Writing at the end of his career, Joseph Schumpeter advised: 'Nobody can hope to understand the economic phenomena of any, including the present, epoch who has not an adequate command of the historical *facts* and an adequate amount of historical *sense* or of what may be described as *historical experience*.'[38] By 'historical experience' Schumpeter, who more than any other economist argued for the centrality of innovation for understanding a capitalist economy, meant the ability of the economist to integrate theory and history. For theory to be relevant to real-world phenomena, it must be derived from the rigorous study of historical reality. To develop relevant theory requires an iterative methodology; one derives theoretical postulates from the study of the historical record, and uses the resultant theory to analyse history as an ongoing and, viewing the present as history, unfolding process. Theory, therefore, serves as an abstract explanation of what we already know, and as an analytical framework for identifying and researching what we need to know.

The constrained-optimisation methodology that has been so central to the training of economists *is* a useful analytical tool: an understanding of the industrial, organisational and institutional conditions that 'constrain' economic activity at a point in time can enable integrative research to be more systematic in analysing how, why and under what conditions certain 'constraints' are, or are not, transformed over time.[39] As a dominant methodology, however, constrained optimisation is typically an excuse for ignoring history, when what is required is a methodology that both uses theory to explore history and uses history to reshape theory.

As Edith Penrose, author of the seminal *The Theory of the Growth of the Firm*,[40] put it in an article written late in her career:

'Theory' is, by definition, a simplification of 'reality' but simplification is necessary in order to comprehend it at all, to make sense of 'history'. If each event, each institution, each fact, were really unique in all aspects, how could we understand, or claim to understand, anything at all about the past, or indeed the present for that matter? If, on the other hand, there are common characteristics, and if such characteristics are significant in the determination of the course of events, then it is necessary to analyse both the characteristics and their significance and 'theoretically' to isolate them for that purpose.

92

If we need theory to make sense of history, so we also need history to make sense of theory. As Penrose concluded: 'universal truths without reference to time and space are unlikely to characterise economic affairs'.[41]

Obviously, rigorous historical analysis is essential if an economic theory is to have descriptive value. But in contrast to the 'positive' economic methodology proposed in the 1950s by Milton Friedman, rigorous historical analysis is also essential if a theory is to have predictive value. Friedman argued that, because all theories involve abstraction from reality, one's choice of theoretical assumptions does not matter as long as one's predictions prove to be correct.[42]

There are two basic problems with this methodological position. First, if one's predictions do not prove to be correct (as has often been the case with neoclassical economists), then one requires a methodology that entails rigorous empirical analysis in order to discover what assumptions would yield correct predictions. Given their ahistorical constrained-optimisation approach, neoclassical economists lack such a methodology. Second, even when one's predictions do prove to be correct at one point in time, they may prove to be incorrect at another point in time, because the underlying model takes as given one or more variables that are in fact integral to the changes that have occurred over the time period. Put differently, two very different theoretical models may yield the same predictions at a point in time, but only one of the models may be able to account for changes in outcomes over time.[43] If a theory is to have predictive (and hence prescriptive) value, rigorous historical analysis (brought up to the present) is a precondition for rigorous logical analysis.

Basic to overcoming the intellectual constraints of a conventional training in economics is the ability to do rigorous analysis of a dynamic historical process. To do historical analysis (again brought up to the present if one wants to inform current policy debates) does not mean, however, that one neglects theory. Rather, it means that one makes theory the servant of comprehending reality rather than an excuse for ignoring it.

In line with Schumpeter's notion of 'historical experience', historical analysis provides us with the knowledge required to make theoretical abstractions that are relevant and to modify our adherence to abstractions previously adopted that fail to comprehend a changing reality. At the same time, theory provides us with a framework that directs our historical research to ask the relevant questions and explore the relevant facts to provide answers. The analysis with which we answer these questions is rigorous because it is based on the systematic investigation of reality.

In a world of economic change, theory without history can never be rigorous. It can only be wrong. Economists require a methodology that brings history and theory into dynamic interaction with one another so that our theoretical deductions remain anchored in our understanding of historical reality. And when that historical reality is of an *innovative* economy, it will by definition be a reality that is always in the process of change.

Notes

1 See W. Lazonick, 'The theory of the market economy and the social foundations of innovative enterprise', *Economic and Industrial Democracy*, vol. 24, no. 1, 2003, pp. 9–44.
2 E. Wais, 'Trained incapacity: Thorstein Veblen and Kenneth Burke', *The Journal of the Kenneth Burke Society*, vol. 2, no. 1, 2005, http://kbjournal.org/wais (accessed 28 March 2016).
3 On the methodologies of Marx and Schumpeter, see W. Lazonick, *Competitive Advantage on the Shop Floor*, Cambridge MA, Harvard University Press, 1990, chs. 1 and 2; 'The integration of theory and history: methodology and ideology in Schumpeter's economics', in L. Magnusson, ed., *Evolutionary Economics: The Neo-Schumpeterian Challenge*, Boston, MA, Kluwer, 1994, pp. 245–63; 'Innovative enterprise and historical transformation', *Enterprise & Society*, vol. 3, no. 1, 2002, pp. 35–54.
4 J. A. Schumpeter, *Capitalism, Socialism, and Democracy*, 3rd edn, New York, Harper, p. 106.
5 It is beyond the scope of this chapter to explore the relation between the theory of innovative enterprise and other theories of the firm such as those contained in transaction-cost theory, resource-based theory, agency theory, dynamic-capability theory and evolutionary theory. For consideration of these alternative theories, see W. Lazonick, *Business Organisation and the Myth of the Market Economy*, Cambridge, Cambridge University Press, 1991; 'Integration of theory and history'; 'Innovative enterprise and historical transformation'; 'The Chandlerian corporation and the theory of innovative enterprise', *Industrial and Corporate Change*, vol. 19, no. 2, 2010, pp. 317–49; 'The theory of innovative enterprise: methodology, ideology, and institutions', in J. K. Moudud, C. Bina and P. L. Mason, eds., *Alternative Theories of Competition: Challenges to the Orthodoxy*, New York, Routledge, 2012, pp. 127–59; 'Innovative enterprise and shareholder value', *Law and Financial Markets Review*, vol. 8, no. 1, 2014, pp. 52–64; 'Innovative enterprise or sweatshop economics? In search of foundations of economic analysis', *Challenge*, vol. 59, no. 2, 2016, pp. 1–50.
6 In the history of economics, Alfred Marshall, whose followers created the theory of the firm in perfect competition, recognised that for a firm to become a monopolist it would have to develop superior productive resources that would permit it to produce more output at a lower cost than a competitive firm: A. Marshall, *Principles of Economics*, 9th (variorum) edn, New York, Macmillan, 1961, pp. 484–5. As Marshall concluded: 'This argument does indeed assume the single firm to be managed with ability and enterprise, and to have an unlimited command of capital—an assumption which cannot always be fairly made. But where it can be made, we may generally conclude that the supply schedule for the commodity, if not monopolised, would show higher supply prices than those of our monopoly supply schedule; and therefore the equilibrium amount of the commodity produced under free competition would be less than that for which the demand price is equal to the monopoly supply price.'

7 In the first edition of *Economics*, Samuelson wrote: 'After the overhead has been spread thin over many units, fixed costs can no longer have much influence on average costs. Variable costs become important, and as average costs begin to rise because of limitations of plant space and management difficulties, average costs finally begin to turn up': P. A. Samuelson, *Economics*, New York, McGraw-Hill, 1948, p. 497. Samuelson does not explain why the economy benefits when all firms experience an increase in variable costs that offsets the decrease in fixed costs at such a low level of output that each firm is so small that it can sell all the output it wants to produce to maximise profits with no discernible impact on the product price—the definition of 'perfect competition'.

8 Given that the theory of the firm in perfect competition and its comparison with the monopoly model have been reproduced in introductory economics textbooks for more than six decades, the implication is that the economists who write these textbooks do not spend much time pondering the relevance of their assumptions. Why should they? Since the 1950s neoclassical economists have accepted Milton Friedman's notion of positive economics in which the assumptions of a theoretical model do not matter as long as the model's predictions are correct. See Milton Friedman, *Essays in Positive Economics*, Chicago, University of Chicago Press, 1953. I take up the severe intellectual limits of this methodological stance in the conclusion to this chapter.

9 Karl Marx's *Das Kapital: Kritik der politischen Ökonomie* was published in German in 1867 as Volume 1 of a multi-volume work. The first English translation, *Capital: A Critique of Political Economy*, vol. 1, appeared in 1887, four years after Marx's death. When, in the text, I refer to Marx's *Capital*, I am referring to *Capital*, Volume 1.

10 D. Ricardo, *On the Principles of Political Economy and Taxation*, London, John Murray, 1817.

11 M. Friedman, *Capitalism and Freedom*, Chicago, University of Chicago Press, 1962.

12 K. Marx, *Capital: A Critique of Political Economy*, vol. 1, p. 121, https://www.marxists.org/archive/marx/works/download/pdf/Capital-Volume-I.pdf (accessed 28 March 2016).

13 Ibid.

14 Ibid., ch. 25.

15 Lazonick, *Competitive Advantage*, chs. 1 and 2.

16 See W. Lazonick, 'Marxian theory and the development of the labour force in England', PhD thesis, Harvard University Department of Economics, November 1975; 'Industrial relations and technical change: the case of the self-acting mule', *Cambridge Journal of Economics*, vol. 3, no. 3, 1979, pp. 231–62; 'Theory and history in Marxian economics', in A. J. Field, ed., *The Future of Economic History*, Boston, Kluwer-Nijhoff, 1987, pp. 255–312; *Competitive Advantage*, chs. 1 and 2.

17 Lazonick, 'Industrial relations and technical change'.

18 Lazonick, *Competitive Advantage*, chs. 3–5.

19 B. Elbaum and W. Lazonick, eds., *The Decline of the British Economy*, Oxford, Oxford University Press, 1986.

20 Ibid.; W. Lazonick, *Organisation and Technology in Capitalist Development*, Aldershot, Edward Elgar, 1992; 'Varieties of capitalism and innovative enterprise', *Comparative Social Research*, vol. 24, 2007, pp. 21–69.

21 W. Lazonick, *Sustainable Prosperity in the New Economy: Business Organisation and High-Tech Employment in the United States*, Kalamazoo, Upjohn Institute for Employment Research, 2009.

22 W. Lazonick, *The Theory of Innovative Enterprise: A Foundation of Economic Analysis*, AIR Working Paper #13-0201, August 2015, http://www.theairnet.org/v3/back-bone/uploads/2015/08/Lazonick.TIE-Foundations_AIR-WP13.0201.pdf (accessed 28 March 2016). See also Lazonick, 'The Chandlerian corporation'.

23 W. Lazonick, *Entrepreneurial Ventures and the Developmental State: Lessons from the Advanced Economies*, World Institute of Development Economics Research, dp2008/01, January 2008, https://www.wider.unu.edu/publication/entrepreneurial-ventures-and-developmental-state (accessed 28 March 2016); F. Block and M. R. Keller, eds., *The State of Innovation: The U.S. Government's Role in Technology Development*, Boulder, Paradigm Publishers, 2011; M. Mazzucato, *The Entrepreneurial State*, London, Anthem Press, 2013; M. Hopkins and W. Lazonick, *Who Invests in the High-Tech Knowledge Base?* Institute for New Economic Thinking Working Group on the Political Economy of Distribution Working Paper No. 6, October 2014, http://ineteconomics.org/ideas-papers/research-papers/who-invests-in-the-high-tech-knowledge-base (accessed 28 March 2016).

24 W. Lazonick, 'Organisational learning and international competition', in J. Michie and J. Grieve Smith, eds., *Globalisation, Growth, and Governance*, Oxford, Oxford University Press, 1998, pp. 204–38; M. O'Sullivan, 'The innovative enterprise and corporate governance', *Cambridge Journal of Economics*, vol. 24, no. 4, 2000, pp. 393–416.

25 Lazonick, *The Theory of Innovative Enterprise*.

26 J. Corbett and T. Jenkinson, 'The financing of industry, 1970–1989: an international comparison', *Journal of the Japanese and International Economies*, vol. 10, no. 1, 1996, pp. 71–96.

27 W. Lazonick, 'Profits without prosperity: stock buybacks manipulate the market and leave most Americans worse off', *Harvard Business Review*, September 2014, pp. 46–55; 'Labor in the twenty-first century: the top 0.1 percent and the disappearing middle class', in C. E. Weller, ed., *Financial Market Development and Labor Relations Inequality, Uncertainty, and Opportunity: The Varied and Growing Role of Finance in Labor Relations*, Cornell, Cornell University Press, 2015, pp. 143–92.

28 W. Lazonick, 'The new economy business model and the crisis of US capitalism', *Capitalism and Society*, vol. 4, no. 2, 2009, article 4.

29 W. Lazonick and M. O'Sullivan, 'Maximising shareholder value: a new ideology for corporate governance', *Economy and Society*, vol. 29, no. 1, 2000, pp. 13–35; W. Lazonick, 'The financialisation of the US corporation: what has been lost, and how it can be regained', *Seattle University Law Review*, vol. 36, no. 2, 2013, pp. 857–909; 'Profits without prosperity'; 'Labor in the twenty-first century'.

30 W. Lazonick, 'Innovative business models and varieties of capitalism: financialisation of the US corporation', *Business History Review*, vol. 84, no. 4, 2010, pp. 675–702.

31 R. A. Burgelman, 'Fading memories: a process theory of strategic exit in dynamic environments', *Administrative Science Quarterly*, vol. 39, no. 1, 1994, pp. 24–56; D. L. Okimoto and Y. Nishi, 'R&D organisation in Japanese and American semiconductor firms', in M. Aoki and R. Dore, eds., *The Japanese Firm: The Sources of Competitive Strength*, Oxford, Oxford University Press, 1994, pp. 178–208.

32 Lazonick, *Sustainable Prosperity*; 'The new economy business model'; 'Financialisation'; 'Profits without prosperity'; *Stock Buybacks: From Retain-and-Reinvest to Downsize-and-Distribute*, Brookings Institution Center for Effective Public Management, April 2015, http://www.brookings.edu/research/papers/2015/04/17-stock-buybacks-lazonick (accessed 28 March 2016).
33 G. E. Moore, 'Some personal perspectives on research in the semiconductor industry', in R. Rosenbloom and W. Spencer, eds., *Engines of Innovation: U.S. Industrial Research at the End of an Era*, Boston, Harvard Business School Press, 1996, p. 171.
34 Hopkins and Lazonick, *Who Invests*.
35 W. Lazonick, *Taking Stock: Why Executive Pay Results in an Unstable and Inequitable Economy*, Roosevelt Institute White Paper, 5 June 2014, http://www.rooseveltinstitute.net/taking-stock-executive-pay (accessed 28 March 2016).
36 Lazonick, 'Financialisation'; 'Profits without prosperity'.
37 Standard & Poor's Compustat database. The figure of 9,000 companies is an annual average over the decade 2004–2013.
38 J. A. Schumpeter, *History of Economic Analysis*, Oxford, Oxford University Press, 1954, pp. 12–13.
39 See, for example, W. Lazonick, 'Factor costs and the diffusion of ring spinning in Britain prior to World War I', *Quarterly Journal of Economics*, vol. 96, no. 1, 1981, pp. 89–109; 'Production relations, labor productivity, and choice of technique: British and U.S. cotton spinning', *Journal of Economic History*, vol. 41, no. 3, 1981, pp. 491–516.
40 E. T. Penrose, *The Theory of the Growth of the Firm*, Oxford, Blackwell, 1959.
41 E. T. Penrose, 'History, the social sciences and economic "theory," with special reference to multinational enterprise', in A. Teichova, M. Lévy-Leboyer and H. Nussbaum, eds., *Historical Studies in International Corporate Business*, Cambridge, Cambridge University Press, 1989, p. 11.
42 Friedman, *Essays in Positive Economics*.
43 Lazonick, *Organisation and Technology*, ch. 4.

6. Innovation, the State and Patient Capital

MARIANA MAZZUCATO

Introduction

GOVERNMENTS IN developed countries all around the world say they want 'smart', innovation-led growth.[1] But very few are achieving it. On the contrary, since the financial crisis the majority of advanced economies have been marked by low growth rates, historically low investment rates and poor productivity performance. The rate of productivity-enhancing innovation appears to have slowed down markedly over the last decade,[2] a trend likely to be exacerbated in the future by declining rates of investment in research and development by both public and private sectors. This is one factor generating concerns that the developed world has entered a period, not of sustained growth, but of 'secular stagnation'.[3] Some economists see the risk of secular stagnation as a quasi-inevitable consequence of demographic change and savings behaviour in high-income countries. This chapter will instead highlight its endogenous character: the result of problematic *choices* that are being made by both businesses and governments. It will focus on how a different understanding of the origins of innovation—and, in particular, the role of public investment in the process of wealth creation—creates a different set of policy imperatives for countries seeking 'smart' growth.

Public debate about innovation—where it comes from, and how it can be stimulated and supported—is frequently mired in out-dated economic ideas. Orthodox economic analysis has tended to see innovation as an essentially private sector process driven by 'exogenous' technological opportunities. Drawing on conventional theories of markets and market failure, government is viewed to have little role in the innovation process beyond the funding of basic scientific research, which as a 'public good' is characterised by too little private investment.[4] Insofar as policy can stimulate innovation, it is thought that this should largely consist in correcting such market failures, 'incentivising' private investment and ensuring sufficient competition between firms.

But the orthodox view is not consistent with the evidence. In fact, as this chapter will show, governments have been widely involved in the innovation process. This has not just been in supporting scientific research and addressing other types of positive and negative externalities, but also in more active and strategic ways. This has included investing across the *entire* innovation chain: from basic research to applied research and early stage financing of new companies. Furthermore, governments have been critical in

Published by John Wiley & Sons Ltd, 9600 Garsington Road, Oxford OX4 2DQ, UK and 350 Main Street, Malden, MA 02148, USA

determining not only the *rate* of innovation, but also in shaping its *direction*. Computing, information and communication technologies were chosen as a direction in the US in the 1960s, 1970s and 1980s, as 'green' technology is being chosen today in countries like Germany, Denmark and China. And in an increasingly financialised economy where only a low share of private companies' profits is being reinvested back into productive investments the need for committed and long-term—or 'patient'—capital from public finance is only increasing.

Thus understanding the role of public investment in innovation requires a more sophisticated understanding of how innovation occurs. Analysing the inadequacies of the orthodox model of markets and market failure, the chapter draws on the insights of Schumpeterian and evolutionary economics to present an alternative framework. Accelerating the rate of innovation is crucial to long-term growth and for meeting some of the great challenges—such as climate change, natural resource scarcity and improved healthcare—which societies today face. This means rethinking the role of public policy in the economy, and the relationship between public and private sectors. The role of the state cannot just be to only fix market failures as the orthodox model would prescribe. It must also be to actively *shape* and *create* markets to drive stronger more sustainable and more inclusive forms of economic growth.

Headed in the wrong direction

One of the few things that economists agree on is that technological innovation produces long-term economic growth.[5] It is widely recognised that public and private investments in research and development (R&D), human capital formation and the ensuing technological and organisational changes have led to long-term increases in productivity and output. However, how this occurs is an area of hot debate. The orthodox neoclassical model sees the role of innovation as shifting a production function from one equilibrium to another. By contrast, evolutionary, Schumpeterian models focus on the disequilibrating effects of innovation, which make production functions less meaningful. The evolutionary emphasis on transformation and structural change has led to the concept of 'systems of innovation', which posits that firms are embedded in a national network of institutions—in both public and private sectors—'whose activities and interactions initiate, import, modify and diffuse new technologies'.[6] Such systems comprise 'the elements and relationships which interact in the production, diffusion and use of new, and economically useful, knowledge'.[7] In this systems view, what drives national innovation performance is not simply the level of R&D spending in a country, but the circulation of knowledge and its diffusion throughout the economy as a whole. The systems view sees the innovation process not as linear but as full of feedback loops between markets and technology, applications and science, and policy and investments.

It is this understanding of how national innovation systems work which makes recent evidence on patterns of R&D spending so worrying. In the US, for example, while the total amount of R&D investment as a share of GDP is still relatively high (around 2.8 per cent), its composition has changed dramatically. First, the share of public R&D investment has decreased; it peaked at 67 per cent in 1964, fell to as low as 25 per cent in 2000, and increased to 30 per cent in 2012, due mainly to the temporary stimulus introduced by the US Government after the financial crash (discussed in Stephanie Kelton's chapter in this book).[8] The same pattern has been seen in several European countries. For example, in the UK the share of government in R&D spending decreased from 43.5 per cent in 1985 to 30.2 per cent in 2000 and 28.8 per cent in 2014. In Italy it was still at 50.7 per cent in 2005, but fell to 41.4 per cent in 2013. In the Eurozone as a whole it decreased by 3.4 points between 2003 and 2013 (from 36.7 per cent to 33.3 per cent).[9]

Second, while private sector R&D has to some extent filled the gap, it is increasingly concentrated on *applied* areas that are narrower in scope.[10] In the US, the share of basic research carried out by industry fell from 33–35 per cent in the 1950s to 15–20 per cent in the 2000s.[11] Firms have been engaged in more D and less R, so to speak. The result has been a fundamental shift in the composition of R&D away from basic research.[12] This seems highly likely to reduce future innovation opportunities, which have always been driven by a strong interaction between basic and applied research in *both* industry and government.

Indeed, research by Arora, Belenzon and Patacconi provides evidence that since the 1980s, large corporations have shifted away from scientific research. They showed that this trend is consistently displayed by different indicators of firms' investment in research and, importantly, is not driven by any decline in the usefulness of science as an input into innovation. They concluded that firms still profit from the fruits of scientific research as much as before, but have become less willing to invest in it.[13]

Why is this happening? One of the reasons the private sector has been disinvesting in the difficult R side of R&D is the increasing short-termism of corporations. The rise of the 'shareholder-value' model of corporate governance (discussed in William Lazonick's chapter in this book) has played an important role in the reduced propensity of firms to undertake long-term investment projects. Increased shareholder pressure can limit the ability of firms to invest in areas of long-term innovation, reducing their willingness to take up the kind of risks that innovation requires. The impact of greater short-termism in contemporary shareholder capitalism has been found in studies looking both across countries (for example, Japan vs. the US) and across different sectors.[14] Andrew Haldane's chapter in this book provides further firm-level evidence, showing that in recent decades capital markets have become excessively focused on short-term profits, with a negative impact on the investment rate of publicly-quoted firms.

As Lazonick and O'Sullivan argue, 'maximizing shareholder value' is in effect a managerial ideology that has enabled top executives to get extremely rich in many countries (particularly in the US).[15] Financialised companies have been spending a large and increasing share of their revenues on buying back their own stocks, thus manipulating share prices and boosting the value of stock options, which are closely linked to executive pay. And more recently, Lazonick has shown that between 2003 and 2012, publicly listed companies included in the S&P 500 index used 54 per cent of their earnings (around $2.4 trillion in total) to buy back their own shares.[16] Such spending has occurred at the expense of investment and innovation, as can also be seen from the rising ratio of repurchases (share buybacks) to R&D spending for the Fortune 500 companies.[17]

Such short-termism in corporate behaviour is sometimes discussed as if it was imposed on firms by the unavoidable forces of 'the market'. But it is important to recognise that short-termism is not a characteristic of capitalism or markets *per se*, but a result of particular kinds of corporate governance structures, ownership models and financial cultures.[18] Indeed, as Jacobs and Mazzucato argue in the Introduction to this book, markets are best understood as the *outcomes* of the interactions between different economic actors. Short-termism is a reflection of powerful shifts which have occurred, particularly in the US and UK, over the last two decades, but there is nothing inevitable or universal in such changes. Indeed, the 'varieties of capitalism' literature has shown that business and finance have traditionally been structured very differently in Japan and Germany, for example; and companies with long-term investment perspectives can be found in all economies.[19] It is only by understanding the concrete ways in which firms are governed and why this results in different forms of market behaviour that we can explain how these may contribute to, or undermine, long-term growth.[20]

This question relates not just to the private sector on its own, but also to its relationship with the state: the 'deal' that is struck between government and business. Over recent years this relationship has increasingly exhibited what might be described as 'parasitic' features, with the private business sector lobbying governments to weaken regulations and cut capital gains taxes, but at the same time reducing its share of investment in basic research and thus relying even more on public spending in this area.[21] As we shall show below, future growth will require a very different form of collaboration between public and private sectors, characterised by a healthy symbiosis that is sustainable over the long-term.

Orthodox economic theory and the 'market failure' approach

To meet these challenges and achieve the goal of smart, innovation-led growth, we need to develop a new conceptual framework. For this we need to look beyond the narrow assumptions of mainstream economics, which has paid too little attention to the disequilibrating process of innovation. These models continue to assume that innovation is (a) driven mainly by the individual genius of single entrepreneurs, at best 'facilitated' by the public sector; (b) only characterised by predictable risk (which can be precisely quantified ex-ante by means of well-defined probability distributions, as in lotteries) rather than true uncertainty; and (c) has the same probability of occurrence at any moment in time.

In fact, innovation, as observed in the real world, is of a very different nature. Grounded in empirical observation, the evolutionary approach to understanding economic change has emphasised the following features of innovation: (a) it is *collective*, characterised by a system of heterogeneous public and private actors, interacting in different ways; (b) it is *uncertain* in the Knightian sense,[22] with potentially unpredictable outcomes whose probability is not known ex-ante; (c) it is based on routines which are difficult to emulate even when patents expire as routines are often tacit (hence hard to imitate), and embedded in organisational practices and memory, and (d) it is *path dependent* and cumulative with a 'fat-tailed distribution'.[23] This means that, rather than having an equally likely probability of occurring at any time, innovation occurs in waves and clusters, a feature emphasised in the work of Schumpeter. Grasping the collective, uncertain, tacit and persistent nature of innovation is crucial to asking the right policy questions on how to achieve smart, innovation-led growth. It also means that economic models must be able to account for heterogeneity and path-dependency, something that traditional statistical tools that assume 'normally distributed' variables cannot.[24]

The orthodox economic view sees a particularly limited role for the state in the innovation process. In general state intervention is justified by orthodox economics only if it is aimed at fixing situations in which markets fail to efficiently allocate resources.[25] This *market failure theory* suggests that the role of governments is to 'correct' or 'fix' markets by investing in public goods (such as scientific research and defence), and by devising market mechanisms to internalise external costs (such as pollution) or external benefits (such as herd immunity).

While market failure theory provides valuable insights, it is most useful for constructing policies aimed at adjusting existing trajectories provided by markets. This perspective takes the thought experiment of neoclassical general equilibrium as its reference point, assuming the existence and stability of an exogenously determined 'equilibrium'. This view admits that actual economies can deviate from this theoretical benchmark and points to the imperfections that prevent real markets from reaching this deterministic bliss point. But this ignores Schumpeter's main insight that in a neoclassical competitive equilibrium (with complete markets and perfect information), there would be no scope at all for innovation and economic development; in fact, innovation means disequilibrating structural changes. A framework that sees policy as simply fixing imperfections in order to let markets achieve an exogenously determined equilibrium state is of little use when policy is needed to dynamically create and shape new markets in processes of evolution and transformation.

Within the orthodox framework, the existence of some market failure is a necessary but not sufficient condition for state intervention.[26] If government is to step in, it is claimed that gains from the intervention must outweigh the associated costs due to 'governmental failures'[27] such as capture by private interests (cronyism, corruption, rent-seeking),[28] misallocation of resources (for example, 'picking losers')[29] or undue competition with private initiatives ('crowding out').[30] There is thus a presumed trade-off between two inefficient outcomes, one of which is generated by free markets (market failure) and the other by public intervention (government failure). Neo-Keynesian economists tend to emphasise market failures, especially those related to imperfect information,[31] and thus to advocate more extensive government intervention, while public choice theorists[32] tend to see the market as usually able to 'self-correct' and worry more about government failures.

The 'crowding-out' criticism refers to the way in which public investment is said to displace private initiative. Managed long-term interest rates, it is claimed, crowd-out credit that would otherwise be supplied (at a higher rate of interest) by private agents in a free market, thereby inhibiting private capital markets. In 2010, for instance, the German development bank KfW was accused of crowding-out private finance institutions issuing short-term debt.[33] Theoretically, this facet of the crowding-out criticism is associated with mainstream (neo-Keynesian or new classical) models in which public investments displace private ones, particularly if government deficits are financed through debt.[34] However, the crowding-out hypothesis rests on very particular assumptions. It assumes that: (a) the economy is in a state of continuous full employment of resources, which (as Stephany Griffith-Jones and Giovanni Cozzi point out in their chapter in this book) is not the case in current circumstances; and (b) ignores the way in which the state often does precisely what the private sector does not, such as financing long-term infrastructure projects and innovation. As we see below, this role is more about creating and shaping markets than just 'fixing' them.

A second type of critique based on the idea of crowding out is often directed at public institutions, such as the BBC, which have historically invested in activities bolder and more strategically directed than market failure theory would allow.[35] When they do this they are often criticised for being too active, taking up a share of the market that should be reserved for private firms. Should the BBC include popular light entertainment in its programme portfolio? Should a government R&D agency invest in applied research and commercial ventures? The answers to these questions are often 'No' because they fall outside the traditional justification for public investment. But this is a problematic view. It ignores the fact that those countries that have achieved innovation-led growth have often required this very type of strategic, directed investment that has gone beyond classical definitions of the 'public good'. Indeed, they point to the need for a broader concept of public value altogether.

A third common criticism attacks public investments in particular technologies and sectors, which attempt to 'pick winners'. Critics argue that the state is poor at doing this because politicians and bureaucrats lack the capability, information and incentives provided by the market, which are necessary for success.[36] However, it is notable that the inability of the state to pick winners is usually an *a priori* assumption; very few studies have attempted systematically to evaluate industrial policy of this kind.[37] The preconception that the state is structurally unable to target technologies and sectors is widespread also because governments tend to take full blame when things go wrong (as in the cases of the loss-making supersonic aircraft Concorde or the failed solar manufacturer Solyndra, discussed further below), while the big successes of state support (such as the internet or various forms of biotechnology, described in the following section) are often attributed exclusively to the private actors that ultimately profited from them.

The state as a key actor in the innovation system

In fact—contrary to the claims of the traditional 'market failure' approach—the state has been a central player in many of the most important innovations of the recent past. The real story behind Silicon Valley and other dynamic centres of innovation is not the one told by the orthodox view, of the state getting out of the way so that risk-taking venture capitalists and garage inventors could do their thing. From the Internet to nanotechnology, most of the fundamental technological advances of the past half century—in both basic research and downstream commercialisation—were funded by government agencies, with private businesses moving into the game only once the returns were in clear sight.[38] For example, in both biotechnology and nanotechnology most of the private actors entered only after the public sector invested in these areas. And entrepreneurs like Bill Gates and Steve Jobs were able to create great products because they surfed the waves of government-funded technologies. Indeed, all of the technologies that make the iPhone a smart phone were funded by the state, including the internet, GPS, touchscreen display and the voice-activated Siri personal assistant.[39]

The story here is in fact of an 'entrepreneurial state'.[40] This was not just about the government funding 'basic' upstream research, a typical 'public good' in market failure theory. US government agencies funded both the basic and applied research and, in some cases, went as far downstream as to provide early-stage risk finance to companies deemed too risky by the private financial sector. In its early years Apple received $500,000 from the

Small Business Investment Corporation (SBIC), a financing arm of the US government. Likewise, Compaq and Intel received early-stage funding (to set up the companies), not from venture capital but from the public Small Business Innovation Research (SBIR) programme, which has been particularly active in providing early stage finance to risk-taking companies.[41]

It is sometimes assumed that such investments are only characteristic of the 'military industrial complex', with the Department of Defence playing the leading role. In fact, similar strategic investments have been made by the US government through the Department of Health and the Department of Energy. Around 75 per cent of the most innovative drugs on the market today (the so-called 'new molecular' entities with priority rating) owe much of their funding to the publicly funded National Institutes of Health (NIH).[42] Since 2000, the NIH has invested more than $400 billion (2013 dollars) in the biotech-pharma knowledge base, $29 billion in 2013 alone. In energy, the US government has been behind some of the biggest advances in renewable energy through innovation in agencies like ARPA-E, the sister organisation of DARPA in the Department of Energy, as well as the recent revolution in shale gas.[43]

Timing is important. Although venture capital entered the biotech industry in the late 1980s and early 1990s, all the heavy investments in this sector occurred in the 1950s, 1960s and 1970s—and were mostly made by the state.[44] Venture capitalists only entered 20 years after the state had funded the most high-risk and capital-intensive stages of development. The same pattern is being repeated in the areas of renewable energy technology. In many of the leading countries in the field, including the US, China, Germany and Denmark, the state funds those areas within the sector that are characterised by the highest degree of technological risk and capital intensity.[45] Business typically waits for future returns to become more certain before entering. Indeed, evidence shows that the early high-risk stage of the innovation chain, characterised by high capital intensity, is disproportionately occupied by public actors. It is these early direct public investments that prepare the ground, creating a new landscape which businesses later develop. This also suggests that those policies which are overly focused on indirect support to business, through different types of tax incentives, ignore the need for direct policies which create the technological and market opportunities that are required for businesses to exercise their 'animal spirits'.[46] It also means that if business admits that it waits for the state to do the early heavy lifting, a sharing of the rewards is required downstream, to enable the state to continue playing this role in the future. We come to this in the next section.

These examples show that the role of the state has been much broader and more fundamental than just fixing market failures. It's important to note that this is not just a criticism of neoclassical theory. In Keynesian models, state investment has a largely counter-cyclical function: it is necessary during slumps to support aggregate demand and prevent a recessionary spiral. This role, too, can be seen as a response to a market failure, in particular a coordination failure that leads private agents to simultaneously withdraw their spending during recessions. But many successful public investments, such as those behind these major technological breakthroughs, were put in place during economic upswings. The lesson is that it is not simply in recession that the state has a valuable public investment role.

A further crucial aspect of these public investments in innovation is that they did not just provide finance to private actors to do something that was already in their minds. Rather, they created and shaped entirely new markets and sectors. That is, the public role was not limited to facilitating and de-risking the private sector for something that it already wanted to do; it made things happen that otherwise would not have. In financing the race into space, for example, and then by initiating the development of the internet and the biotechnology and nanotech sectors, public agencies actively envisioned a new direction of change, defining new 'missions' to be tackled.[47] Such 'mission orientation' of public policy did not necessarily occur top-down, through centralised ministries, but was often set through the decentralised activities of different public agencies and departments that selected particular sectors, technologies and broadly defined areas to develop. Block and Keller have described this decentralised directionality as a 'developmental network state'.[48] This required the state to take on risk and uncertainty: some choices win (such as the internet) while others fail. Failure in some cases is inevitable, but should then become a source of policy evaluation. Indeed, the success of state R&D organisations such as DARPA, in the US Department of Defense, has been attributed to the attention it pays to experimental processes to enable organisational learning.[49] It is an example of what Albert Hirschman called the use of 'policy as a process' to foster learning within the public sector.[50]

The question we should be asking is not whether the state should seek to pick winners or not, but how to foster more debate and transparency on *which directions* should be taken. Missions set up grand challenges, which are, however, concrete enough to enable actors to know when the mission is nearly complete. Missions require different sectors to work together (going to the moon involved a dozen sectors), and different forms of public–private collaborations. They are not based on choosing single technologies, but a host of different ones in a portfolio approach. Germany's *Energiewende* mission, to eliminate all non-renewable energy sources in the country, includes an investment portfolio in different types of renewable energy, as well as strong demand-pull policies. In the US, energy policies have also included fracking for shale gas, promoted by decades of explorative innovation by the Department of Energy. While fracking was later criticised by environmentalists, opening up debates about directionality would enable such criticisms to be located more in the beginning of the mission-oriented investment process, when such choices are being made.

Karl Polanyi, who envisioned this role of the state in creating and shaping markets, was an economic historian and sociologist who understood markets as being deeply embedded in social institutions, with policy not standing on the sidelines but within the very *market creation* process. In his seminal work, *The Great Transformation*, Polanyi described the way in which capitalist markets are deeply 'embedded' in social and political institutions, rendering meaningless the usual static juxtaposition of state vs. market: 'The road to the free market was opened and kept open by an enormous increase in continuous, centrally organized and controlled interventionism'.[51] Polanyi's description, to some degree, complements John Maynard Keynes' challenge for governments to think big: 'The important thing for government is not to do things which individuals are doing already, and to do them a little better or a little worse; but to do those things which at present are not done at all'.[52] The list of what is not being done does not only include areas characterised by positive and negative externalities, but also the vision behind the creation of new market landscapes. This view of policy, as creating new landscapes, has implications for the transformational effect of government policies, which is not found in macroeconomic interpretations of Keynes' work.

Public rewards for public risk-taking

By ignoring the entrepreneurial role of the state as lead investor and risk taker, and focusing only on the role of the public sector as setting the background (horizontal) conditions, orthodox economic theory has also ignored the way in which the socialisation of risks should be accompanied by the socialisation of rewards. Indeed, the more downstream the public investments, into particular technologies and firms, the higher the risk that one of those technologies or firms will fail. But this is indeed normal, as any venture capitalist would admit: for every success there are many failures. The US government has recently experienced this, with a big success, the Tesla S car (which received a $465 million loan guaranteed by the taxpayer), occurring in the same period as a big loss, a $535 million guaranteed loan to the solar manufacturer Solyndra, which later went bankrupt. In reality, the most successful capitalist economies have had active states that made risky investments, some of them contributing to technological revolutions. The Finnish public innovation agency SITRA has had some great successes, but also some failures. Likewise Israel's public venture capital fund Yozma. In the Anglo-Saxon economies public debate has been too quick to criticise public investments when they go wrong and too slow to acknowledge the state's role in those that succeed.

But this then raises a more fundamental question: how to make sure that, like private venture capital funds, the state can reap back some return from the successes (the 'upside'), in order to cover the inevitable losses (the 'downside') and finance the next round of investments. This is especially important given the path-dependent and cumulative nature of innovation. Returns arise slowly; they are negative in the beginning and gradually build up, potentially generating huge rewards after decades of investments. Indeed companies in areas like information technology, biotechnology and nanotechnology had to accept many years of zero profits before any returns were in sight. If the collective process of innovation is not properly recognised, the result will be a narrow group of private corporations and investors reaping the full returns of projects which the state helped to initiate and finance.

So who gets the reward for innovation? Some economists argue that returns occur to the public sector through the knowledge spillovers that are created (new knowledge that can benefit various areas of the economy), and via the taxation system (due to new jobs generated, as well as taxes paid by companies benefiting from the investments). But the evolution of the patenting system, in which it has become easier to take out patents on upstream research, mean that knowledge dissemination can effectively be blocked and spillovers cannot be assumed. At the same time the global movement of capital means that the particular country or region funding initial investments in innovation is by no means guaranteed to reap the wider economic benefits, such as to employment or taxation. Indeed, corporate taxation has been falling globally, and corporate tax avoidance and evasion rising. Some of the technology companies which have benefited significantly from public support, such as Apple and Google, have also been among those accused of using their international operations to avoid paying tax.[53] Perhaps most importantly, while the spillovers that occur from upstream 'basic' investments, such as education and research, should not be thought of as needing to earn a *direct* return for the state, downstream investments targeted at specific companies and technologies are qualitatively different. Precisely because some investments in firms and technologies will fail, the state could treat these downstream investments as a portfolio, and enable some of the upside success to cover the downside risk.

In particular, there is a strong case for arguing that—where technological breakthroughs have occurred as a result of targeted state interventions benefiting specific companies—the state should reap some of the financial rewards over time by retaining ownership of a small proportion of the intellectual property it had a hand in creating. This is not to say the state should ever have exclusive licence or hold a large enough proportion of the value of an innovation to deter its diffusion (and this is almost never the case). The role of government is not to run commercial enterprises, it is to spark innovation elsewhere. But by owning some of the value it has created, which over time has the potential for significant growth, funds can be generated for reinvestment into new potential innovations. By adopting a 'portfolio' approach to public investments in innovation, success from a few projects can then help cover the losses from other projects.[54] In this way, *both* risks and rewards are socialised.

There are various ways to consider a direct return to the state for its investments in innovation. One is to ensure that loans and guarantees given by the state to business come with conditions, like the 'income-contingent loans' given to students. If a company receives a loan or grant from the state, it could be required to pay back a portion if and when it makes profits above a certain threshold. The state could also retain equity or royalties in the companies it supports. This already occurs in some countries which have public venture capital funds, including Israel (through the Yozma public venture capital fund) and Finland (through its public innovation funds in SITRA and the Finnish Industry Investment fund.). Equity stakes are also retained by state investment banks, for example in Germany, Brazil and China, as we shall discuss below. The key here is to allow risks and rewards to be realigned. And this won't happen until it is acknowledged that the state's role in the process generating economic growth is not just one of administration and incentives, but also one of active risk-taking and investment. Indeed, Keynes believed that 'socialization of investment', through such participation, could be a way to stabilize both investment and growth.[55]

Patient capital: the role of state on how to better align risks and rewards investment banks

All the dynamics described above—the investment slowdown in Western economies, growing short-termism and the historical 'entrepreneurial' role of the state—raise a fundamental question for capitalism: how to make 'patient long-term capital' available to finance innovation. Schumpeter, who put innovation at the centre of his understanding of capitalism, called the banker the 'ephor' of the exchange economy (a Latin term for the magistrates that supervised the Spartan kings) because he recognised that innovation must be financed.[56] And he thought that it was the banks that had to bring such finance into the 'circular flow' of existing capital. What he did not foresee, however, was that in reality the banking system—indeed the entire private financial system—would find ways to make money simply from speculation rather than from financing the productive economy. That is, finance is financing itself—banks financing mortgage backed securities, which use credit default swaps, for example—rather than what Hyman Minsky called the 'capital development' of the economy.[57] The speculative and short-term character of the financial system means that the banker is now more the problem than the solution Schumpeter assumed.[58]

Even when finance does pay attention to the real economy, the relationship is not always beneficial. This is because finance is not neutral: the kind of finance received by companies may affect their future investment patterns.[59] For example, venture capital (VC) was initially created to allow innovative companies to receive finance in their early-stage, high-risk phases. But the evidence shows that in industries particularly reliant on VC finance, such as biotechnology, many firms have suffered from the VC model. Most VC funds are 'exit-driven' and their exits occur usually within three to five years of initial investment, either via a buyout to a large company or an initial public offering (IPO). Lazonick and Tulum argue that this has led to a prevalence of many 'product-less' public companies in the biotech field (what they call PLIPOS, or product-less IPOs), a sign that the VC model is often not able to nurture and support the underlying complex and uncertain knowledge base.[60] This problem is especially relevant in the emerging clean-technology sector, where venture capital—where it invests at all—produces the quick in/out funding dynamics that result in bankruptcies such as that of Solyndra in 2012. Indeed, Solyndra's key business backers were venture capitalists, and, like all venture capitalists, they eagerly awaited an IPO, merger or acquisition to provide an 'exit' from their investments. But a successful 'exit' is not always possible in uncertain markets. When Solyndra's key investors abandoned their $1.1 billion investment, 1,000 jobs were lost, and a $535 million government-guaranteed loan was wasted. Rather than staying the course, in other words, Solyndra's investors jumped ship. The irony is that government support often makes companies like Solyndra more attractive to investors, who seek the State's 'patient capital' and respond to its signals. Is this a symbiotic eco-system? Hardly. Arguing that 'science is not a business', Gary Pisano suggests that the VC model is especially problematic for science-based sectors characterised by complex and interdisciplinary knowledge bases.[61]

It is precisely due to the short-term nature of private finance that the role of public finance is so important in nurturing the parts of the innovation chain subject to long lead times and high uncertainty. While in some countries this has occurred through public agencies, such as DARPA and NIH (discussed above), in others patient finance has been provided through publicly owned development banks, otherwise known as state investment banks.

State investment banks (SIBs) have their historical roots in the monetary agreements of Bretton Woods and the reconstruction plans for Europe following World War II. The idea was to create an institution that promoted financial stability through a permanent flow of finance to fund the reconstruction plan and unleash agricultural production potential, thus preventing the deleterious effects that speculative private finance could have on post-World War II economic recovery. Following this rationale, the International Bank for Reconstruction and Development (IBRD) was created, providing its first loan to France in 1947.[62] Other national development banks were founded around that time, such as KfW in Germany (1948),[63] with the aim of channelling international and national funds to the promotion of long-term growth, infrastructure and modern industry. While in industrialised countries these institutions focused on niche areas (such as aiding specific sectors), in developing countries SIBs such as the Brazilian BNDES initially promoted a catching-up agenda, with heavy investments in infrastructure.[64]

In subsequent decades, SIBs diversified their operations and focus. In the mid-1950s, KfW assumed the responsibility to provide finance for environmental protection and small and medium-sized enterprises (SMEs), roles that were intensified in the 1970s when it also began to target energy efficiency and innovation.[65] Other development banks followed suit: BNDES, for instance, created new credit lines for SMEs in the 1980s, and in the following decade began to experiment with financing programs targeted at high-tech firms and innovation development.[66] By the 2000s, China Development Bank (CDB) was one of the most active SIBs, investing in regional economic development and industrial catching-up; supporting and nurturing new ventures and innovation development; and, later in the decade, targeting finance to projects aimed at 'green growth'.[67] After the outbreak of the global financial crisis in 2007, SIBs across the world significantly promoted countercyclical credit, increasing their loan portfolio by 36 per cent on average between 2007 and 2009, with some increasing their loans by more than 100 per cent.[68]

While the traditional functions of state investment banks were in infra-structure investment and counter-cyclical lending during recessions when private banks restrained credit (thus playing a classic Keynesian role) they have over time become more active as key players in the innovation system. They have provided the patient capital for innovative firms, and also focused on modern societal challenges with technological 'missions'. For example, SIBs have notably filled the vacuum left behind by private commercial banks since the outbreak of the crisis, more than trebling their investments in clean energy projects between 2007 and 2012 (Figure 1).[69] A recent report by Bloomberg New Energy Finance finds that in 2013

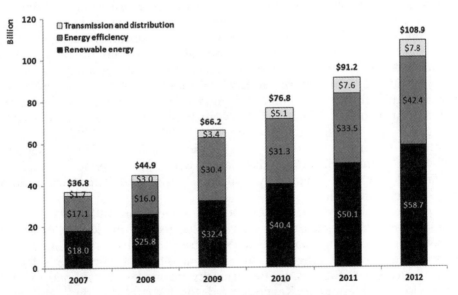

Figure 1: *Renewable energy investments financed by SIBs, by sector*
Source: Mazzucato and Penna (2014), 'Beyond market failures: The market creating and shaping roles of state investment banks', SPRU Working Paper Series, 2014-21, 2014, http://www.sussex.ac.uk/spru/documents/2014-21-swps-mazzucato-and-penna.pdf (accessed 22 April 2016); FS-UNEP/BNEF, Global Trends in Renewable Energy Investment 2013, BNEF, 2013.

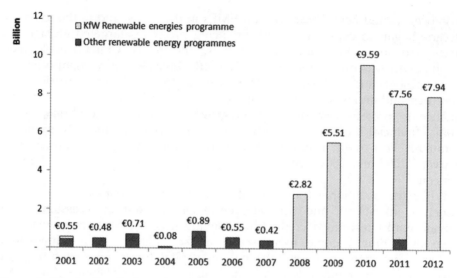

Figure 2: *Kfw funding for 'green' projects*
Source: Mazzucato and Penna (2014), based on data from KfW's annual reports

state investment banks were the largest funders of the deployment and diffusion phase of renewable energy, outpacing investment from the private sector.[70] The four most active banks are (in order) the China Development Bank, the German KfW, the European Investment Bank (EIB) and the Brazilian BNDES. Examples of 'mission-oriented' investments include the EIB's €14.7 billion commitment to sustainable city projects in Europe,[71] the efforts of KfW to support Germany's *Energiewende* policies through the greening and modernisation of German industries and infrastructures,[72] China Development Bank's investments in renewable energies,[73] and the technology fund put in place by BNDES to channel resources toward selected technologies in Brazil (FUNTEC).[74] Figure 2 below, for example, illustrates the way in which KfW has not only played a classical Keynesian counter-cyclical role, but also directed that funding towards 'climate financing'.

But when state investment banks actively finance innovation and promote transformational objectives, are they just correcting market failures? The lesson from recent 'mission-oriented' programs of SIBs is that in practice they are actively creating and shaping markets, not only fixing them.[75] When successful, they have the capacity to make things happen that otherwise would not, as Keynes called for the state to do.[76] But more importantly, they are paving the way for the kind of 'Great Transformation' that Polanyi referred to when arguing that market-based mechanisms cannot be expected to provide the solution to societal and environmental challenges.[77]

At a time in which countries need not only to promote growth but also to address key challenges of this kind, SIBs seem well positioned to effectively promote the much needed capital development of the economy in a smart, inclusive and sustainable direction. This, however, requires monitoring and assessing the degree to which public investments are pushing the market frontier, and in what direction. Analysing, theorising and constructively criticising what is being done, using a market shaping policy framework in combination with a market fixing one, presents a new agenda for pubic policy in economics.

Conclusion

Long run growth has been highly dependent on public and private investments in innovation. Areas like Silicon Valley, hubs of modern day innovation, have required public institutions that not only fix market failures but which also actively seek to create and shape markets. They have needed the organisations of an 'entrepreneurial state', willing to take risks along the entire innovation chain and driven by missions, from putting a man on the moon (where NASA's investments spilled over to many of the technologies in smart phones), to today's imperative to develop the green economy. They have also required an engaged private sector, willing to reinvest profits back into production, and undertaking downstream innovation. Yet today Western capitalist economies are suffering from a crisis in long-term investment, due to increasing short-termism in the private sector, and increasing austerity in the public sector. Economies are not getting the kind of long-term patient finance that is needed for innovation to flourish.

Indeed, as the private financial system has become obsessed with itself rather than nurturing growth in the productive economy we have witnessed the rise of active strategic 'mission-oriented' state investment banks. Some of these banks are playing a key role today in the 'green transformation' of countries like Germany and China, even though these countries are very different in terms of their development challenges.

Yet it is not enough to have such active public agents. It is also necessary to have the right policy framework that guides their investments and that can also assess and evaluate them. Rather than framing such assessments within a static approach that inevitably argues that any public institution which does more than fixing failures is 'crowding out' private investment, it is essential to build a new framework for policy analysis.

A market-shaping/creating framework can start by recognising that markets are outcomes of choices being made within both public and private institutions. This is not novel—public policy has always provided directionality. The winning IT revolution was 'picked' in the US in just the same way that the green revolution is being chosen by some countries today. For such transformations to occur, patient finance is required. How that patient finance is organised, and how it interacts with broadly defined missions to set directions, is a key challenge. As Carlota Perez discusses in her chapter in this book, the 'green' direction is not only about renewable energy, but also about new production, distribution and consumption systems in all sectors.[78] This is not about prescribing specific technologies, but providing directions of change with which bottom-up solutions can then experiment. As Andy Stirling has recently put it, 'The more demanding the innovation challenges like poverty, ill health or environmental damage, the greater becomes the importance of effective policy. This is not a question of "picking winners"—but about investing across a host of different areas (with a portfolio approach) with the objective of achieving societal missions. And building the most fruitful conditions for deciding what 'winning' even means.'[79]

This sort of agenda requires an emphasis on diversity, as emphasised in the framework of evolutionary economics, but also a belief in the role of the public sector. In turn that would lead to a strengthening of its internal capacity to understand and interact with new technological opportunities when they appear. In sum, this chapter has argued that to approach the innovation challenge of the future, we must open up the discussion, away from worries about picking winners and crowding out, and instead ask four big questions:[80]

1. *Direction.* How can public policy set the direction and route of change? What can be learned from the ways in which directions were set in the past, and how can we stimulate more democratic debate about such directionality?
2. *Evaluation.* How can a conceptualisation of the role of the public sector in the economy (providing an alternative to market failure theory) translate into new indicators and assessment tools for evaluating public policies, beyond static cost/benefit analysis? How does this alter the crowding in/out narrative?
3. *Organisational change.* How should public organisations be structured so they promote risk-taking and explorative capacity and the capabilities needed to envision and manage contemporary challenges?
4. *Risks and rewards.* How should we frame investment tools in such a way as to socialise not only the risks but also the rewards, allowing for growth to be more inclusive?

Notes

1 See Innovation Union Flagship Initiative in the Europe 2020 strategy, http://ec.europa.eu/research/innovation-union/index_en.cfm (accessed 7 September 2015).
2 R. J. Gordon, 'Is US economic growth over? Faltering innovation confronts the six headwinds', Centre for Economic Policy Research, Policy Insight No 63, September 2012. Available at: http://www.cepr.org/sites/default/files/policy_insights/PolicyInsight63.pdf (accessed 13 June 2015).

3 See for example C. Teulings and R. Baldwin, eds, *Secular Stagnation: Facts, Causes and Cures*, London, CEPR Press, 2014. Available at http://www.voxeu.org/content/secular-stagnation-facts-causes-and-cures (accessed 20 May 2015).

4 A public good is a good that is both non-excludable and non-rivalrous so the use by one individual does not exclude the use by another. This means it is hard to appropriate privately the return from public goods, and hence they are characterised by too little private investment. Public goods might include clean air, national defence, basic research, all of which create benefits, positive externalities, for the wider community besides the agent investing in it.

5 R. Nelson and S. Winter, 'An Evolutionary Theory of Economic Change', 1984, Cambridge, MA, Harvard University Press; P. M. Romer, 'The Origins of Endogenous Growth', *The Journal of Economic Perspectives*, vol. 8, no. 1, 1994, pp. 3–22.

6 C. Freeman, *Technology Policy and Economic Performance: Lessons from Japan*, London, Pinter, 1987.

7 B.-A. Lundvall, 'Introduction', in B.-A. Lundvall, ed. *National Systems of Innovation: Towards a Theory of Innovation and Interactive Learning*, London, Pinter, 1992, pp. 1–20.

8 SSTI, 'The Changing Nature of U.S. Basic Research: Trends in Funding Sources' http://ssti.org/blog/changing-nature-us-basic-research-trends-funding-sources (accessed 8 August 2015).

9 Eurostat, 'Science, Technology and Innovation Database', R&D Expenditure at National and Regional Level, Key Indicators—GERD by Source of Funds (%) [rd_e_fundgerd] (extracted on 23 December 2015).

10 A. Arora, S. Belenzon and A. Patacconi, 'Killing the Golden Goose? The Decline of Science in Corporate R&D', *NBER*, January 2015.

11 SSTI, 'The Changing Nature of U.S. Basic Research'.

12 See M. Muro and S. Andes, 'U.S. R&D: A Troubled Enterprise', Metropolitan Policy Program, Brookings Institute, May 2015.

13 Arora et al., 'Killing the Golden Goose?'.

14 W. Lazonick and M. O'Sullivan, 'Maximizing Shareholder Value: A New Ideology for Corporate Governance', *Economy and Society*, vol. 29, no. 10, 2000, pp. 13–35.

15 Ibid.

16 W. Lazonick, 'Profits without Prosperity', *Harvard Business Review*, vol. 92, no. 9, 2014, pp. 46–55.

17 M. Mazzucato, 'Financing innovation: creative destruction vs. destructive creation', in special issue of *Industrial and Corporate Change*, M. Mazzucato, ed., vol. 22, no. 4, 851–67, See repurchases/R&D in Figure 1, p. 857.

18 J. Kay, 'The Kay review of UK Equity Markets and Long-term Decision Making', Final Report (July 2012).

19 P. A. Hall and D. Soskice, *Varieties of Capitalism and Institutional Complementarities* (pp. 43–76), New York, Springer US, 2001.

20 Lazonick and O'Sullivan, 'Maximizing Shareholder Value'.

21 The share of basic research funded by the private sector has fallen, causing the public sector to focus more on basic research, and in the process cut its applied research budget (Arora et al., 'Killing the Golden Goose?').

22 Frank Knight (and later John Maynard Keynes) emphasised the difference between risk and uncertainty. See F. H. Knight, *Risk, Uncertainty and Profit* New York, Hart, Schaffner and Marx, 1921.

23 Nelson and Winter *An Evolutionary Theory of Economic Change.*
24 This is why evolutionary theory has made use of advances in complexity science, such as agent-based modeling, and non-parametric techniques in statistics which allow fat-tailed distributions to be explored.
25 A classic reference is K. Arrow, 'An Extension of the Basic Theorems of Classical Welfare Economics', paper presented at the Second Berkeley Symposium on Mathematical Statistics and Probability, Berkeley, 1951.
26 C. Wolf, *Markets or Governments: Choosing between Imperfect Alternatives*, Cambridge, MA, MIT Press, 1988.
27 G. Tullock, A. Seldon and G. L. Brady, *Government Failure: A Primer in Public Choice*, Washington, DC, Cato Institute, 2002.
28 A. Krueger, 'The Political Economy of the Rent-seeking Society', *The American Economic Review*, vol. 64, no. 3, 1974, pp. 291–303.
29 O. Falck, C. Gollier and L. Woessmann, 'Arguments for and against Policies to Promote National Champions', in O. Falck, C. Gollier and L. Woessmann, eds, *Industrial Policy for National Champions*, Cambridge, MA, MIT Press, 2001, pp. 3–9.
30 M. Friedman, 'Crowding Out or Crowding In? The Economic Consequences of Financing Government Deficits', *Brookings Papers on Economic Activity*, no. 3, 1979, pp. 593–654.
31 J. Stiglitz and A. Weiss, 'Credit Rationing in Markets with Imperfect Information', *American Economic Review*, vol. 3, no. 71, 1981, pp. 393–410.
32 See, for example, J. M. Buchanan, 'Public Choice: The Origins and Development of a Research Program', *Champions of Freedom*, vol. 31, 2003, pp. 13–32.
33 See EuroWeek, 'KfW Domination of ECP Ends Fears of SSA Crowding-out', *EuroWeek*, March 2011.
34 See Friedman, 'Crowding Out or Crowding In?'.
35 As explored in this blog by Mazzucato in 2016, as part of the debate on the BBC charter renewal http://blog.britac.ac.uk/the-future-of-the-bbc-the-bbc-as-market-shaper-and-creator/ (accessed 9 May 2016).
36 J. A. Hanson, 'Public Sector Banks and Their Transformation', in *6th Annual Financial Markets and Development Conference: The Role of State-Owned Financial Institutions—Policy and Practice* Washington, DC, Brookings Institute Press, 2004.
37 M. Mazzucato, 'From market-fixing to market-creating: a new framework for economic policy', forthcoming in a special issue of Industry and Innovation: 'Innovation policy – can it make a difference?' DOI 10.1080/13662716.1146124.
38 F. L. Block and R. M. Keller, *State of Innovation: The U.S. Government's Role in Technology Development* Boulder, CO, Paradigm Publishers, 2011.
39 Mazzucato, 'Financing innovation'.
40 M. Mazzucato, *The Entrepreneurial State*, London, Anthem Press, 2013.
41 M. R. Keller and F. Block, 'Explaining the transformation in the US innovation system: the impact of a small government program', *Socio-Economic Review*, mws021, 2012.
42 M. Angell, *The Truth about the Drug Companies* New York, Random House, 2004.
43 A. Trembath, T. Nordhaus, M. Shellenberger and J. Jenkins, 'US government role in shale gas fracking history: an overview'. Breakthrough Institute Report, http://thebreakthrough.org/archive/shale_gas_fracking_history_and (accessed 13 April 2016).
44 M. Mazzucato and G. Dosi, eds, *Knowledge Accumulation and Industry Evolution: The Case of Pharma-biotech* Cambridge, UK, Cambridge University Press, 2006;

S. P. Vallas, D. L. Kleinman and D. Biscotti, 'Political Structures and the Making of US Biotechnology', in Block and Keller, State of Innovation: pp. 57–76.

45 M. Mazzucato and G. Semieniuk, 'Financing renewable energy: who is financing what and why it matters', paper presented at Bloomberg New Energy Finance conference, 11 February 2016. http://missionorientedfinance.com/wp-content/uploads/2016/02/SemMaz_ESRC-SPRU_feb11.pdf (accessed 9 May 2016).

46 Indeed, countries like the US, Finland and Israel which have a higher proportion of 'direct' public financing for business R&D (verus indirect) tend to achieve higher business spending on R&D (BERD). This suggests the direct spend crowds in the private spend. See OECD figures, http://www.oecd.org/site/innovation-strategy/45188105.pdf (accessed 12 December 2015).

47 D. Foray, D. Mowery and R. R. Nelson, 'Public R&D and social challenges: What lessons from mission R&D programs?' Research Policy, vol. 41, no. 10, 2012, pp. 1697–902.

48 Block and Keller, State of Innovation.

49 J. Abbate, Inventing the Internet Cambridge, MA, MIT Press, 1999.

50 A. O. Hirschman, Development Projects Observed Washington, DC, Brookings Institute Press, 1967; D. Rodrik, 'From Welfare State to Innovation State', 2014, https://www.project-syndicate.org/commentary/labor-saving-technology-by-dani-rodrik-2015-01?barrier=true (accessed 11 October 2015).

51 K. Polanyi, The Great Transformation: The Political and Economic Origins of Our Time (2nd ed.), Boston, MA, Beacon Press, 2001 [1944], p. 144.

52 J. M. Keynes, The End of Laissez-faire London, England, Prometheus Books, 1926, p. 46.

53 See for example D. C. Johnston, 'How Google and Apple make their taxes disappear', Newsweek, 14 December 2014, http://www.newsweek.com/2014/12/26/how-google-and-apple-make-their-taxes-disappear-291571.html (accessed 22 April 2016).

54 For an argument on how a public sector portfolio approach can address risks and rewards see, Mazzucato 'The Innovative State', Foreign Affairs, January/February 2015, pp. 61–8 and Rodrik, 'From Welfare State to Innovation State'.

55 J. M. Keynes, The Collected Writings of John Maynard Keynes, vol. 7, Cambridge, UK, Cambridge University Press, 1973, pp. 164, 378.

56 J. A. Schumpeter, The Theory of Economic Development: An Inquiry into Profits, Capital, Credit, Interest, and the Business Cycle, Cambridge, MA, Harvard University Press, 1934 [1912], p. 74.

57 H. P. Minsky, 'The Capitalist Development of the Economy and the Structure of Financial Institutions', The Jerome Levy Economics Institute Working Paper, no. 72, 1992, p. 2.

58 A. Turner, Between Debt and the Devil: Money, Credit, and Fixing Global Finance, Princeton, NJ, Princeton University Press, 2015.

59 Mazzucato, 'Financing innovation'.

60 W. Lazonick and Ö. Tulum, 'US biopharmaceutical finance and the sustainability of the biotech business model', Research Policy, vol. 40, 2011, pp. 1170–87.

61 G. P. Pisano, 'Can Science Be a Business? Lessons from Biotech', Harvard Business Review, October 2006, pp. 114–25.

62 World Bank, History. Available online, http://go.worldbank.org/65Y36GNQB0 (accessed 15 December 2015).

63 M. Schröder, P. Ekins, A. Power, M. Zulauf and R. Lowe, 'The Kfw experience in the reduction of energy use in Co2 emissions from buildings: Operation, impacts and lessons for the UK', London, UCL Energy Institute, University College London and LSE Housing and Communities, London School of Economics, 2011.
64 E. T. Torres Filho and F. N. D. Costa, 'BNDES E O Financiamento Do Desenvolvimento', *Economia e Sociedade*, vol. 21, 2012, pp. 975–1009.
65 KfW, *Annual Report 2008*, Frankfurt am Main, KfW Group, 2009.
66 C. E. Branco, 'Apoio às Pequenas e Médias Empresas de Base Tecnológica: A Experiência do Contec', *Revista do BNDES*, vol. 1, 1994, pp. 129–142; F. L. D. Sousa, ed., 'Bndes 60 Anos: Perspectivas Setoriais', Rio de Janeiro, BNDES, 2012.
67 H. Sanderson and M. Forsythe, 'China's superbank: Debt, oil and influence – how China Development Bank is rewriting the rules of finance', Singapore, John Wiley & Sons, 2013.
68 D. Luna-Martinez and L. Vicente, 'Global Survey of Development Banks', World Bank Policy Research Working Paper, 2012.
69 L. S. Fried, S. Shukla and S. Sawyer, eds, *Global Wind Report: Annual Market Update 2011*, Brussels, Global Wind Energy Council, March 2012.
70 A. Louw, 'Development banks: less for green in 2013?' Renewables Research note, Bloomberg New Energy Finance, 2012.
71 S. Griffith-Jones and J. Tyson, 'The European Investment Bank and Its Role in Regional Development and Integration', in M. A. Cintra and K. D. R. Gomes, eds, *The Transformations of the International Financial System*, Brasília, IPEA, 2012.
72 T. Duve, 'Financing Environmental Protection & Energy Efficiency', KfW Institutional Presentation, 2007; Schröder et al., 'The Kfw Experience in the Reduction of Energy Use'.
73 Sanderson and Forsythe, 'China's Superbank'.
74 BNDES 2012. *Apoio À Inovação*, Rio de Janeiro, BNDES, 2012.
75 M. Mazzucato and C. Penna, 'State investment banks and mission-oriented finance for innovation', in L. Burlamaqui, R. Sobreira and M. Vianna, eds, *The Present and the Future of Development Financial Institutions: Theory and History*, Minds, Rio de Janeiro, 2015.
76 Keynes, *The End of Laissez-faire*.
77 Polanyi, *The Great Transformation*.
78 M. Mazzucato and C. Perez, 'Innovation as Growth Policy', in J. Fagerberg, S. Laestadius and B. Martin, eds, *The Triple Challenge: Europe in a New Age*, Oxford, Oxford University Press, 2015.
79 A. Stirling, 'Making Choices in the Face of Uncertainty', Themed Annual Report of the Government Chief Scientific Adviser, Chapter 2, June 2014, draft mimeo.
80 See M. Mazzucato, 'Innovation Systems: From Fixing Market Failures to Creating Markets', *Intereconomics*, vol. 50, no. 3, 2015, pp. 120–25.

7. Investment-led Growth: A Solution to the European Crisis

STEPHANY GRIFFITH-JONES AND GIOVANNI COZZI

Introduction

EUROPE IS suffering from growth that is too low and unemployment that is too high. This is especially, but not only, true in the southern euro zone countries. While European institutions, and the European Central Bank in particular, had by the end of 2015 at last succeeded in taming financial turmoil (although the situation in Greece may return as a source of uncertainty), they have been far less successful in dealing with economic stagnation. There is no sign suggesting a return to robust growth and full employment in Europe within the next decade.

In this chapter we argue that low investment is at the root of European stagnation, and that a sustained (and sustainable) recovery can only be investment-driven. Investment is necessary to cure insufficient demand and unemployment in the short run, but also to introduce innovative technologies and increase potential output in the long run. Moreover, only higher investment can reverse the disquieting trend of de-industrialisation that can be observed throughout Europe.

However, the measures that the European institutions have so far put in place to revive investment—in particular the 'Growth Compact' and President Jean-Claude Juncker's 'Investment Plan for Europe'—are likely to prove inadequate to deliver the desired outcomes. This chapter argues that a two-pronged approach is needed to achieve a significant increase in European investment. One is to use the European Investment Bank (EIB) and national development banks to help catalyse private investment. The other is to reduce the pace of fiscal consolidation, so that public investment does not continue to fall. As we will show through model simulations, it is the combined impact of public and private investment that will lead to sufficient total investment in Europe. Private investment can be discouraged by lack of public investment and lack of sufficient demand, especially in times of very slow growth: there is strong evidence that public investment 'crowds in' private investment under such circumstances.

In this chapter we make specific proposals on how the EIB, the European Union's regional development bank, can significantly expand its lending to stimulate growth, investment and innovation, particularly in the countries that have suffered most during the sovereign debt crisis. This would help

Published by John Wiley & Sons Ltd, 9600 Garsington Road, Oxford OX4 2DQ, UK and 350 Main Street, Malden, MA 02148, USA

deal with the fragmentation of financial and banking markets that has emerged in Europe since the crisis and has caused enterprises to be severely credit-rationed, particularly in the periphery of the continent.

The role of the EIB, and in parallel of national State Investment Banks (SIBs), is crucial to our proposal, for the reasons set out by Mariana Mazzucato in her chapter in this volume.[1] First, SIBs are able to leverage public funds, enabling them to mobilise large amounts of private investment from relatively limited initial public resources. Second, they can play a stabilising role: while private financial actors tend to expand credit during booms and restrict it during downturns, exacerbating cyclical swings, SIBs are able to 'lean against the wind', playing a countercyclical role. This is especially relevant in the present context of economic stagnation and pervasive macroeconomic uncertainty. Third, and perhaps most important, well-managed SIBs with a clear mandate are able to provide the kind of patient, long-term and mission-oriented finance that is needed to support investment in infrastructure and new technologies. Many of these long-term, capital-intensive and risky projects, which are necessary to deal with great challenges like climate change and energy security, will not be given credit by a private financial sector increasingly oriented towards the short term.[2]

This chapter starts by outlining the weak macroeconomic conditions currently exhibited in the EU, in particular in the euro zone. We then discuss the main EU policy measures that have been implemented in recent years to counteract the decline in productive fixed investment. After illustrating their limited effectiveness, we set out our proposed investment plan for Europe, comprising an expansion of lending by the EIB and slower fiscal consolidation. By estimating the impact of this investment plan on the European economy using the Cambridge Alphametrics Model (CAM), and comparing it with an alternative 'business-as-usual' scenario, we show the potential for stronger investment to stimulate renewed growth and reduce unemployment.

Underinvestment and economic stagnation in Europe

Few would deny that the EU, and the euro zone in particular, are suffering from too low economic growth and too high unemployment. This is most evident and urgent in southern Europe, where Italy and Spain, for example, saw GDP fall by more than 5 per cent between 2008 and 2014, Portugal by 6 per cent over the same period, and Greece by over 25 per cent, a decline larger than in any country during peacetime since the Great Depression of the 1930s. But in Germany, too, output growth averaged little more than 1 per cent per year in the same period. Recovery from the global and European crises was short-lived, as displayed in Figure 1, and there is little sign of a return to robust growth within the next decade.

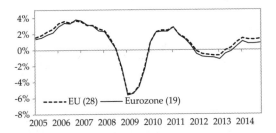

Figure 1: GDP growth (% change on same quarter of previous year)
Source: Eurostat

Another remarkable and disquieting trend is de-industrialisation, which has accelerated during the crisis. In 2013 alone, the share of industry in GDP fell by 1 percentage point at the EU level—from 15 per cent to 14 per cent. In Germany, Europe's major industrial champion, in 2014 the share of industry was 25.1 per cent, or 30.7 per cent including construction activities. This is down from 30.2 per cent (36.8 per cent) in 1991, the first year of common statistics after German reunification: it has been decreasing, on average, by 0.2 per cent per year. A continuation of the present EU trend would imply a 12 per cent share of industry in GDP in 2020, which would be strikingly small for a rich economic zone. To complete the discomforting picture, productivity growth has been extremely low, averaging just 0.8 per cent per year in the EU in the period 2011–2014 (Figure 2).

To reverse these worrying trends, powerful action will be needed. The key to recovery and positive structural transformation in Europe is a significant increase in investment, particularly if linked to innovation. Higher investment accelerates recovery in the short term by expanding aggregate demand and—most importantly—it increases future output and encourages structural transformation. Sustained investment is necessary to incorporate innovative technologies and reignite productivity growth. In a world with growing globalisation and increasing competition, de-industrialisation can only be reversed through higher investment.[3]

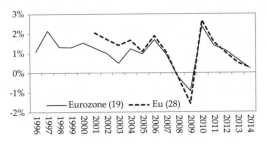

Figure 2: Output per hour worked (% change)
Source: OECD

121

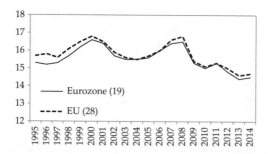

Figure 3: Gross non-residential fixed capital formation as a % of GDP
Source: Eurostat

Indeed in the EU, and especially in the euro zone, an already relatively low level of private investment has fallen further since the beginning of the financial crisis (Figure 3). Particularly dramatic has been the decline in the investment-to-GDP ratio in the south euro zone, from 21.7 per cent in 2007 to only 14 per cent in 2014. In the UK the fall was also sharp, from 15.9 per cent in 2007 to a mere 11.0 per cent in 2012, though this subsequently increased to 13 per cent by 2014. An investment ratio of 19–21 per cent of GDP can be considered normal for a mature country with some industrial strength.[4] Even in countries that are doing rather well, investment is much too low with respect to this benchmark. Indeed, in Germany it was just above 17.5 per cent in 2014.

Countries seeking to return to trend growth after the crisis, and 'convergence' countries with a GDP per capita less than 75 per cent of the EU average, should show a significantly higher investment activity; if not, they will not catch up. In fact, before the crisis, the share of investment was above 20 per cent in countries such as Spain, Greece, Ireland and Portugal. There was certainly misallocation and over-investment in certain sectors during the boom (creating asset bubbles), but the order of magnitude of investment was right. In these four countries investment fell during the crisis, declining by 2014 to less than 15 per cent of GDP.[5] At around 15 per cent de-industrialisation occurs rapidly, as existing stock is depreciated and no replacement or new formation of capital takes place.

Low investment has been dragging down growth and industrial development in Europe, and increasing it is a necessary condition for a real and sustainable recovery. Strategies that try to circumvent this central problem, seeking to revive demand largely by increasing consumer debt, as observed in the UK, or to increase profit margins by indiscriminately cutting labour costs, are not going to work in the medium run.

It is not only the size, but also the timing, of a major boost in investment which is key. The acute phase of the financial part of the euro zone sovereign debt crisis is hopefully over, though the Greek situation remains precarious and may reignite uncertainty in the future. This gives renewed urgency for a less austere and more expansionary fiscal policy, particularly to increase public investment levels and to facilitate private investment.

One of the justifications for fiscal austerity has been the orthodox economic view that public investment does not ultimately boost demand because it merely 'crowds out' private investment, as government borrowing leads to higher interest rates and taxation. This thesis, drawing on the work of Robert Barro,[6] appeared to receive empirical support from the experiences of Ireland and Denmark in the late 1980s. Giavazzi and Pagano's analysis of these countries' fiscal consolidation policies suggested that reductions in government spending have a positive impact on investors' confidence and that reduced public investment enables greater private investment.[7] Alesina and Ardanga went further, arguing that spending reductions accompanied by modest tax cuts are expansionary and therefore were the appropriate policy mix in times of economic crisis.[8]

But the economic environment of the 1980s was not the same as now. It was a period of significant economic expansion. Denmark and Ireland in particular were special cases, as subsequent analysis showed. Fiscal consolidation occurred at the same time as other, favourable economic circumstances, including currency devaluation prior to linking to the European Exchange Rate Mechanism, the opening up of the single European market and (in Ireland's case) new European fiscal revenues.[9] These examples did not in fact make the case for 'expansionary austerity'.

Today, with private investment low even at record low interest rates, the case for 'crowding out' is particularly weak. With significant under-utilised resources in the European economy, there is no constraint on the availability of physical or human capital which would squeeze private investment, and interest rates are likely to remain at historically low levels. On the contrary, as Stiglitz has argued, public investment, particularly in infrastructure, is much more likely to 'crowd in' private investment.[10] Infrastructure investment, such as in energy, transport or telecommunications, creates demand in the short term for a wide range of goods and services in construction and installation supply chains, and in the medium term stimulates growth through an expanded stock of physical capital and greater efficiency. In joint public–private investment projects, the public sector can take on risks which improve the risk–reward ratios for private investors. In both these ways public investment will stimulate and complement, rather than compete with, private investment.

Indeed, when interest rates are low, the enhanced growth in GDP from such investment will almost certainly offset the increased cost of government borrowing, thereby lowering the ratio of debt to GDP. In turn, higher growth with a lower debt ratio, generating expectations of lower future interest and tax rates, and higher consumption may induce further private investment today. In this way public investment under current economic conditions is likely to increase the effective fiscal multiplier.[11]

A recent International Monetary Fund paper has provided empirical evidence for this proposition.[12] Identifying the causal effect of government investment in seventeen OECD economies since 1985, it finds that increased public investment raises output, both in the short term and in the long term; crowds in private investment; and reduces unemployment. Several factors shape the macroeconomic effects of public investment: when there is economic slack and monetary policy accommodation, the demand effects are stronger, and the public-debt-to-GDP ratio may actually decline.

A well-designed pan-European public investment financing strategy would therefore have the potential to crowd in private investment and increase aggregate demand, with long-term positive effects on growth and employment. It should be designed to enhance productive capacity, encouraging present and future sustainable growth by financing economically sustainable projects and activities, in the context of a vision of innovation and structural transformation towards a greener economy. It should support the growth of both existing and new competitive enterprises, especially ones in innovative fields. To have a real chance of success, such a strategy needs to be implementable quickly; have sufficient size to have a significant economic impact; be cost-effective in terms of impact relative to limited additional public resources; ensure significant leverage; and drive the kind of investments that will help to make the European economy more dynamic and equitable. The additional finance, which could be generated by expanding the lending capacity of the European Central Bank and by a better allocation of funds within the EU budget, should provide resources not only for working capital to generate greater employment today, but—above all—for investment in innovation and increased productivity, including in new sectors, strategic for future growth, which will generate jobs in the future.

The current EU policy framework

In June 2012 the European Council approved the so-called 'Growth Compact', a set of measures aimed at encouraging European growth.[13] From the point of view of national fiscal policies, it prescribed continued austerity (though this was described as 'growth-friendly fiscal consolidation'[14]). At the European level, however, the strategy outlined was twofold: first, the Compact stressed the need for further reforms in various fields to deepen the Single Market; second, it required member states to provide €10 billion of additional capital to the EIB. According to the Growth Compact this would unlock, through leverage, up to €180 billion of additional private investment. In addition to this, the Compact proposed a reallocation of the EU budget, shifting funds towards programmes aimed at fighting stagnation and unemployment.

By the end of 2015 an *ex post* assessment could be made. The results show a half-hearted implementation of insufficient measures. The main problems have been suboptimal utilisation of the EU budget, with not enough shift to programmes to fight stagnation, as well as further overall restrictions of the EU budget in the years following approval. In terms of outcomes, the Growth Compact did not deliver the revival of investment and the reduction of unemployment rates that it had promised. Increasing the capital of the EIB was a good idea and yielded some positive results in terms of increased lending since 2013. But this positive measure was not implemented on a sufficient scale, and it was accompanied by further austerity measures at the national level, which more than offset its positive effects on growth.

The main focus of the EU Compact was on unleashing market potential through a deeper common market. Experience shows that the results of such reforms take time; forecasts of impact tend to be over-optimistic and impacts are not neutral in terms of income distribution. Additional means to compensate for the 'collateral damage' of income effects would have improved the policy.

In November 2014, when it was clear that the Growth Compact had not delivered the desired boost to the European economy, European Commission President Juncker proposed the mobilisation of up to €315 billion in additional public and private investment in the following three years.[15] Juncker argued that additional investment was needed in infrastructure, notably in broadband, renewable energy, distribution and energy efficiency and transport in industrial centres, and in education, research and innovation. Juncker called for a significant amount to be channeled towards projects that could counter youth unemployment.[16] The Juncker plan proposed that the EIB and national development banks should play a central role in financing and catalysing this additional investment.

Specifically, the plan was to relocate €21 billion from the existing EU budget and EIB resources into a new fund, with the hope of achieving a leverage large enough to mobilise €315 billion in total investment. Even if this leverage ratio of 15 were achieved (many observers fear it will not be, as much of the money contributed is not an addition to fiscal resources), €315 billion over three years represents an annual investment boost of approximately 0.75 per cent of EU GDP, which is far short of what is needed to kick-start sufficient growth. By comparison, in 2009–2010 the US government's stimulus package amounted to around 2.8 per cent of GDP per annum over two years.[17] An order of magnitude closer to this is needed today in Europe. The Juncker plan is not of sufficient size to provide a significant and sustainable stimulus to the European economy.

A proposal for investment-led European recovery

We propose three major measures to boost investment in the European economy, with a particular focus on the countries that have suffered most in the crisis. These measures should be seen as additional to the proposed Investment Plan for Europe and are based on the recognition that public investment is essential in order to crowd in private investment.

125

The first is an expansion of lending by the EIB, based on an increase in its paid-in capital provided by EU members. The EIB's ability to leverage its own financing to attract private co-investment enables a significant economic impact to be achieved from fairly limited public resources. Using the proven EIB would enable the programme to be implemented quickly and effectively.

Since 2013 the EU has doubled the EIB's paid-in capital. This has led to a significant increase in lending. If we assume a leverage ratio of 8, as accepted by the rating agencies to maintain the bank's triple-A status, an extra €10 billion provided would allow the EIB to expand its lending by up to €80 billion. Given that EIB-funded projects are typically 50 per cent co-financed by the private sector or in some cases by national development banks, this may result in additional investment of around €160 billion. Even if a more conservative leverage ratio of 6 is assumed, a €10 billion increase in paid-in capital would result in a total of €120 billion of additional lending in coming years.

Such additional lending should be focused especially on investment linked to innovation and structural transformation, particularly in infrastructure. As Carlota Perez argues in her chapter in this volume, there are particular opportunities in the field of renewable energy and environmental technologies, where digitalisation offers the potential of a radical increase in the efficiency of resource use. A range of innovative proposals are already available, such as the linking of European energy markets through new grid transmission lines, to maximise the use of solar power in the south of the continent and wind in the north.[18] Employment creation, especially for the young, should also be a priority: the direct and indirect labour intensity of investments could be a criterion for choosing projects.

Second, we propose that funds from the EU budget are used to mitigate investment risk for the private sector. Today many institutional investors such as pension funds and insurance companies do not fund large investment projects, particularly in infrastructure, due to a perception that the risks are too high. Before the financial crisis, these risks were typically absorbed by large mono-line insurers (such as AIG), which enabled the financing of such projects through triple-A-rated bonds. Since the crisis, such insurance has no longer been available. We therefore propose that around €5 billion a year (a very small proportion of the EU budget) should be allocated to a risk mitigation fund. Such resources could come from the existing EU budget, with a small restructuring of expenditure areas such as the EU Structural Funds, including the European Regional Development Fund (ERDF), which already focuses on investment in comparable areas. The figure of €5 billion a year would allow the EIB to lend an additional €10 billion annually both for financing infrastructure projects (through project bonds) and for investments in research and development of new technologies and innovative enterprises. In turn this would likely leverage around €40 billion of project finance annually, or around €200 billion over five years. Some small steps have already been taken to mitigate risk in this way, but there is an urgent need to scale them up.[19]

Third, we suggest the creation of a new European Fund for Investment (EFI), as proposed by former Polish Finance Minister Mateusz Szczurek.[20] A special purpose vehicle sitting under the umbrella of the EIB, such a Fund would focus on equity investment in large-scale, long-term infrastructure projects, particularly in energy, transportation and information and communication technology (ICT), and particularly at a pan-European scale. Such projects typically carry too much risk for the private sector to finance on their own, but with co-investment by a triple-A rated, government-backed fund, considerable private investment currently seeking long-term returns could be leveraged. The assets created through these investments could eventually be privatised, generating ongoing revenues for the Fund.

The EFI would be financed by paid-in capital from EU member states, complementary to that of the EIB. This would be excluded from the calculation of budget deficits and its borrowing on financial markets would be recorded as EFI debt, not re-routed to member states. This would be the same treatment as for the European Stability Mechanism currently under the rules of the Stability and Growth Pact. With paid-in capital of around €20–30 billion, such a fund could leverage total investment of around €170 billion over the five years to 2020.

These three measures would generate an additional €530 billion of investment in the EU economy over the 2015–2020 period, which represents an annual investment boost of 0.75 per cent of EU GDP. Added to the Juncker Investment Plan's €315 billion for the first three years, this would provide an average investment boost in the EU of the order of 1.2 per cent of GPD per annum, sustained over five years. In addition, as we argue below, we would propose that Europe follows a more expansionary fiscal stance in order to halt the fall in public investment.

In the next section we assess the impact of this significant investment boost on EU growth, employment and investment, as well as on debt-to-GDP ratios and fiscal deficits to GDP. We present results at the aggregate level for the European Union and also for the north euro zone (which comprises Germany, the Netherlands, Finland, Austria and Belgium) and the south euro zone (which comprises Spain, Portugal, Italy and Greece).

Projected impacts of the proposals

Using the Cambridge Alphametrics Model (CAM), we examined two alternative scenarios for Europe for the period 2015–2020 (more information on the CAM model can be found in the Appendix to the chapter). In the first scenario—'business as usual'—we attempt to model the impact of the €315 billion Juncker Investment Plan for Europe. We assume that as a result of the Plan, private investment in the EU increases from 15.7 per cent of GDP in 2015 to 17 per cent of GDP by 2020. This represents an optimistic assumption that, over the next five years, all of the resources allocated under the Investment Plan will feed into higher investment rates across the EU. In addition, the business-as-usual scenario assumes that austerity policies in Europe are maintained in an attempt to reduce national debt-to-GDP ratios to around 60 per cent. In other words, governments will continue to cut their expenditures to reduce government debt. This is translated into a negative effect on public investment, which would continue to fall.

We contrast this scenario with an investment-led recovery scenario for Europe. In this scenario investment (both government and private) is considered as the key strategy to increase employment and economic growth. Based on the proposals set out above, we assume additional resources for investment, compared to the business-as-usual scenario, of approximately €530 billion by 2020 in nominal terms. This enables private investment in the EU to increase significantly to 19 per cent of GDP by 2020, while public investment would stop falling.

Table 1 summarises the estimates for private investment for the 'business as usual' scenario and the 'investment-led' scenario for the EU as a whole and for the north and south euro zone. With regard to the distribution of the investment funds, we assume that more funds will be directed to the south euro zone compared to the north euro zone.

The second important aspect of our investment-led scenario is the implementation of a more expansionary (or in some cases less contractionary) fiscal policy stance at the EU level. In this respect, we assume that EU governments either maintain or increase public expenditure as a share of GDP, in an attempt to create the economic momentum required to substantially increase investment, employment and economic growth. The more significant increase in government expenditure occurs in the south euro zone, from 22.8 per cent of GDP in 2014 to 23.8 per cent by 2020. The north euro zone experiences a more marginal increase in government expenditure, from 23 per cent of GDP in 2014 to 23.5 per cent of GDP in 2020. The key is to maintain levels of public investment, particularly in infrastructure and innovation, as a vital basis to support long-term growth and structural transfor-

Table 1: Private investment as % of GDP

	Scenario	Actual		Projected		
		2007	2014	2015	2018	2020
European Union	Business as usual	19.0	15.3	15.7	16.8	17.2
	Investment-led			16.0	18.0	19.1
North euro zone	Business as usual	17.5	15.9	16.2	17.0	17.3
	Investment-led			16.5	18.2	19.4
South euro zone	Business as usual	22.1	14.2	14.5	15.8	16.2
	Investment-led			14.8	17.6	18.8

mation and to complement and crowd in private investment. In the modelling these increases in government expenditure are mainly funded by higher tax revenues, from additional output generated under the investment-led strategy, along with some increases in direct taxation and stronger action to curb tax evasion.

The impact of our alternative investment-led scenario on fiscal deficits is particularly important. Alternatives to current investment policy proposals are often criticised on the grounds of economic viability, with the claim that they would lead to higher government debt and larger fiscal deficits. However, our simulations demonstrate that a much stronger pan-European investment strategy coupled with expansionary fiscal policies can have positive effects, not only on European GDP and employment, but on the fiscal deficits and debt position of European economies.

Table 2 summarises the projected average GDP growth for the business-as-usual scenario and the investment-led scenario. Under the assumption that 85 per cent of resources from the Juncker plan will be allocated towards investment, projected average GDP growth for the EU as a whole in the business-as-usual scenario reaches only 1.5 per cent over the 2015–2020 period. This is much lower than the 2.3 per cent average growth recorded in the period 2000–2008. By contrast, in the investment-led scenario, average growth in the same period is projected to be 3 per cent.

In the south euro zone, average GDP growth increases from 2.3 per cent in 2000–2008 to 3.3 per cent in 2015–2020 under the investment-led scenario, compared with 1.2 per cent in the business-as-usual scenario. In the north euro zone average growth is 2.9 per cent in the investment-led scenario and 1.5 per cent in the business-as-usual scenario.

Our simulations also reveal some improvement, albeit still insufficient, in the level of unemployment (Table 3). Under both scenarios, unemployment in the EU falls. The highest reduction occurs in the investment-led scenario, where unemployment falls by 5.2 million from 2014 to 2020. In the north euro zone unemployment does not experience any significant variation between the two scenarios over the period, although it increases slightly from 3.4 to 3.8

Table 2: Projected average GDP growth (%)

	Scenario	Actual		Projected
		2000–2008	2009–2014	2015–2020
European Union	Business as usual	2.3	0.1	1.5
	Investment-led			3.0
North euro zone	Business as usual	1.8	0.6	1.5
	Investment-led			2.9
South euro zone	Business as usual	2.3	−1.3	1.2
	Investment-led			3.3

STEPHANY GRIFFITH-JONES AND GIOVANNI COZZI

Table 3: Unemployed workers (millions of people)

	Scenario	Actual			Projected	
		2000	2008	2014	2015	2020
European Union	Business as usual	21.7	17.9	27.3	26.7	24.3
	Investment-led				26.3	22.1
North euro zone	Business as usual	3.9	4.0	3.4	3.5	3.8
	Investment-led				3.4	3.4
South euro zone	Business as usual	5.9	5.3	12.0	11.6	9.5
	Investment-led				11.4	8.5

million from 2014 to 2020. Finally, in the south euro zone, under the more positive investment-led scenario, unemployment falls by 3.5 million.

Despite these important reductions, the level of unemployment in the European Union and in the euro zone does not decline to pre-crisis levels. To further reduce the level of unemployment in Europe, an investment-led strategy would have to be complemented by other policies, such as better educational programmes, training and research.

The investment-led scenario also leads to more favourable results in terms of debt-to-GDP ratios compared to the business-as-usual scenario. While debt levels for both scenarios are projected to remain above the 60 per cent level prescribed by the Stability and Growth Pact, the important gains achieved in terms of GDP growth in the investment-led scenario lead to lower debt-to-GDP ratios. Table 4 presents the debt-to-GDP ratio for the EU, as well as the north and south euro zone. Overall, the debt-to-GDP ratio in the EU under the investment-led scenario declines from 92 per cent in 2014 to 90 per cent in 2020, whereas it continues to increase under the business-as-usual scenario, where debt-to-GDP reaches 103 per cent by 2020. In the south euro zone, the block with the highest level of debt, government debt as a ratio to GDP continues to rise in both scenarios. However, the increase

Table 4: Debt-to-GDP ratio, south euro zone

	Scenario	Actual			Projected	
		2000	2008	2014	2015	2020
European Union	Business as usual	61.9	62.4	91.9	92.8	102.7
	Investment-led				90.5	89.6
North euro zone	Business as usual	63.3	66.8	82.6	81.5	82.3
	Investment-led				79.2	71.4
South euro zone	Business as usual	86.6	78.5	133.4	138.1	172.7
	Investment-led				133.5	144.1

Table 5: Net government lending as % of GDP

	Scenario	Actual			Projected	
		2000	2008	2014	2015	2020
European Union	Business as usual	0.4	−2.4	−3.5	−3.1	−2.6
	Investment-led				−2.7	−2.0
North euro zone	Business as usual	0.9	−1.6	−1.8	−1.5	−1.5
	Investment-led				−1.2	−1.1
South euro zone	Business as usual	−1.0	−4.0	−6.5	−5.9	−5.1
	Investment-led				−4.9	−4.0

in debt-to-GDP in the investment-led scenario is much more moderate compared to the business-as-usual scenario.

In the south euro zone, projected levels of government debt-to-GDP ratios increase from 133 per cent of GDP in 2014 to 173 per cent by 2020 under the business-as-usual scenario. On the other hand, the increase in government debt-to-GDP ratio under the investment-led scenario is more modest, projected to reach 144 per cent of GDP by 2020. In the north euro zone, under the business-as-usual scenario government debt as a ratio to GDP remains virtually unchanged, whereas it declines from 83 per cent in 2014 to 71 per cent in 2020 under the investment-led scenario.

More positive results in terms of fiscal deficit reduction are also achieved under the investment-led scenario in comparison with the business-as-usual scenario. Table 5 shows net government lending for the EU, the north and the south euro zone. In the EU as a whole, under the investment-led scenario, fiscal deficits significantly reduced from −3.5 per cent of GDP in 2014 to −2 per cent in 2020. In the north euro zone, under the investment-led scenario, net government lending falls to −1.1 per cent of GDP. The fiscal deficit in the south euro zone also significantly improves. Under the investment-led scenario fiscal deficits decline on average from −6.5 per cent in 2014 to −4 per cent in 2020. Under the business-as-usual scenario, fiscal deficits remain above 5 per cent of GDP in 2020.

Conclusion

Europe's core economic problem is insufficient investment. At current levels of investment, European economies are not generating enough demand in the short term, and are not laying down the basis for future growth and structural transformation. Private investment will not return to adequate levels without complementary public investment and measures to mitigate risk. While current EU policy, in the form of the Juncker Investment Plan, is a step in the right direction, it is too small, and is offset by continued national austerity. A larger investment plan is needed, based on expanded lending from the EIB, and accompanied by a slower pace of fiscal consolidation in national economies.

Modelling such a recovery package, simulation results suggest an important conclusion. Not only does an investment-led strategy of this kind lead to an average growth rate in the EU of around 3 per cent during the period 2015–2020, with a reduction in unemployment of 5.2 million; in addition, such a package leads to lower debt-to-GDP ratios and lower fiscal deficits compared to a business-as-usual scenario. In other words, stimulating investment is not only good for growth and employment. It is also a more successful way of bringing down deficits and debt than continued austerity.

Appendix: The Cambridge Alphametrics Model (CAM)

The Cambridge Alphametrics Model (CAM) of the world economy is a non-conventional macroeconomic model that is primarily used to make medium- to long-term projections of historical trends of the global economy, blocs of countries and major individual countries. This macro model does not have any single, well-defined equilibrium path to which the economy tends to return. Being an open disequilibrium system, a wide variety of outcomes may be simulated with different growth rates and end points.[21] CAM projections draw on continuous historical data from 1970 to the latest year available (2014 for this exercise).

In CAM the world economy is regarded as an integrated system in which the behaviour of different countries and blocs differs and changes progressively through time because of their specific situation in terms of geography, level of development, financial position, etc. The macro model has a common set of identities and behavioural equations for all blocs to reflect they are part of the same world economy. This allows for panel estimation methods.

In the model aggregate demand and technical progress are the principal drivers of growth. Thus the long-term growth rate is best understood as reflecting the growth of aggregate investment and government spending in the world as a whole. These variables in turn reflect confidence, expectations and policy.[22]

Acknowledgements

We thank Mariana Mazzucato and Michael Jacobs for very valuable comments on a previous draft, as well as Ernst Stetter, Secretary General of the Foundation for European Progressive Studies (FEPS), for his crucial support for this work. We are grateful to Matthias Kollatz and Signe Hansen for their very good comments, as well as valuable previous collaboration on this topic. We thank Edward Griffith-Jones and Daniele Girardi for excellent research and editorial assistance.

Notes

1 See also S. Griffith-Jones and G. Cozzi, 'The role of development banks', in A. Noman and J. E. Stiglitz, eds., *Efficiency, Finance and Varieties of Industrial Policy*, New York, Columbia University Press, forthcoming summer 2016.

2 See M. Mazzucato and C. Penna, *The Rise of Mission-oriented State Investment Banks: The Cases of Germany's KfW and Brazil's BNDES*, SPRU Working Paper Series, 2015, for a detailed illustration of the role of state investment banks with relevant case studies.

3 See B. Eichengreen, *Lessons from the Marshall Plan*, World Development Report 2011, Background Case Note, April 2010.

4 See discussion in E. Klär, *Die Eurokrise im Spiegel der Potenzialsähtzungen*, Wiso Diskurs, Friedrich Ebert Stiftung, April 2014, pp. 31–3.

5 Ibid.

6 R. Barro, 'Are government bonds net wealth?', *Journal of Political Economy*, vol. 82, no. 6, 1974, pp. 1095–17.

7 F. Giavazzi and M. Pagano, 'Can severe fiscal contractions be expansionary? Tales of two small European economies', *NBER Macroeconomics Annual*, vol. 5, 1990, pp. 75–111, http://www.nber.org/chapters/c10973.pdf%20 (accessed 26 November 2015).

8 A. Alesina and S. Ardanga, 'Tale of fiscal adjustment', *Economic Policy*, vol. 13, no. 27, 1998, pp. 489–585.

9 S. Konzelmann, 'The political economics of austerity', *Cambridge Journal of Economics*, vol. 38, no. 4, 2014, pp. 701–41; S. Kinsella, 'Is Ireland really the role model of austerity?', *Cambridge Journal of Economics*, vol. 36, 2012, pp. 223–35

10 J. Stiglitz, 'Stimulating the economy in an era of debt and deficit', *The Economists' Voice*, vol. 9, pp. 1–6, March 2015, http://academiccommons.columbia.edu/item/ac:157963 (accessed 26 November 2015).

11 Ibid.

12 A. Abiad, D. Furceri and P. Topalova, *The Macroeconomic Effects of Public Investment: Evidence from Advanced Economies*, IMF Discussion Paper, WP15/95, 2015.

13 European Council, 'Compact for growth and jobs', Annex to the *Conclusions of the European Council*, EUCO 76/12, 28–29 June 2012, pp. 8–15, http://www.consilium.europa.eu/uedocs/cms_Data/docs/pressdata/en/ec/131388.pdf (accessed 30 November 2015).

14 Ibid., p. 9.

15 European Commission, *An Investment Plan for Europe*, COM(2014) 903, 26 November 2014, https://ec.europa.eu/transparency/regdoc/rep/1/2014/EN/1-2014-903-EN-F1-1.PDF (accessed 30 November 2015).

16 See ibid., which also provides details on the financial mechanisms through which the Plan would work.

17 IMF, 'Update on Fiscal Stimulus and Financial Sector Measures'. Note to update the information in the paper *The State of Public Finances: Outlook and Medium-term Policies After the 2008 Crisis*, http://www.imf.org/external/np/fad/2009/042609.htm (accessed 30 November 2015).

18 See http://www.renewables-grid.eu/ (accessed 30 November 2015).

19 See M. Kollatz-Ahnen, S. Griffith-Jones and U. Bullmann, 'Industrial policy as a contribution to overcome the crisis in Europe', in G. Cozzi, S. Newman and J. Toporowski, eds., *Finance and Industrial Policy. Beyond Financial Regulation in Europe*, Oxford, Oxford University Press, forthcoming 2016.

20 M. Szczurek, 'Investing for Europe's future', speech delivered at the Bruegel Institute, September 2014, http://www.voxeu.org/article/investing-europe-s-future (accessed 30 November 2015).

21 F. Cripps, 'Macro-model scenarios and implications for European policy. Technical Appendix', in J. Eatwell, T. McKinley and P. Petit, eds., *Challenges for Europe in the World, 2030*, 2013, Farnham, Ashgate.

22 Ibid.

8. Inequality and Economic Growth

JOSEPH E. STIGLITZ

Introduction

IN THE middle of the twentieth century, it came to be believed that 'a rising tide lifts all boats': economic growth would bring increasing wealth and higher living standards to all sections of society. At the time, there was some evidence behind that claim. In industrialised countries in the 1950s and 1960s every group was advancing, and those with lower incomes were rising most rapidly.

In the ensuing economic and political debate, this 'rising-tide hypothesis' evolved into a much more specific idea, according to which regressive economic policies—policies that favour the richer classes—would end up benefiting everyone. Resources given to the rich would inevitably 'trickle down' to the rest. It is important to clarify that this version of old-fashioned 'trickle-down economics' did not follow from the postwar evidence. The 'rising-tide hypothesis' was equally consistent with a 'trickle-up' theory—give more money to those at the bottom and everyone will benefit; or with a 'build-out from the middle' theory—help those at the centre, and both those above and below will benefit.

Today the trend to greater equality of incomes which characterised the postwar period has been reversed. Inequality is now rising rapidly. Contrary to the rising-tide hypothesis, the rising tide has only lifted the large yachts, and many of the smaller boats have been left dashed on the rocks. This is partly because the extraordinary growth in top incomes has coincided with an economic slowdown.

The trickle-down notion—along with its theoretical justification, marginal productivity theory—needs urgent rethinking. That theory attempts both to *explain* inequality—why it occurs—and to *justify* it—why it would be beneficial for the economy as a whole. This chapter looks critically at both claims. It argues in favour of alternative explanations of inequality, with particular reference to the theory of rent-seeking and to the influence of institutional and political factors, which have shaped labour markets and patterns of remuneration. And it shows that, far from being either necessary or good for economic growth, excessive inequality tends to lead to weaker economic performance. In light of this, it argues for a range of policies that would increase both equity and economic well-being.

The great rise of inequality

Let us start by examining the ongoing trends in income and wealth. In the past three decades, those at the top have done very well, especially in the

Published by John Wiley & Sons Ltd, 9600 Garsington Road, Oxford OX4 2DQ, UK and 350 Main Street, Malden, MA 02148, USA

US. Between 1980 and 2014, the richest 1 per cent have seen their average real income increase by 169 per cent (from $469,403, adjusted for inflation, to $1,260,508) and their share of national income more than double, from 10 per cent to 21 per cent. The top 0.1 per cent have fared even better. Over the same period, their average real income increased by 281 per cent (from $1,597,080, adjusted for inflation, to $6,087,113) and their share of national income almost tripled, from 3.4 to 10.3 per cent.[1]

Over the same thirty-four years, median household income grew by only 11 per cent. And this growth actually occurred only in the very first years of the period: by 2014 it was only .7 per cent higher than in 1989, after peaking in 1999.[2] But even this underestimates the extent to which those at the bottom have suffered—their incomes have only done as well as they have because hours worked have increased. Median hourly compensation (adjusted for inflation) increased by only 9 per cent from 1973 to 2014, even though at the same time productivity grew by 72.2 per cent (Figure 1). (To understand how significant this divergence of productivity and wages is, consider that from 1948 to 1973 both increased at the same pace, about doubling over the period.)[3] And these statistics underestimate the true deterioration in workers' wages, for education levels have increased (the percentage of Americans who are college graduates has nearly doubled since 1980, to more than 30 per cent),[4] so that one should have expected a significant increase in wage rates. In fact, average real hourly wages for all Americans with only a high school diploma have decreased in the past three decades.[5, 6]

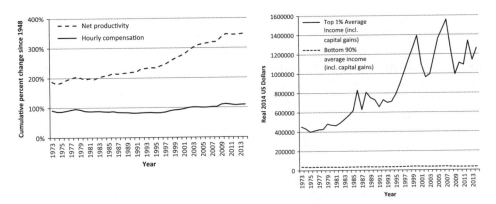

Figure 1: Wages, productivity and average incomes in the US (1973–2014)
Notes: (left panel) Data are for average hourly compensation of production/nonsupervisory workers in the private sector and net productivity of the total economy. 'Net productivity' is the growth of output of goods and services minus depreciation per hour worked. EPI analysis of data from the BEA and BLS (see technical appendix for more detailed information).
Sources: Economic Policy Institute (left panel); The World Wealth and Income Database. Facundo Alvaredo, Tony Atkinson, Thomas Piketty, Emmanuel Saez and Gabriel Zucman (right panel)

In the first three years of the so-called recovery from the Great Recession of 2008–2009—in other words, since the US economy returned to growth—fully 91 per cent of the gains in income went to the top 1 per cent. By 2014, the rest of the income distribution had experienced a bit more of a boost, but even accounting for that, 58 per cent of the gains in total income have gone to the top 1 per cent since 2009. (During that period, the income of the bottom 99 per cent has grown by just 4 per cent.)[7] Presidents Bush and Obama both tried a trickle-down strategy—giving large amounts of money to the banks and the bankers. The idea was simple: by saving the banks and bankers, all would benefit. The banks would restart lending. The wealthy would create more jobs. This strategy, it was argued, would be far more efficacious than helping homeowners, businesses or workers directly. The US Treasury typically demands that when money is given to developing countries, conditions be imposed on them to ensure not only that the money is used well, but also that the country adopts economic policies that (according to the Treasury's economic theories) will lead to growth. But no conditions were imposed on the banks—not even, for example, requirements that they lend more or stop abusive practices. The rescue worked in enriching those at the top; but the benefits did not trickle down to the rest of the economy.

The Federal Reserve, too, tried trickle-down economics. One of the main channels by which quantitative easing was supposed to rekindle growth was by leading to higher stock market prices, which would generate higher wealth for the very rich, who would then spend some of that, which in turn would benefit the rest.

As Yeva Nersisyan and Randall Wray argue in their chapter in this volume, both the Fed and the Administration could have tried policies that more directly benefited the rest of the economy: helping homeowners, lending to small and medium-sized enterprises and fixing the broken credit channel. These trickle-down policies were relatively ineffective—one reason why seven years after the US slipped into recession, the economy was still not back to health.

Wealth is even more concentrated than income—by one estimate more than ten times so. The wealthiest 1 per cent of Americans hold 41.8 per cent of the country's wealth; the top 0.1 per cent alone control more than 22 per cent of total wealth.[8] Just one example of the extremes of wealth in America is the Walton family: the six heirs to the Walmart empire command a wealth of $145 billion, which is equivalent to the net worth of 1,782,020 average American families.[9]

Wealth inequality too is on the upswing. For the four decades before the Great Recession, the rich were getting wealthier at a more rapid pace than everyone else. Between 1978 and 2013 the share of wealth owned by the top 1 per cent rose dramatically, from less than 25 per cent to its current level above 40 per cent; the share of the top 10 per cent from about two-thirds to well over three-quarters.[10] By 2010, the crisis had depleted some of the richest Americans' wealth because of the decline in stock prices, but many Americans also had had their wealth almost entirely wiped out as their homes lost value. After the crisis, the average wealthiest 1 per cent of households still had 165 times the wealth of the average American in the bottom 90 per cent—more than double the ratio of thirty years ago.[11] In the years of 'recovery', as stock market values rebounded (in part as a result of the Fed's lopsided efforts to resuscitate the economy through increasing the balance sheet of the rich), the rich have regained much of the wealth that they had lost; the same did not happen to the rest of the country.[12]

Inequality plays out along ethnic lines in ways that should be disturbing for a country that had begun to see itself as having won out against racism. Between 2005 and 2009, a huge number of Americans saw their wealth drastically decrease. The net worth of the typical white American household was down substantially, to $113,149 in 2009, a 16 per cent loss of wealth from 2005. But the recession was much worse for other groups. The typical African American household lost 53 per cent of its wealth—putting its assets at a mere 5 per cent of the median white American's. The typical Hispanic household lost 66 per cent of its wealth.[13]

Probably the most invidious aspect of America's inequality is that of opportunities: in the US a young person's life prospects depend heavily on the income and education of his or her parents, even more than in other advanced countries.[14] The 'American dream' is largely a myth.

A number of studies have noted the link between inequality of outcomes and inequality of opportunities.[15] When there are large inequalities of income, those at the top can buy for their offspring privileges not available to others, and they often come to believe that it is their right and obligation to do so. And, of course, without equality of opportunity those born in the bottom of the distribution are likely to end up there: inequalities of outcomes perpetuate themselves. This is deeply troubling: given our low level of equality of opportunity and our high level of inequality of income and wealth, it is possible that the future will be even worse, with still further increases in inequality of outcome and still further decreases in equality of opportunity.

A generalised international trend

While the US has been winning the race to be the most unequal country (at least within developed economies), much of what has just been described for it has also been going on elsewhere. In the past twenty-five to thirty years the Gini index—the widely used measure of income inequality—has increased by roughly 29 per cent in the United States, 17 per cent in Germany, 9 per cent in Canada, 14 per cent in UK, 12 per cent in Italy and 11 per cent in Japan (Figure 2).[16] The more countries follow the American economic model, the more the results seem to be consistent with what has occurred in the United States. The UK has now achieved the second highest level of inequality among the countries of Western Europe and North

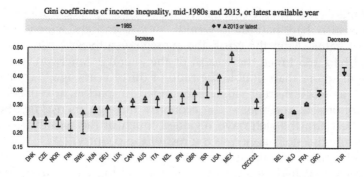

Figure 2: Gini coefficient of income inequality in OECD countries (after-tax and transfer)

Note: income refers to disposable income adjusted for household size.

Source: OECD, *In It Together: Why Less Inequality Benefits All*, OECD, Paris, 2015, p. 24

America, a marked change from its position before the Thatcher era (Figures 2 and 3). Germany, which had been among the most equal countries within the OECD, now ranks in the middle.

The enlargement of the share of income appropriated by the richest 1 per cent has also been a general trend, and in Anglo-Saxon countries it started earlier and it has been more marked than anywhere else (Figure 3). In rich countries, such as the US, the concentration of wealth is even more pronounced than that of income, and has been rising too. For instance, in the UK the income share of the top 1 per cent went up from 5.7 per cent in 1978 to 14.7 per cent in 2010, while the share of wealth owned by the top 1 per cent surged from 22.6 per cent in 1970 to 28 per cent in 2010 and the

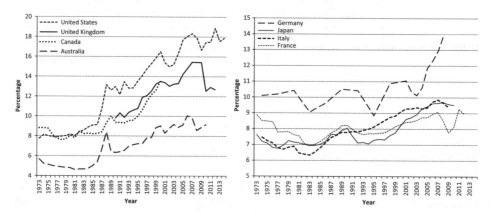

Figure 3: Income share of the richest 1 per cent in some major industrialised countries

Source: The World Wealth and Income Database (latest data available at http://www.wid.world/ (accessed 12 May 2016))

top 10 per cent's wealth share increased from 64.1 per cent to 70.5 per cent over the same period.[17]

Also disturbing are the patterns that have emerged in transition economies, which at the beginning of their movement to a market economy had low levels of inequality in income and wealth (at least according to available measurements). Today, China's inequality of income, as measured by its Gini coefficient, is roughly comparable to that of the United States and Russia.[18] Across the OECD, since 1985 the Gini coefficient has increased in seventeen of twenty-two countries for which data is available, often dramatically (Figure 2).

Moreover, recent research by Piketty and his co-authors has found that the importance of inherited wealth has increased in recent decades, at least in the rich countries for which we have data. After displaying a decreasing trend in the first postwar period, the share of inheritance flows in disposable income has been increasing in the past decades.[19]

Explaining inequality

How can we explain these worrying trends? Traditionally, there has been little consensus among economists and social thinkers on what causes inequality. In the nineteenth century, they strived to explain and either justify or criticise the evident high levels of disparity. Marx talked about exploitation. Nassau Senior, the first holder of the first chair in economics, the Drummond Professorship at All Souls College, Oxford, talked about the returns to capital as a payment for capitalists' abstinence, for their not consuming.[20] It was not exploitation of labour, but the just rewards for their forgoing consumption. Neoclassical economists developed the marginal productivity theory, which argued that compensation more broadly reflected different individuals' contributions to society.

While exploitation suggests that those at the top get what they get by taking away from those at the bottom, marginal productivity theory suggests that those at the top only get what they add. The advocates of this view have gone further: they have suggested that in a competitive market, exploitation (e.g. as a result of monopoly power or discrimination) simply couldn't persist, and that additions to capital would cause wages to increase, so workers would be better off thanks to the savings and innovation of those at the top.

More specifically, marginal productivity theory maintains that, due to competition, everyone participating in the production process earns remuneration equal to her or his marginal productivity. This theory associates higher incomes with a greater contribution to society. This can justify, for instance, preferential tax treatment for the rich: by taxing high incomes we would deprive them of the 'just deserts' for their contribution to society, and, even more importantly, we would discourage them from expressing their talent.[21] Moreover, the more they contribute—the harder they work and the more they save—the better it is for workers, whose wages will rise as a result.

139

The reason why these ideas justifying inequality have endured is that they have a grain of truth in them. Some of those who have made large amounts of money have contributed greatly to our society, and in some cases what they have appropriated for themselves is but a fraction of what they have contributed to society. But this is only a part of the story: there are other possible causes of inequality. Disparity can result from exploitation, discrimination and exercise of monopoly power. Moreover, in general, inequality is heavily influenced by many institutional and political factors—industrial relations, labour market institutions, welfare and tax systems, for example—which can both work independently of productivity and affect productivity.

That the distribution of income cannot be explained just by standard economic theory is suggested by the fact that the *before*-tax and transfer distribution of income differs markedly across countries. France and Norway are examples of OECD countries that have managed by and large to resist the trend of increasing inequality (Figures 2 and 3). The Scandinavian countries have a much higher level of equality of opportunity, regardless of how that is assessed. Marginal productivity theory is meant to have universal application. Neoclassical theory taught that one could explain economic outcomes without reference, for instance, to institutions. It held that a society's institutions are simply a façade; economic behaviour is driven by the underlying laws of demand and supply, and the economist's job is to understand these underlying forces. Thus, the standard theory cannot explain how countries with similar technology, productivity and per capita income can differ so much in their *before*-tax distribution.

The evidence, though, is that institutions do matter. Not only can the effect of institutions be analysed, but institutions can themselves often be explained, sometimes by history, sometimes by power relations and sometimes by economic forces (like information asymmetries) left out of the standard analysis.[22] Thus, a major thrust of modern economics is to understand the role of institutions in creating and shaping markets. The question then is: what is the relative role and importance of these alternative hypotheses? There is no easy way of providing a neat quantitative answer, but recent events and studies have lent persuasive weight to theories putting greater focus on rent-seeking and exploitation. We shall discuss this evidence in the next section, before turning to the institutional and political factors which are at the root of the recent structural changes in income distribution.

Rent-seeking and top incomes

The term 'rent' was originally used to describe the returns to land, since the owner of the land receives these payments by virtue of his or his ownership and not because of anything he or she *does*. The term was then extended to include monopoly profits (or monopoly rents)—the income that one receives simply from control of a monopoly—and in general returns due to similar ownership claims. Thus, rent-seeking means getting an income not as a reward for creating wealth but by grabbing a larger share of the wealth that would have been produced anyway. Indeed, rent-seekers typically destroy wealth, as a by-product of their taking away from others. A monopolist who overcharges for her or his product takes money from those whom she or he is overcharging and at the same time destroys value. To get her or his monopoly price, she or he has to restrict production.

Growth in top incomes in the past three decades has been driven mainly in two occupational categories: those in the financial sector (both executives and professionals) and non-financial executives.[23] Evidence suggests that rents have contributed on a large scale to the strong increase in the incomes of both.

Let us first consider executives in general. That the rise in their compensation has not reflected productivity is indicated by the lack of correlation between managerial pay and firm performance. As early as 1990 Jensen and Murphy, by studying a sample of 2,505 CEOs in 1,400 companies, found that annual changes in executive compensation did not reflect changes in corporate performance.[24] Since then, the work of Bebchuk, Fried and Grinstein has shown that the huge increase in US executive compensation since 1993 cannot be explained by firm performance or industrial structure and that, instead, it has mainly resulted from flaws in corporate governance, which enabled managers in practice to set their own pay.[25] Mishel and Sabadish examined 350 firms, showing that growth in the compensation of their CEOs largely outpaced the increase in their stock market value. Most strikingly, executive compensation displayed substantial positive growth even during periods when stock market values decreased.[26]

There are other reasons to doubt standard marginal productivity theory. In the United States the ratio of CEO pay to that of the average worker increased from around 20 to 1 in 1965 to 354 to 1 in 2012.[27] There was no change in technology that could explain a change in relative productivity of that magnitude—and no explanation for why that change in technology would occur in the US and not in other similar countries. Moreover, the *design* of corporate compensation schemes has made it evident that they are not intended to reward effort: typically, they are related to the performance of the stock, which rises and falls depending on many factors outside the control of the CEO, such as market interest rates and the price of oil. It would have been easy to design an incentive structure with less risk, simply by basing compensation on relative performance, relative to a group of comparable companies.[28] The struggles of the Clinton administration to introduce tax systems encouraging so-called performance pay (without imposing conditions to ensure that pay was actually related to performance) and disclosure requirements (which would have enabled market participants to better assess the extent of stock dilution associated with CEO stock option plans) clarified the battle lines: those pushing for favourable tax treatment and against disclosure understood well that these arrangements would have facilitated greater inequalities in income.[29]

For specifically the rise in top incomes in the financial sector, the evidence is even more unfavourable to explanations based on marginal productivity theory. An empirical study by Philippon and Reshef shows that in the past two decades workers in the financial industry have enjoyed a huge 'pay-premium' with respect to similar sectors, which cannot be explained by the usual proxies for productivity (such as the level of education or unobserved ability). According to their estimates, financial sector compensations have been about 40 per cent higher than the level that would have been expected under perfect competition.[30]

It is also well documented that banks deemed 'too big to fail' enjoy a rent due to an implicit state guarantee. Investors know that these large financial institutions can count, in effect, on a government guarantee, and thus they are willing to provide them funds at lower interest rates. The big banks can thus prosper not because they are more efficient or provide better service but because they are in effect subsidised by taxpayers. There are other reasons for the super-normal returns to the large banks and their bankers. In certain of the activities of the financial sector, there is far from perfect competition. Anti-competitive practices in debit and credit cards have amplified pre-existing market power to generate huge rents. Lack of transparency (e.g. in over-the-counter Credit Default Swaps (CDSs) and derivatives) too have generated large rents, with the market dominated by four players.[31] It is not surprising that the rents enjoyed in this way by big banks translated into higher incomes for their managers and shareholders.

In the financial sector even more than in other industries, executive compensation in the aftermath of the crisis provided convincing evidence against marginal productivity theory as an explanation of wages at the top: the bankers who had brought their firms and the global economy to the brink of ruin continued to receive high rates of pay—compensation which in no way could be related either to their social contribution or even their contribution to the firms for which they worked (both of which were negative). For instance, a study that focused on Bear Sterns and Lehman Brothers in 2000–2008 has found that the top executive managers of these two giants had brought home huge amounts of 'performance-based' compensations (estimated at around $1 billion for Lehman and $1.4 billion for Bear Stearns), which were not clawed back when the two firms collapsed.[32]

Still another piece of evidence supporting the importance of rent-seeking in explaining the increase in inequality is provided by those studies that have shown that increases in taxes at the very top do not result in decreases in growth rates. If these incomes were a result of their *efforts*, we might have expected those at the top to respond by working less hard, with adverse effects on GDP.[33]

The increase in rents[34]

Three striking aspects of the evolution of most rich countries in the past thirty-five years are (a) the increase in the wealth-to-income ratio; (b) the stagnation of median wages; and (c) the failure of the return to capital to decline. Standard neoclassical theories, in which 'wealth' is equated with 'capital', would suggest that the increase in capital should be associated with a decline in the return to capital and an increase in wages. The failure of unskilled workers' wages to increase has been attributed by some (especially in the 1990s) to skill-biased technological change, which increased the premium put by the market on skills. Hence, those with skills would see their wages rise, and those without skills would see them fall. But recent years have seen a decline in the wages paid even to skilled workers. Moreover, as my recent research shows,[35] *average* wages should have increased, even if some wages fell. Something else must be going on.

There is an alternative—and more plausible—explanation. It is based on the observation that rents are increasing (due to the increase in land rents, intellectual property rents and monopoly power). As a result, the value of those assets that are able to provide rents to their owners—such as land, houses and some financial claims—is rising proportionately. So overall wealth increases, but this does not lead to an increase in the productive capacity of the economy or in the mean marginal productivity or average wage of workers. On the contrary, wages may stagnate or even decrease, because the rise in the share of rents has happened at the expense of wages.

The assets which are driving the increase in overall wealth, in fact, are not produced capital goods. In many cases, they are not even 'productive' in the usual sense; they are not directly related to the production of goods and services.[36] With more wealth put into these assets, there may be less invested in real productive capital. In the case of many countries where we have data (such as France) there is evidence that this is indeed the case: a disproportionate part of savings in recent years has gone into the purchase of housing, which has not increased the productivity of the 'real' economy.

Monetary policies that lead to low interest rates can increase the value of these 'unproductive' fixed assets—an increase in the value of wealth that is unaccompanied by any increase in the flow of goods and services. By the same token, a bubble can lead to an increase in wealth—for an extended period of time—again with possible adverse effects on the stock of 'real' productive capital. Indeed, it is easy for capitalist economies to generate such bubbles (a fact that should be obvious from the historical record,[37] but which has also been confirmed in theoretical models.[38]) While in recent years there has been a 'correction' in the housing bubble (and in the underlying price of land), we cannot be confident that there has been a *full* correction. The increase in the wealth–income ratio may still have more to do with an increase in the value of rents than with an increase in the amount of productive capital. Those who have access to financial markets and can get credit from banks (typically those already well off) can purchase these assets, using them as collateral. As the bubble takes off, so does their wealth and society's inequality. Again, policies amplify the resulting inequality: favourable tax treatment of capital gains enables especially high after-tax returns on these assets and increases the wealth especially of the wealthy, who disproportionately own such assets (and understandably so, since they are better able to withstand the associated risks).

The role of institutions and politics

The large influence of rent-seeking in the rise of top incomes undermines the marginal productivity theory of income distribution. The income and wealth of those at the top comes at least partly at the expense of others—just the opposite conclusion from that which emerges from trickle-down economics. When, for instance, a monopoly succeeds in raising the price of the goods which it sells, it lowers the *real* income of everyone else. This suggests that institutional and political factors play an important role in influencing the relative shares of capital and labour.

As we noted earlier, in the past three decades wages have grown much less than productivity (Figure 1)—a fact which is hard to reconcile with marginal productivity theory[39] but is consistent with increased exploitation. This suggests that the weakening of workers' bargaining power has been a major factor. Weak unions and asymmetric globalisation, where capital is free to move while labour is much less so, are thus likely to have contributed significantly to the great surge of inequality.

The way in which globalisation has been managed has led to lower wages in part because workers' bargaining power has been eviscerated. With capital highly mobile—and with tariffs low—firms can simply tell workers that if they don't accept lower wages and worse working conditions, the company will move elsewhere. To see how asymmetric globalisation can affect bargaining power, imagine, for a moment, what the world would be like if there was free mobility of labour, but no mobility of capital. Countries would compete to attract workers. They would promise good schools and a good environment, as well as low taxes on workers. This could be financed by high taxes on capital. But that's not the world we live in.

In most industrialised countries there has been a decline in union membership and influence; this decline has been especially strong in the Anglo-Saxon world. This has created an imbalance of economic power and a political vacuum. Without the protection afforded by a union, workers have fared even more poorly than they would have otherwise. Unions' inability to protect workers against the threat of job loss by the moving of jobs abroad has contributed to weakening the power of unions. But politics has also played a major role, exemplified in President Reagan's breaking of the air traffic controllers' strike in the US in 1981 or Margaret Thatcher's battle against the National Union of Mineworkers in the UK.

Central bank policies focusing on inflation have almost certainly been a further factor contributing to the growing inequality and the weakening of workers' bargaining power. As soon as wages start to increase, and especially if they increase faster than the rate of inflation, central banks focusing on inflation raise interest rates. The result is a higher average level of unemployment and a downward ratcheting effect on wages: as the economy goes into recession, real wages often fall; and then monetary policy is designed to ensure that they don't recover.

Inequalities are affected not just by the legal and formal institutional arrangements (such as the strength of unions) but also by social custom, including whether it is viewed as acceptable to engage in discrimination.

At the same time, governments have been lax in enforcing anti-discrimination laws. Contrary to the suggestion of free-market economists, but consistent with even casual observation of how markets actually behave, discrimination has been a persistent aspect of market economies, and helps explain much of what has gone on at the bottom. The discrimination takes many forms—in housing markets, in financial markets (at least one of America's large banks had to pay a very large fine for its discriminatory practices in the run-up to the crisis) and in labour markets. There is a large literature explaining how such discrimination persists.[40, 41]

Of course, market forces—the demand and supply for skilled workers, affected by changes in technology and education—play an important role as well, even if those forces are partially shaped by politics. But instead of these market forces and politics balancing each other out, with the political process dampening the increase in inequalities of income and wealth in periods when market forces have led to growing disparities, in the rich countries today the two have been working together to increase inequality.

The price of inequality

The evidence is thus unsupportive of explanations of inequality solely focused on marginal productivity. But what of the argument that we *need* inequality to grow?

A first justification for the claim that inequality is necessary for growth focuses on the role of savings and investment in promoting growth, and is based on the observation that those at the top save, while those at the bottom typically spend all of their earnings. Countries with a high share of wages will thus not be able to accumulate capital as rapidly as those with a low share of wages. The only way to generate savings required for long-term growth is thus to ensure sufficient income for the rich.

This argument is particularly inapposite today, where the problem is, to use Bernanke's term, a global savings glut.[42] But even in those circumstances where growth would be increased by an increase in national savings, there are better ways of inducing savings than increasing inequality. The government can tax the income of the rich, and use the funds to finance either private or public investment; such policies reduce inequalities in consumption and disposable income, and lead to increased national savings (appropriately measured).

A second argument centres on the popular misconception that those at the top are the job creators, and giving more money to them will thus create more jobs. Industrialised countries are full of creative entrepreneurial people throughout the income distribution. What creates jobs is *demand*: when there is demand, firms will create the jobs to satisfy that demand (especially if we can get the financial system to work in the way it should, providing credit to small and medium-sized enterprises).

In fact, as empirical research by the IMF has shown, inequality is associated with economic instability. In particular, IMF researchers have shown that growth spells tend to be shorter when income inequality is high. This result holds also when other determinants of growth duration (like external shocks, property rights and macroeconomic conditions) are taken into account: on average, a 10-percentile decrease in inequality increases the expected length of a growth spell by one half.[43] The picture does not change if one focuses on medium-term average growth rates instead of growth duration. Recent empirical research released by the OECD shows that income inequality has a negative and statistically significant effect on medium-term growth. It estimates that in countries like the US, the UK and Italy, overall economic growth would have been six to nine percentage points higher in the past two decades had income inequality not risen.[44]

There are different channels through which inequality harms the economy.[45] First, inequality leads to weak aggregate demand. The reason is easy to understand: those at the bottom spend a larger fraction of their income than those at the top.[46] The problem may be compounded by monetary authorities' flawed responses to this weak demand. By lowering interest rates and relaxing regulations, monetary policy too easily gives rise to an asset bubble, the bursting of which leads in turn to recession.[47]

Many interpretations of the current crisis have indeed emphasised the importance of distributional concerns.[48] Growing inequality would have led to lower consumption but for the effects of loose monetary policy and lax regulations, which led to a housing bubble and a consumption boom. It was, in short, only growing debt that allowed consumption to be sustained.[49] But it was inevitable that the bubble would eventually break. And it was inevitable that, when it broke, the economy would go into a downturn.

Second, inequality of outcomes is associated with inequality of opportunity. When those at the bottom of the income distribution are at great risk of not living up to their potential, the economy pays a price not only with weaker demand today, but also with lower growth in the future. With nearly one in four American children growing up in poverty,[50] many of them facing not just a lack of educational opportunity but also a lack of access to adequate nutrition and health, the country's long-term prospects are being put into jeopardy.

Third, societies with greater inequality are less likely to make public investments which enhance productivity, such as in public transportation, infrastructure, technology and education. If the rich believe that they don't need these public facilities, and worry that a strong government which could increase the efficiency of the economy might at the same time use its powers to redistribute income and wealth, it is not surprising that public investment is lower in countries with higher inequality. Moreover, in such countries tax and other economic policies are likely to encourage those activities that benefit the financial sector over more productive activities. In the United States today returns on long-term financial speculation (capital gains) are taxed at approximately half the rate of labour, and speculative derivatives are given priority in bankruptcy over workers. Tax laws encourage job creation abroad rather than at home. The result is a weaker and more unstable economy. Reforming these policies—and using other policies to reduce rent-seeking—would not only reduce inequality; it would improve economic performance.

It should be noted that the existence of these adverse effects of inequality on growth is itself evidence against an explanation of today's high level of inequality based on marginal productivity theory. For the basic premise of marginal productivity is that those at the top are simply receiving just deserts for their efforts, and that the rest of society benefits from their activities. If that were so, we should expect to see higher growth associated with higher incomes at the top. In fact, we see just the opposite.

Reversing inequality

A wide range of policies can help reduce inequality. Policies should be aimed at reducing inequalities both in market income and in the post-tax-and-transfer incomes. The *rules of the game* play a large role in determining market distribution—in preventing discrimination, in creating bargaining rights for workers, in curbing monopolies and the powers of CEOs to exploit firms' other stakeholders and the financial sector to exploit the rest of society. These rules were largely rewritten during the past thirty years in ways which led to more inequality and poorer overall economic performance. Now they must be rewritten once again, to reduce inequality and strengthen the economy, for instance, by discouraging the short-termism that has become rampant in the financial and corporate sector.[51]

Reforms include more support for education, including pre-school; increasing the minimum wage; strengthening earned-income tax credits; strengthening the voice of workers in the workplace, including through unions; and more effective enforcement of anti-discrimination laws. But there are four areas in particular that could make inroads in the high level of inequality which now exists.[52]

First, executive compensation (especially in the US) has become excessive, and it is hard to justify the design of executive compensation schemes based on stock options. Executives should not be rewarded for improvements in a firm's stock market performance in which they play no part. If the Federal Reserve lowers interest rates, and that leads to an increase in stock market prices, CEOs should not get a bonus as a result. If oil prices fall, and so

147

profits of airlines and the value of airline stocks increase, airline CEOs should not get a bonus. There is an easy way of taking account of these gains (or losses) which are not attributable to the efforts of executives: basing performance pay on the relative performance of firms in comparable circumstances. The design of good compensation schemes that do this has been well understood for more than a third of a century,[53] and yet executives in major corporations have almost studiously resisted these insights. They have focused more on taking advantages of deficiencies in corporate governance and the lack of understanding of these issues by many shareholders to try to enhance their earnings—getting high pay when share prices increase, and also when share prices fall. In the long run, as we have seen, economic performance itself is hurt.[54]

Second, macroeconomic policies are needed that maintain economic stability and full employment. High unemployment most severely penalises those at the bottom and the middle of the income distribution. Today, workers are suffering thrice over: from high unemployment, weak wages and cutbacks in public services, as government revenues are less than they would be if economies were functioning well.

As we have argued, high inequality has weakened aggregate demand. Fuelling asset price bubbles through hyper-expansive monetary policy and deregulation is not the only possible response. Higher public investment—in infrastructures, technology and education—would both revive demand and alleviate inequality, and this would boost growth in the long-run and in the short-run. According to a recent empirical study by the IMF, well-designed public infrastructure investment raises output both in the short and long term, especially when the economy is operating below potential. And it doesn't need to increase public debt in terms of GDP: well-implemented infrastructure projects would pay for themselves, as the increase in income (and thus in tax revenues) would more than offset the increase in spending.[55]

Third, public investment in education is fundamental to address inequality. A key determinant of workers' income is the level and quality of education. If governments ensure equal access to education, then the distribution of wages will reflect the distribution of abilities (including the ability to benefit from education) and the extent to which the education system attempts to compensate for differences in abilities and backgrounds. If, as in the United States, those with rich parents usually have access to better education, then one generation's inequality will be passed on to the next, and in each generation, wage inequality will reflect the income and related inequalities of the last.

Fourth, these much-needed public investments could be financed through fair and full taxation of capital income. This would further contribute to counteracting the surge in inequality: it can help bring down the net return to capital, so that those capitalists who save much of their income won't see their wealth accumulate at a faster pace than the growth of the overall economy, resulting in growing inequality of wealth.[56] Special provisions providing for favourable taxation of capital gains and dividends not only distort the economy, but, with the vast majority of the benefits going to the very top, increase inequality. At the same time they impose enormous budgetary costs: 2 trillion dollars from 2013 to 2023 in the US, according to the Congressional Budget Office.[57] The elimination of the special provisions for capital gains and dividends, coupled with the taxation of capital gains on the basis of accrual, not just realisations, is the most obvious reform in the tax code that would improve inequality and raise substantial amounts of revenues. There are many others,[58] such as a good system of inheritance and effectively enforced estate taxation.

Conclusion: redefining economic performance

We used to think of there being a trade-off: we could achieve more equality, but only at the expense of overall economic performance. It is now clear that, given the extremes of inequality being reached in many rich countries and the manner in which they have been generated, greater equality and improved economic performance are complements.

This is especially true if we focus on appropriate measures of growth. If we use the wrong metrics, we will strive for the wrong things. As the international Commission on the Measurement of Economic Performance and Social Progress argued, there is a growing global consensus that GDP does not provide a good measure of overall economic performance.[59] What matters is whether growth is sustainable, and whether most citizens see their living standards rising year after year.

Since the beginning of the new millennium, the US economy, and that of most other advanced countries, has clearly not been performing. In fact, for three decades, real median incomes have essentially stagnated. Indeed, in the case of the US, the problems are even worse and were manifest well before the recession: in the past four decades average wages have stagnated, even though productivity has drastically increased.

As this chapter has emphasised, a key factor underlying the current economic difficulties of rich countries is growing inequality. We need to focus not on what is happening on average—as GDP leads us to do—but on how the economy is performing for the typical citizen, reflected for instance in median disposable income. People care about health, fairness and security, and yet GDP statistics do not reflect their decline. Once these and other aspects of societal well-being are taken into account, recent performance in rich countries looks much worse.

The economic policies required to change this are not difficult to identify. We need more investment in public goods; better corporate governance, antitrust and anti-discrimination laws; a better regulated financial system; stronger workers' rights; and more progressive tax and transfer policies. By 'rewriting the rules' governing the market economy in these ways, it is possible to achieve greater equality in both the pre- and post-tax and transfer distribution of income, and thereby stronger economic performance.[60]

149

Acknowledgements

The author is indebted to Eamon Kircher-Allen and Deberati Ghosh for research assistance. Financial support from INET and the Roosevelt Institute Project on Inequality, supported by the Ford Foundation, the Bernard and Irene Schwartz Foundation, and the John D. and Catherine T. MacArthur Foundation, is gratefully acknowledged.

Notes

1 Source: T. Piketty and E. Saez, 'Income inequality in the United States, 1913–1998', *Quarterly Journal of Economics*, vol. 118, no. 1, 2003, pp. 1–39, Tables A3 and A6 – Updated version downloaded from http://eml.berkeley.edu/~saez/ (accessed 22 December 2015). Figures are in real 2014 dollars and include capital gains.
2 Source: US Census Historical Table H-6. It should be clear that median wages could have declined, even though in a panel study, most individuals (families) would have seen an increase in their wages, if there were a sufficiently large number of new entrants into the labour force, and if these new entrants had much lower skills/education than those previously in the labour force.
3 See J. Bivens, L. Mishel and H. Shierholz, *Understanding the Historic Divergence Between Productivity and a Typical Worker's Pay*, Economic Policy Institute briefing paper No. 406, 2 September 2015.
4 US Census Data on educational attainment, http://www.census.gov/hhes/socdemo/education/ (accessed 22 December 2015).
5 See *The State of Working America, 12th ed* by the Economic Policy Institute, http://www.stateofworkingamerica.org/chart/swa-wages-table-4-14-hourly-wages-education/ (accessed 22 December 2015).
6 At one time, such results were explained as a result of skill-biased technical change (see G. Violante, 'Skill-biased technical change', in S. Durlauf and L. Blume, eds, *The New Palgrave Dictionary of Economics*, New York, Palgrave Macmillan, 2008, http://www.dictionaryofeconomics.com/article?id=pde2008_S000493&goto=skillbiased&result_number=3340 (accessed 6 May 2016) in which case those without skills would see their wages decline, but those with skills should see their wages increase. But an (appropriately) weighted average wage should still rise. (See J. E. Stiglitz, *New Theoretical Perspectives on the Distribution of Income and Wealth among Individuals*, paper presented at an IEA/World Bank Roundtable on Shared Prosperity, Jordan, 10–11 June 2014 and to be published in *Inequality and Growth: Patterns and Policy, Volume 1: Concepts and Analysis*, New York, Palgrave Macmillan, 2016. Data over the past fifteen years, however, during which even the wages of skilled workers have stagnated, implies that something else is going on.
7 Piketty and Saez, 'Income inequality' (updated version downloaded from http://eml.berkeley.edu/~saez/ (accessed 22 December 2015)).
8 E. Saez and G. Zucman, 'Wealth inequality in the United States since 1913: evidence from capitalized income tax data', forthcoming in *Quarterly Journal of Economics* (revised October 2015). As the authors show, wealth share estimates vary slightly depending on how and whether capital gains are included in the estimate.

9 J. Harkinson, 'The Walmart heirs are worth more than everyone in your city combined', *Mother Jones*, 3 October 2015, http://www.motherjones.com/politics/2014/10/walmart-walton-heirs-net-worth-cities (accessed 22 December 2015).

10 Saez and Zucman, 'Wealth inequality'.

11 Ibid.

12 That this is the case can be clearly seen by examining what has happened to different kinds of wealth since the end of the crisis. Stocks, which are disproportionately owned by the wealthy, have done very well. Stock market values in the United States increased by \$13 trillion from January 2009 to December 2013, according to data from the Center for Research in Security Prices. Meanwhile, home values, which account for much of middle-class wealth, have not enjoyed a strong recovery: 13.4 per cent of American homes were still underwater as of the third quarter of 2015, according to real estate company Zwillow—their owners owe more on their mortgages than the market says their houses are worth. For a concise discussion of this, see P. Dreier, 'What housing recovery?', *The New York Times*, 8 May 2014, http://www.nytimes.com/2014/05/09/opinion/what-housing-recovery.html?ref=opinion&_r=0 (accessed 22 December 2015).

13 See P. Taylor, R. Kochhar, R. Fry, G. Velasco and S. Motel, 'Wealth gaps rise to record highs between whites, blacks and Hispanics', 2011, Pew Research Center report, http://www.pewsocialtrends.org/files/2011/07/SDT-Wealth-Report_7-26-11_FINAL.pdf (accessed 22 December 2015).

14 M. Corak, 'Income inequality, equality of opportunity, and intergenerational mobility', *Journal of Economic Perspectives*, vol. 27, no. 3, Summer 2013, pp. 79–102.

15 Ibid.

16 OECD Income and Poverty Statistics, http://stats.oecd.org/Index.aspx?DataSetCode=IDD# (accessed 22 December 2015) . See also OECD, *In It Together: Why Less Inequality Benefits All*, Paris, OECD, 2015.

17 Piketty, T., *Capital in the 21st Century*, supplementary materials, Tables S9.2 and S10.1: piketty.pse.ens.fr/en/capital21c2, (accessed 14 April 2016).

18 The comparison is made using World Bank data. Some caution should be exercised in comparing different countries' Gini coefficients: in addition to the well-known flaws in the measure, different databases have used slightly different methodologies or income data to arrive at their respective figures, and thus figures are different depending on the data source. Nevertheless, many different studies confirm these broad trends. One should also be particularly cautious in interpreting differences in Gini coefficients between developed and developing countries: Kuznets ('Economic growth and income inequality', *The American Economic Review*, vol. XLV, no. 1, March 1955, pp. 1–28) put forward a persuasive set of reasons why one might expect inequality to increase in the initial stages of development, as some parts of the country and some groups in the country are better able to seize new opportunities and pull away from others. Eventually, the laggards catch up. China's growth in inequality over the past thirty years is consistent with Kuznets' hypothesis; that of the advanced countries is not.

19 T. Piketty and G. Zucman, 'Wealth and inheritance in the long-run', in A. Atkinson and F. Bourguignon, eds, *Handbook of Income Distribution*, vol. 2, Amsterdam, Elsevier-North Holland, 2015, pp. 1303–1368.

20 See N. Senior's 1836 *An Outline of the Science of Political Economy*, London, Richard Griffin & Co.

21 For a recent application of this argument in defence of inequality, see N. G. Mankiw, 'Defending the one percent', *Journal of Economic Perspectives*, vol. 27, no. 3, Summer 2013, pp. 21–34.

22 I recognised this early in my own work on information asymmetries, in a major controversy with Steven N. S. Cheung over whether the institution of sharecropping (which I argued could be explained by information asymmetries) mattered (see J. E. Stiglitz, 'Incentives and risk sharing in sharecropping', *The Review of Economic Studies*, vol. 41, no. 2, 1974, pp. 219–55 and S. Cheung, 'Transaction costs, risk aversion and the choice of contractual arrangements', *Journal of Law and Economics*, vol. 19, no. 1, 1969). North has perhaps done more to bring institutional analysis into the mainstream than anyone else: see D. C. North, *Institutions, Institutional Change and Economic Performance*, Cambridge, Cambridge University Press, 1990.

23 J. Bakija, A. Cole and B. T. Heim, 'Job and income growth of top earners and the causes of changing income inequality: evidence from U.S. tax return data', 2012, http://web.williams.edu/Economics/wp/BakijaColeHeimJobsIncomeGrowthTop Earners.pdf (accessed 22 December 2015).

24 See M. Jensen and K. Murphy, 'Performance pay and top-management incentives', *The Journal of Political Economy*, vol. 98, no. 2, 1990, pp. 225–64.

25 L. Bebchuk and J. Fried, *Pay without Performance: The Unfulfilled Promise of Executive Compensation*, Cambridge, MA, Harvard University Press, 2006; L. Bebchuk and Y. Grinstein, *The Growth of Executive Pay*, NBER Working Paper No. 11443, June 2005.

26 L. Mishel and N. Sabadish, *CEO Pay and the Top 1 Per Cent*, Economic Policy Institute Brief 332, 2012; J. Bivens and L. Mishel, 'The pay of corporate executives and financial professionals as evidence of rents in the top 1 percent incomes', *Journal of Economic Perspectives*, vol. 27, no. 3, Summer 2013, pp. 57–78.

27 AFL-CIO, *CEO-to-Worker Pay Ratios around the World*, 2013, http://www.aflcio.org/Corporate-Watch/Paywatch-Archive/CEO-Pay-and-You/CEO-to-Worker-PayGap-in-the-United-States/Pay-Gaps-in-the-World (accessed 22 December 2015).

28 I had written a series of theoretical and policy papers arguing this in the 1980s. See e.g. B. J. Nalebuff and J. E. Stiglitz, 'Prizes and incentives: towards a general theory of compensation and competition', *The Bell Journal of Economics*, vol. 14, no. 1, 1983, pp. 21–43 and J. E. Stiglitz, 'The design of labor contracts: economics of incentives and risk-sharing', in H. Nalbantian, ed., *Incentives, Cooperation and Risk Sharing*, Totowa, NJ, Rowman & Allanheld, 1987, pp. 47–68, reprinted in *The Selected Works of Joseph E. Stiglitz, Volume II: Information and Economic Analysis: Applications to Capital, Labor, and Product Markets*, Oxford, Oxford University Press, 2013, pp. 432–46.

29 The author was a participant in some of these battles. For a more extensive discussion of them, and their consequences, see J. E. Stiglitz, *Roaring Nineties*, New York, W. W. Norton, 2003. There were other later battles, for example concerning say in pay and other reforms in corporate governance. For a discussion of the kinds of reforms in tax and corporate governance laws that might make a difference, see J. E. Stiglitz, *Rewriting the Rules*, Hyde Park, NY, The Roosevelt Institute, May 2015.

30 T. Philippon and A. Reshef, 'Wages and human capital in the US financial industry: 1909–2006', *The Quarterly Journal of Economics*, vol. 127, no. 4, 2012, pp. 1551–609.

31 D. Baker and T. McArthur, *The Value of the 'Too Big to Fail' Big Bank Subsidy*, Center for Economic and Policy Social Research Issue Brief, September 2009. For a different view, see United States Government Accountability Office, *Large Bank Holding Companies: Expectations of Government Support*, 2014, GAO-14-621, Washington, DC, United States General Accounting Office, which argues that funding advantages existed before the recent financial crash but disappeared afterwards.

32 See L. Bebchuk, A. Cohen and A. Spamaan, 'The wages of failure: executive compensation at Bear Stearns and Lehman 2000–2008', *Yale Journal on Regulation*, vol. 27, 2010, pp. 257–82.

33 Philippon and Reshef, 'Wages and human capital'.

34 This section is based on J. E. Stiglitz, *New Theoretical Perspectives on the Distribution of Income and Wealth among Individuals*, 2015, NBER Working Paper 21191.

35 Ibid.

36 Though they may be reflected in GDP, and may be related in particular to the value of housing services.

37 See C. Reinhardt and K. Rogoff, *This Time Is Different: Eight Centuries of Financial Folly*, 2009, Princeton, NJ, Princeton University Press.

38 See, for instance, K. Shell and J. E. Stiglitz, 'Allocation of investment in a dynamic economy', *Quarterly Journal of Economics*, vol. 81, no. 4, 1967, pp. 592–609; F. Hahn, 'Equilibrium dynamics with heterogeneous capital goods', *Quarterly Journal of Economics*, vol. 80, no. 4 1966, pp. 633–46; and Stiglitz, *New Theoretical Perspectives*.

39 As we noted earlier, skill-biased technological change might be able to explain declines in unskilled labour; but it is hard to reconcile either the timing of wage changes, or the stagnation even of skilled wages in recent years, with such theories. Moreover, *average* wages should have increased. It is, of course, possible that average productivity increased while marginal productivity did not. (This cannot, of course, happen in the Cobb–Douglas production function so beloved by macroeconomists.) But I have seen no evidence for this sudden change in technology—and no theory for why this might have happened.

40 America's mass incarceration policies have also been an important instrument of discrimination. See M. Alexander, *The New Jim Crow: Mass Incarceration in the Age of Colorblindness*, New York, The New Press, 2010.

41 For a recent account of this literature, see K. Basu, *Beyond the Invisible Hand: Groundwork for a New Economics*, Princeton, NJ, Princeton University Press, 2010. See also J. E. Stiglitz, 'Approaches to the economics of discrimination', *American Economic Review*, vol. 62, no. 2, 1973, pp. 287–95 and J. E. Stiglitz, 'Theories of discrimination and economic policy', in G. von Furstenberg, Ann R. Horowitz, and Bennett Harrison, eds, *Patterns of Racial Discrimination*, Lexington, MA, D. C. Heath and Company Lexington Books, 1974, pp. 5–26.

42 I have argued elsewhere ('Monetary policy in a multipolar world', in J. E. Stiglitz and R. S. Gurkaynak, eds, *Taming Capital Flows: Capital Account Management in an Era of Globalization*, IEA Conference Volume No. 154, New York, Palgrave Macmillan, 2015) that the problem is not really a savings glut: there are huge needs for investment on the global level. Unfortunately, the global financial system is unable to intermediate—to ensure that the available savings is used to finance the real global investment needs. The consequence is the 'paradox of thrift': savings leads to inadequate aggregate demand.

43 A. Berg and J. Ostry, *Inequality and Unsustainable Growth: Two Sides of the Same Coin?* IMF Staff Discussion Note No. 11/08, April 2011, International Monetary Fund.

44 F. Cingano, *Trends in Income Inequality and Its Impact on Economic Growth*, OECD Social, Employment and Migration Working Papers, no. 163, Dec. 2014, OECD Publishing.

45 The discussion below emphasises three channels. There are others. The increased instability noted earlier has adverse consequences for growth. Extremes of inequality, especially when they seem unjustified, undermine societal trust, and this hurts growth. To the extent that inequality arises from distortionary rents, these distortions also hurt economic performance.

46 K. E. Dynan, J. Skinner and S. P. Zeldes, 'Do the rich save more?' *Journal of Political Economy*, vol. 112, no. 2, 2004, pp. 397–444.

47 This and other arguments in this section are developed at greater length in my book *The Price of Inequality: How Today's Divided Society Endangers Our Future*, New York, W. W. Norton, 2012.

48 A. Jayadev, 'Distribution and crisis: reviewing some of the linkages', in G. Epstein and M. Wolfson, eds, *Handbook on the Political Economy of Crisis*, Oxford, Oxford University Press, 2013, pp. 95–112. See also *The Stiglitz Report: Reforming the International Monetary and Financial Systems in the Wake of the Global Crisis*, with Members of the Commission of Experts of the President of the United Nations General Assembly on Reforms of the International Monetary and Financial System, New York, The New Press, 2010; and J. E. Stiglitz, *Freefall: America, Free Markets, and the Sinking of the World Economy*, New York, W. W. Norton, 2010.

49 See for example A. Barba and M. Pivetti, 'Rising household debt: its causes and macroeconomic implications—a long period analysis', *Cambridge Journal of Economics*, vol. 33, no. 1, 2009, pp. 113–37.

50 See http://www.childstats.gov/americaschildren/eco1a.asp (accessed 22 December 2015).

51 Stiglitz, *Rewriting the Rules*.

52 In the last chapter of my book *The Price of Inequality*, I outline twenty-one such policies, affecting both the distribution of income before taxes and transfers and after.

53 See, for instance, B. J. Nalebuff and J. E. Stiglitz, 'Prizes and incentives: towards a general theory of compensation and competition', *The Bell Journal of Economics*, vol. 14, no. 1, 1983, pp. 21–43.

54 See e.g. J. E. Stiglitz, *Roaring Nineties*, New York, W. W. Norton, 2003. More recently, I and my colleagues at the Roosevelt Institute have explained how other changes in tax and regulatory policy have contributed to short-sighted and dishonest corporate behaviour (see Stiglitz, *Rewriting the Rules*)

55 IMF, 'Is it time for an infrastructure push? The macroeconomic effects of public investment', *World Economic Outlook*, October 2014, pp. 75–114, http://www.imf.org/external/pubs/ft/weo/2014/02/pdf/c3.pdf (accessed 22 December 2015). Note that the balanced budget multiplier itself provides a framework in which governments can increase investment and stimulate the economy today, without incurring any increase in current deficits—but lowering future deficits and the debt/GDP ratio.

56 T. Piketty, *Capital in the 21st Century*, Cambridge, MA and London, Harvard University Press, 2014.

57 More precisely, these are the estimated costs ('tax expenditures') associated with these special provisions. See Congressional Budget Office, *The Distribution of Major Tax Expenditures in the Individual Income Tax System*, May 2013, p. 31, http://cbo.gov/sites/default/files/cbofiles/attachments/TaxExpenditures_One-Column.pdf (accessed 22 December 2015). This figure includes the effects of the 'step-up of basis at death' provision, which reduces the taxes that heirs pay on capital gains. Not including this provision, the ten-year budgetary cost of preferential treatment for capital gains and dividends is $1.34 trillion. These calculations do not, however, include the value of the fact that the tax on capital gains is postponed until realisation.

58 See J. E. Stiglitz, *Reforming Taxation to Promote Growth and Equity*, Roosevelt Institute White Paper, May 2014, http://rooseveltinstitute.org/sites/all/files/Stiglitz_Reforming_Taxation_White_Paper_Roosevelt_Institute.pdf (accessed 22 December 2015).

59 The Commission's report was released in 2009, and published as J. Stiglitz, A. Sen and J. P. Fitoussi, *Mismeasuring Our Lives*, New York, The New Press, 2010. The OECD has since continued work in this vein with its Better Life Initiative (http://www.oecd.org/statistics/betterlifeinitiativemeasuringwell-beingandprogress.htm (accessed 22 December 2015)) and its High Level Expert Group on the measurement of economic and social progress, convened in 2013.

60 See Stiglitz, *Rewriting the Rules*.

9. The Paradoxes of Privatisation and Public Service Outsourcing

COLIN CROUCH

Introduction

THE PRIVATISATION of former public industries and the outsourcing of public services to private providers has been a hallmark of neoliberal economic strategies to increase the role of markets and reduce the role of the state in the economy. However, certain deeply rooted attributes of these processes have led them to have results almost directly opposite to neoliberalism's claims. There has been a growth of oligopoly and restricted competition, of government economic involvement in some of its least desirable forms, and a concomitant political intervention by firms.

In this chapter I shall argue that these outcomes have created not the economy proclaimed by market neoliberalism, but what will be defined here as 'corporate neoliberalism': an economy in which key industries are dominated by small numbers of large corporations which, because of their size and the importance of their sectors, have a political salience incompatible with the assumptions of neoclassical theory. This is a form of political economy that almost no one defends openly, but which is increasingly prevalent. Privatisation and outsourcing are not the only sources of corporate neoliberalism, which exists more generally in sectors of imperfect competition. However, the fact that many of the activities involved in these strategies concern either collective or citizenship goods, or both, makes them particularly prone to domination by politicised corporations rather than markets. A further consequence of corporate neoliberalism is a reinforcement of inequalities, which I shall argue now threatens the positive relationship between capitalism and democracy.

The limits to competition

Pure or market neoliberalism can be understood to mean the doctrine that efficiency will be maximised if as many activities as possible are governed by perfectly competitive markets, the participants in which pursue profit maximisation as their sole goal, with no interference from governments, except to maintain rights to own property and make private contracts.[1] Efficiency is defined as the performance of a given task at the lowest possible cost, which implies lower prices for consumers. This leaves consumers with more money in their hands than a less efficient performance, and therefore

Published by John Wiley & Sons Ltd, 9600 Garsington Road, Oxford OX4 2DQ, UK and 350 Main Street, Malden, MA 02148, USA

with increased choice, which is in turn defined as maximising consumer welfare. Since market theory cannot recognise any activity other than producing, selling and buying, consumer welfare is identical to overall human welfare, and this can be optimally achieved only by profit-maximising firms in perfect markets. There is some ambiguity in neoliberal thinking over the role of other non-market institutions, such as family and community. For some, these provide a useful adjunct to markets; for others they are a source of inefficiency and would be better off for being incorporated within markets.

The privatisation and outsourcing of industries and services owned by public authorities have been among the hallmarks of the neoliberal agenda. By privatisation one means the full transfer to private ownership of the activity in question. Under outsourcing the activity remains publicly owned, but its performance is contracted out to private profit-making firms or other non-state organisations, the public authority becoming the customer instead of the provider. For reasons that we shall explore below, privatisation rarely, outsourcing almost never, results in true markets of the kind envisaged by neoclassical theory.

There have been broadly four different reasons why industries and services have in the past been provided by or specially protected by public authorities in states with predominantly capitalist economies. First, governments have had political motives for sustaining what they have regarded as key sectors for national economic success. Second, there have been the so-called 'natural monopolies', where competition would be impossible (as with water supply) or very difficult to arrange (gas and electricity supply, railways), or where competition itself had produced markets dominated by too small a number of producers to generate true market competition. Third, some goods and services have been considered to contain an important public or collective goods component (defence, police, public administration itself). Finally have been services that had come to be seen as embodying individuals' basic rights of democratic citizenship (education, health, some aspects of social care). While public goods and citizenship rights are different, in practice there is considerable overlap between them. Collective and public goods can be interpreted as an aspect of citizenship, while several individual citizenship services, including education and health, have a collective component.

Protected firms and sectors

The first of these, the identification of key industries, has sometimes taken a passive form, as when coal industries were widely regarded as having become insufficiently profitable to be sustainable within the private sector, but where there was perceived to be widespread dependence on their products. A more active form was the identification of 'national champion' firms or sectors, seen as important to national economic success. Here the industry was usually profitable and therefore retained in private hands, but with continued protection and support from government. This approach is usually associated with French and Italian protectionist industrial strategy from the end of World War II until the construction of the single European market in the 1990s, but a similar approach was followed in ostensibly liberal economic regimes. Examples were the special place of the chemical and motor industries in the UK, or the steel, military and motor industries of the US.

Eliminating these practices has been a prime target of neoliberal changes to international trade, partly because they have been barriers to competition, and partly because of the politicisation of parts of the economy they imply. However, the neoliberal regime has generated its own equivalents of state-protected firms and sectors. Paradoxically some of this results from globalisation, which induces a competition among states to attract investment from international corporations. This often takes the form of offering tax breaks, exemption from labour and other laws and other special treatment, in deals between public officials and corporate representatives. Large firms threaten to relocate to another country unless they are permitted to negotiate the amount of tax they will pay. These actions distort the level playing field that the market requires, usually privileging very large firms against smaller ones.

Rather different, but with similar outcomes, are the sectors that are 'too big to fail', those that are both dominated by a small number of firms and strategically important for a national (or the global) economy, such that the collapse of a small number of them could provoke a massive shock to the whole system. This was notoriously the case with the banking industry and to a lesser extent the motor industry after the 2008 crash, and some other industries, for example energy, fit this model too.[2] These firms have managed to become defined as a collective good, and therefore as requiring protection from the market, just as much as did the national champions of the protectionist age. They differ from those, in that the latter usually accepted certain responsibilities to the national economies in which they found protection. In neoliberal protection the balance of the relationship is more one-sided, with governments feeling obliged to offer support, but without long-term commitments on the corporate side. Both traditional and current forms imply a close political engagement of the firms concerned, which is contrary to neoliberal pretensions.

'Natural' monopolies

Classic arguments about the difficulty of organising markets in sectors with natural monopolies were weakened by various technical and intellectual developments. For example, changes in radio technology ended earlier limitations on the number of airwaves that could be used for telecommunications in radio, television and telephone services. This made possible the development of competition among large numbers of producers in some sub-sectors, reducing the need for public rationing of access for providers. In other cases developments in economic theories of regulation made it possible for regulators to challenge information asymmetries between dominant firms and their customers, and establish what would be an appropriate competitive price level even in markets dominated by oligopolies.[3]

It is important to note that in almost all cases there has been no passage at all to pure, self-governing markets. Working out what corporate behaviour would look like if there could be a true market, and imposing that on the firms concerned, requires a serious regulatory apparatus. Hence in the UK one finds regulatory agencies covering most privatised industries, and certainly all utilities. Dominant firms have developed in the telecommunications, energy and water sectors partly because of the strong presence of network externalities, so competition remains oligopolistic. Although a call for deregulation is a fundamental part of the neoliberal agenda, in reality it produces a major increase in regulation, but with a changed purpose. In theory neoliberal regulation would only work out what a market would look like if there could be one, not introduce other policy goals. For example, neoliberal regulation of radio and television should be concerned solely with monitoring price behaviour, not with such issues as ensuring political balance or restricting pornographic or violent content. If action on these other issues would contribute to profit maximisation, firms would already have taken it; if not, then the action would by definition reduce inefficiency and detract from consumer choice. Consumer choice, according to the theory, cannot include preferences that consumers might hold but which they cannot express through the market. The central 'choice' with which neoliberal theory is concerned exists at the higher level of the overall capacity for market choices that consumers have if goods and services are provided as efficiently as possible.

Making markets or analogues of them where they do not really exist requires some intellectual acrobatics from regulators. An interesting example is found in gas and electricity supply. It is difficult for domestic customers to see themselves as being in a market here. Whichever supplier they have, the same gas and electrical power come to their pipes and cables. There is no variety of product or quality that enables consumers to exercise the kind of choice they have in normal markets. They also sign up to contracts lasting at least a year, and often of unlimited term, so these markets are not very active. Suppliers compete with each other by trying to develop better forward purchasing strategies and superior advertisements. While a few small suppliers may gain some market entry, an illusion of diversity is produced by third-party firms—typically well-known supermarket brands—doing deals for their customers by buying energy from the primary suppliers, badging it, and selling it on. Given the inelastic nature of consumers' behaviour and dominance of the market by a small number of suppliers, energy firms have little incentive to pass on any benefits of their purchasing strategies to consumers. Regulators therefore try to stimulate more consumer elasticity by persuading firms to make reduced price offers to customers

159

who switch to them. At the end of this introductory contract period the price typically increases considerably. The regulators then urge customers to keep switching contracts so that they are always getting the best introductory offers. In this way regulators hope to generate the mass of transactions that a true market needs, creating artificial differences between identical products in order to do so. Such a market brings gains to both (some) consumers and producers only if large numbers of consumers remain inelastic, paying the higher prices of supplies that are not part of introductory offers. Meanwhile, transaction costs rise: for consumers, who have to keep looking out for new introductory offers and making arrangements to change their suppliers; and for suppliers, who have to keep developing and marketing new introductory offers. This is the main way in which a neoliberal strategy can deal with the tendency for an oligopolistic sector to produce high prices.

Countries vary very considerably in the extent to which they have followed neoliberal precepts on all these issues, and this gives an indicator of the limited extent to which neoliberalism has fully triumphed. But even if regulation is limited to acting on the price level, it is not a purely technical task, but requires assumptions made by human actors, both in government setting the parameters for regulatory agencies and within the agencies setting up and running the regulatory regime. Both neoliberals and leftist critical theorists have identified the potential for 'regulatory capture'.[4] Where there is regulation, those being regulated have a strong incentive to win the favour of regulators. At the very least they have opportunities to do this through the dependence on their knowledge that external regulators usually have. Beyond that there is scope for a range of interventions, from lobbying to straightforward corruption.

Collective goods

States have been the principal owners of major infrastructure goods, like roads, and also of the physical infrastructure of public services, like hospitals. A further major motive for partial privatisation has been a desire by governments to attract private investment to such projects, saving on the taxation burden involved in state funding in exchange for having private firms own parts of national infrastructure. This has severe limits. If projects are undertaken for collective goods or citizenship purposes, they are likely to be less profitable than those undertaken on assessments of pure profitability. Firms therefore have to be offered inducements to create this new market. Also, the economic risk of failure that attends private ventures, and which is in theory the *raison d'être* of the capitalist concept of profit, is difficult to translate into the political risk of failure with a collective or citizenship good. Indeed, as already noted, the response to the financial crisis of 2008 demonstrated that, if a risk includes that of system failure, states may feel impelled to absolve investors from the risks that in theory justify their private sector profits.

As a result, recourse to the private sector for public investment has usually not absolved governments from ultimate responsibility for risk, but rather has required them to offer indemnity to private investors in the case of failure.[5] It has therefore not used the market in one of its most basic meanings. The offer in the UK of higher subsidies to private railway undertakings than were made available to the railways when publicly owned is a case in point. Another concerns public–private investment partnerships (PPP), known in the UK as the Private Finance Initiative (PFI). Under PFI, a firm invests in building or reconstructing a school, hospital or similar facility for a public authority, and then leases it back to the authority for a period of years. The authority acquires a facility that it would not otherwise have afforded for several years, but has to pay back a much larger sum over the lease period.[6] Also, guarantees have to be given to the firm that there will be no substantial changes in use, which can threaten the efficiency of the authority's operation. Perhaps most important, in the wake of the financial crisis, the UK government had to promise to underwrite PFI contracts. The state did not divest itself of risk.

Outsourcing public service delivery

We must finally consider the outsourcing of public service delivery itself to private firms. Virtually by definition, public and collective goods and services cannot be provided by pure markets. The neoliberals' approach is to seek ways of transforming such goods into marketable form. This almost always requires action by a public authority, and therefore opens the door to politicisation.

What I have here called citizenship goods overlap with collective goods. For example, education is regarded as contributing to the human infrastructure of the economy; health includes action to prevent the spread of contagious disease and maintain the physical quality and productivity of the workforce. But many other aspects of these and other services are consumed by and benefit individuals alone. In principle these services could be provided by the market, but democratic politics has led to many of them being seen as rights of citizenship, to be provided outside the framework of market exchanges, even if some kind of payment is sometimes involved. In theory, neoliberalism is opposed to any provision of this kind that cannot be defended as a collective good. In practice, however, the nature of democratic politics in many countries has until now rendered it impossible to achieve full marketisation. Instead a public authority becomes the customer, and only supply is privatised. The end users are not customers, just users, and therefore not part of the market relationship. Any rights they have remain those of citizens, as they had under the previous public regime—though in practice these may be attenuated by aspects of the contract between public authority and provider, such as commercial confidentiality clauses that give citizens less information about the details of a service than they had with a public supplier. By their nature many of these contracts have to run for long periods of time, sometimes over twenty years; one cannot frequently renegotiate contracts to run schools or hospitals. Therefore the market exists only at very separated, discrete points of time when contracts are up for tender.

Perhaps most important, what the public authority customer buys is not the substantive service involved, but the terms of the outsourcing contract. Although a large number of firms is engaged in this business across the whole range of public services being traded, the market is dominated by a small number of very large players. In the UK, over recent years, three firms —G4S, Capita and Serco—have come to account for a very large part of the government outsourcing market.[7] A small number of purchasers in public authorities faces a small number of suppliers. These are therefore oligopolistic markets. An indicator that the market is not working well is the fact that large firms have continued to win new contracts even after having been fined for dereliction of duty with some of their existing ones.[8] Significantly evoking the phrase used about the giant banks that had to be rescued during the financial crisis, one analysis of their operations has suggested that the firms involved in winning contracts to run British public services have become 'too big to fail'.[9] That is, they have become so central to providing Britain's public services and infrastructure that if they were to leave the market there would be a crisis of collapsing provision.

The observation that these major firms are found across a wide range of disparate activities is also significant. Both G4S and Serco started as contractors for public infrastructure projects in defence and security, but are today involved in schools and care services. Another major player, Amey, started in road building, but is now found right across the range of public administration. That firms so successfully win contracts across fields where they had no past track record or prior professional knowledge is explained by the fact that their core business is not a particular field of activity in which they have expertise, but knowing how to win government contracts: how to bid, and how to develop contacts with officials and politicians. This becomes a form of network externality; on its basis they can undertake contracts across virtually any field where government has decided to outsource.[10] Defence and road building were very useful starting points for such firms, as these sectors have long been major areas of government contracting.

This approach is typical of what we might describe as the corporate form of neoliberalism: contracts that run for years, negotiated between a small number of public officials who are not spending their own money, and a small group of corporate representatives of 'buddy' firms[11] on whose continued presence in the market government has come to depend. This is not consistent with the theory of market neoliberalism on which the policy of outsourcing was originally justified. In outsourced public service provision we are confronted by a distinctive organisational form. It is too political and oligopolistic to be considered properly part of the market economy, while its core knowledge base is not that of the substantive services being delivered to their users. In such situations the gap between the meaning of ideas like efficiency and customer choice in neoliberal theory and in their everyday sense becomes heavily stretched.

Several examples can be found in recent debates over the UK National Health Service, which has been subjected to a large programme of outsourcing. This process has been projected as improving consumer choice, and observers have therefore been puzzled by such cases as the government's planned reorganisation of hospitals in South London in 2013. The South London Healthcare Trust, which controlled several hospitals, was making heavy losses, leading it to go into administration. The government's solution was to close the accident and emergency department and some other services at Lewisham Hospital. This hospital was not part of the South London Trust and itself had no financial problems. Its A&E department had recently been refurbished and was very popular in the area. By closing various Lewisham services, people in that area could be required to travel some distance to Woolwich Hospital, which was part of the South London group, boosting its numbers of patients and therefore improving its financial situation. Under the market rules governing the NHS, it is not possible for a trust in one area to receive transfers of funds from another, but it seemed to be possible to transfer patients to it, against their will.[12] This seemed to contradict the neoliberal goal of freedom of choice, which has figured prominently in English NHS reforms. From a corporate neoliberal perspective, however, the reasoning was clear. A reduction in the supply of A&E capacity in the wider area would be a means to protect the profitability of the South London trust. Withdrawing services from Lewisham was the best way of securing that profitability.

Similarly, outsourcing health services and schools to private and other providers has usually meant dismantling consultation mechanisms, local users' watchdog committees and other forms of participative governance. Critics have protested that such moves contradict the promise of greater responsiveness to users that had been proclaimed to be a necessary consequence of moving closer to the market.[13] But the owners of the firms providing health and educational services fear that consultation mechanisms will threaten their profitability, formal customer participation mechanisms being virtually unknown in the private sector. The promise of greater consumer welfare offered by the theoretical neoliberal prospectus has been replaced in reality by the pursuit of a much narrower definition of corporate interest.

It may reasonably be objected that in market neoliberal theory the coincidence of profit maximisation and consumer welfare requires a truly competitive market, which is absent from these public service contracts. This is however not a problem for corporate neoliberalism, which draws on arguments developed in the US by economists and lawyers hostile to the tendency for anti-trust legislation to demand the break-up of large corporations in the interests of creating a true market.[14] They argued that in many sectors advantages flow from imperfect rather than pure competition; that returns to scale are more or less infinite; and that therefore increased efficiency is almost certain to follow the emergence of dominant corporations, whether as an outcome of competitive struggle or through mergers and acquisitions. (Mergers and acquisitions, it is argued, only occur if shareholders consider that they would result in increased profits, and profit maximisation is equivalent to the pursuit of the highest efficiency and therefore to consumer welfare.) There are therefore no reasons on grounds of 'consumer welfare' to seek to establish competitive markets. These arguments can be similarly extended to the outsourcing of contracts to run public services.

The limits to competition: conclusions

Privatisation, public–private financial partnerships, outsourcing of public service delivery and other recent strategies have almost always been promulgated as bringing the advantages of competitive markets and consumer choice to activities previously dominated by state bureaucracy. But this has very rarely been the result. A major aim of neoliberal reforms was to depoliticise the economy. Such hopes have nearly always been disappointed, for two very different reasons. First are the collective and citizenship characteristics of many of the goods and services involved. Where a good is collective, it is both in theory and in practice impossible for it to remain solely within the market. In a democratic society this means that debate about its quality and provision are ongoing.

Second, however, has been the fact that neoliberalism has in practice taken what I have called here its corporate rather than its market form. Rarely has there been full competition of the type understood by neoclassical theory; consumer choice has been possible at only a few points; state involvement changed its form rather than declined, with new forms of regulation and new justifications for government support for individual firms and sectors. A small number of giant firms dominate the new privatised and outsourced sectors, while sectors like banking have come to be seen as vital to the economy and therefore have also acquired a kind of collective good status. When this occurs and a sector is dominated by a small number of firms, governments become dependent on them, and they become central political actors. Really tough-minded neoliberal economists may argue that governments could allow several major banks to collapse, or could allow health and other services to disappear from unprofitable areas. But very few outside their ranks are willing to take the enormous risks that such unpredictable experiments would bring.

The mutual convertibility of economic and political resources

A major casualty of the reality of corporate neoliberalism is therefore the barrier between economic and political resources that neoclassical economic theory would in principle erect. According to the theory, government intervention in the economy should be subject to very serious restrictions, mainly limited to maintaining the property rights, law of contract and prevention of monopoly that are necessary to a market order to function. On the other side of the equation, firms as such are expected to play no political role. This is because in a competitive market-economic resources will not be converted into political ones, as spending money on politics would be a business cost, and a firm engaging in such activity would have to raise its prices and so lose out to firms that did not so engage. The possibility remains that all firms in a sector might agree to combine to establish a fund to lobby for their interests in the political arena, but in a proper market economy such action should fall foul of competition law. Also, coordination among a large number of firms would run into the collective action problem, defection from the coordinated action bringing cost advantages.

However, in the oligopolistic markets that are present in several sectors, including in particular many of those involved in privatisation and outsourcing, a different logic applies. Such firms can both afford to divert resources to political action and have an interest in doing so, because they stand to gain so much from favourable public policies or government contracts. They have direct and strong interests in exercising maximum political influence, and in establishing extensive contacts with politicians and civil servants. The uneven distribution of political influence that this implies, even among businesses in different sectors, let alone in comparison with the rest of the population, embodies part of the asymmetry and inequality that makes business political lobbying highly suspect on both market-economic and democratic grounds.

Therefore, under corporate neoliberalism the barrier between economy and polity becomes rather a semi-permeable membrane: government should not intervene autonomously in the economy, but nothing prevents political activity by corporations. Classic liberalism of the kind that influenced the establishment of civil service rules in many countries in the late nineteenth century was at pains to protect the integrity of both the state and the market by having strict rules govern interactions between public officials and personnel in private business. From this stern perspective, much of the interaction that today does not raise an eyebrow would have been defined as corruption.

The approach of modern corporate neoliberalism to relations between government and corporations is governed, not by those classic rules of separation, but by the modern doctrine of new public management (NPM). This advocates a relaxation of these rules, on the grounds that this enables private business thinking to percolate into government and increase the latter's efficiency. A core characteristic of this new model is the 'revolving door' that develops between public officials and the key outsourcing companies. On leaving office, politicians and civil servants are permitted to join firms that they had been involved in regulating; firms are permitted to second staff to ministries with which they are negotiating contracts. Particularly strong links

165

of this kind exist between firms in the public contracting business and members of their staff or boards of directors who either used to be or are about to become public officials involved in regulating or negotiating contracts with them. In another part of the UK economy the taxation authority (Her Majesty's Revenue and Customs) received advice on dealing with tax avoidance from the four leading accountancy firms, which subsequently advised clients on how to continue their avoidance. Finding these connections does not require extensive research. No one is concealing them, because it is part of NPM that such links are not to be seen as corruption but are to be encouraged.

It is difficult to demonstrate to what extent firms' political activities affect the behaviour of public commissioning staff and regulators, partly because one lacks counterfactuals of what contracts and regulator behaviour would have looked like in the absence of such action; partly because there is virtually by definition no paper trail of evidence. One can only measure the input side, the extent of the resources devoted to political activity, and draw the conclusion that, if these firms are rational actors, they would not continue to devote resources in this way were there to be no outcomes. Tamsin Cave and Andy Rowell,[15] who have tracked in detail the work of corporate lobbyists in the UK, have estimated that firms spend £2 billion a year on this activity, and they provide details of it and its successes. Jacky Davis and her colleagues[16] have detailed the role of revolving-door secondments as well as lobbying activities in the outsourcing of NHS contracts to private firms. Similar accounts could be given for a number of other countries, the European Union and particularly the US.

The expansion of corporate political power is well exhibited in proposals for a general trade treaty between the EU and the US, the Transatlantic Trade and Investment Partnership (TTIP). TTIP is a plan for a major relaxation of barriers to trade between member states of the EU and the US. Most tariff barriers have already been negotiated away in various global agreements. What remain are the so-called non-tariff barriers. These extend from rules designed to keep international competitors out of domestic markets, to regulations to protect health, labour rights and various concepts of public and collective goods. What marks TTIP out from previous trade agreements is the attempt to end the exemption of public services from trade provisions.

Under current EU competition law governments can declare certain areas of social policy to be outside the market economy, defining them as services of general economic interest. But the proposed terms of TTIP would undermine this by allowing firms to claim redress against actions by governments that could be said to threaten their profits. Assume that a neoliberal government declared its health service to be tradable within TTIP, only to be followed by a social democratic one that wanted to keep health provision public. TTIP would give overseas health firms grounds to sue the government because that policy change had damaged their investments. The proposal in TTIP that such claims for redress would be heard not through normal law courts with established judges, but through arbitration panels composed solely of corporate lawyers (a procedure called Investor–State Dispute Settlement (ISDS)), makes this particularly controversial. It reinforces the sense that corporate power is effectively challenging the authority of governments to decide how public services should be provided.[17]

Conclusion: capitalism and democracy

We have already seen how the reality of corporate neoliberalism presents a challenge to the theoretical idea of an efficiently functioning market economy, especially the idea that such an economy is free from entanglements between firms and governments. The TTIP case shows that there are similar problematic implications for democracy. Since World War II capitalism and democracy have often been depicted as being two sides of the same liberal coin, and the main theories of liberal democracy have made it virtually an analogy of the market.[18] But a polity in which large corporations have both sufficient market presence to enable them to afford political activity, and sufficient dependence on government assistance of various kinds to make that activity worthwhile, becomes highly unbalanced, with corporations in a position to exercise considerably more influence than most other interests.

This growing imbalance contributes to the growing inequality that has become a feature of most advanced societies in recent years. This can be seen particularly clearly in taxation, where policy changes in recent decades have done much to drive growing inequality. Across the OECD area as a whole, the highest income tax rates declined from 66 per cent to 42 per cent between 1981 and 2010.[19] The bottom 90 per cent of the income distribution receive between 70 and 85 per cent of their income in the form of wages and salaries; the top 0.01 per cent receive only 40 per cent of their income in this form, the majority coming as corporate income, dividends and capital gains. These kinds of income have increasingly been taxed more lightly than wages and salaries. The average corporate income tax in the OECD area has declined from 47 per cent to 25 per cent from 1981 to 2010, dividend tax from 75 per cent to 42 per cent. These changes have taken place during a period when pre-tax income inequality was increasing. One can hypothesise that in the face of growing pre-tax income inequality, democratically responsive governments would improve the progressivity of taxation, while those influenced by corporate power would make regressive changes. The fiscal changes of the neoliberal period have been consistent with the latter hypothesis.

The reality of contemporary capitalism is therefore that economic resources can and do concentrate in ways that make possible the exercise of corporate power within the polity. Indeed, in the US such activity has been explicitly accepted by the Supreme Court. In 2010 it rejected a ruling by the Federal Election Commission that there were limits to the sums of money that organisations could spend on election campaigns, on the grounds that the US Constitution should be seen as having granted the same rights to organisations as to individuals, though it maintained the existing limits on such donations to individual candidates.[20] Four years later, however, in 2014, it also removed the ban on the second kind of donation.[21] It is of course primarily owners of large corporations that are in a position to make donations of this kind. For example, the Koch Brothers, owners of major corporations in petroleum, chemicals and several other politically sensitive sectors, were reported to have budgeted to spend $889 million on supporting candidates in the 2016 US presidential and congressional elections.[22] The *Washington Post* calculated this to be $300 million more than spent by all external funders of all stages of the 2012 elections.

Democracy necessarily implies a certain kind of political equality. This is usually guaranteed through highly elaborate rules to ensure that each citizen has one and only one vote that (s)he is fully able to exercise. Outside that narrow frame, inequalities in the power to exercise political persuasion and influence are tolerated to varying degrees. Countries differ in the extent to which they regulate spending on election campaigns and lobbying of governments in general. If, as is happening at the present time, inequalities of income and wealth increase, then inequalities in the ability to exercise influence of these kinds will also increase. If policies of privatisation and public service outsourcing, and other factors that politicise various sectors of the economy (such as the role of being 'too big to fail') grow, then incentives to use those inequalities for political purposes will also grow. There comes a point where the disparity between the rhetoric and formal rules of democratic equality and real political inequality throws into serious question the ability of a regime to be described as democratic at all. It is not surprising that serious commentators have begun to question whether democracy and capitalism are any longer mutually compatible.[23]

Such a development is important for many aspects of social life, but does democracy matter for neoliberal capitalism? Major neoliberal writers, in particular Friedrich von Hayek,[24] have been highly ambiguous in their commitment to democracy, but overall it is usually assumed that there are elective affinities between democracy and the market order. Both require free competition among contenders for, respectively, votes and customers. Modern democracy more or less guarantees the rule of law and the protection of property rights, which capitalism needs, along with clear procedures for changing law and lobbying around proposed changes. On the other hand, democracy can also produce a mass of regulations to protect non-market, non-corporate interests. Capitalists' preferred regime is probably what I have elsewhere called 'post-democracy', where all the forms of democracy continue, including importantly the rule of law, but where the electorate has become largely passive, and civil society too weak to challenge corporate interests in influencing government.[25] An example of post-democratic politics has been provided by the Transparency of Lobbying, Non-Party

Campaigning and Trade Union Administration Act 2014 in the UK. This imposed restrictions on the spending and other activities of organised lobbying and pressure groups, but did not touch the lobbying activities of individual corporations. Thus, for instance, in a political dispute between a supermarket chain and a group of a town's small shopkeepers, the lobbying activities of the latter, but not the former, would be subject to regulation.

Post-democratic capitalism does not require a formal renunciation of democracy any more than corporate neoliberalism requires a renunciation of the market; indeed, democracy and the market continue to be used as the primary sources of legitimation of the evolving political system of dominant corporate power. Other sources are then used in a supplementary way.[26] For example, anti-anti-trust theory provided a justification for protecting market-dominating corporations from market-making competition law. New public management theory legitimates the abolition of boundaries between public officials and corporate personnel seen as so important to an earlier age of liberal economy. Corporate social responsibility gives business leaders a social legitimation going beyond their role as profit-maximisers and suggests that public policy is not needed to tackle many market failures. In the absence of Keynesian demand management, the widespread desire for a high level of employment gives priority to the policy preferences of business interests. A discussion of the paradoxical and troublesome relationships between the market economy and the strategies of privatisation and public service outsourcing that apparently arise from it reveals broader tensions within contemporary political economy. The corporate dominance involved in actually existing neoliberalism challenges its compatibility with both the market order and political democracy.

Notes

1 The leading neoliberal theorists dominate the economics departments of the world's universities, particularly in the US and especially the University of Chicago. They have been particularly prominent among winners of the Swedish National Bank's economics prize, generally known as the economics Nobel Prize. To some extent neoliberal thinkers are organised within the Mont Pèlerin Society founded by Friedrich von Hayek and his colleagues. A highly critical but thorough guide to the leading members of the school and the range of their contributions will be found in P. Mirowski, *Never Let a Good Crisis Go to Waste: How Neoliberalism Survived the Financial Meltdown*, London, Verso, 2013.

2 C. Crouch, *The Strange Non-Death of Neoliberalism*, Cambridge, Polity Press, 2011, ch. 5.

3 See the works of J.J. Laffont and J. Tirole, for example 'Using cost observation to regulate firms', *Journal of Political Economy*, vol. 94, no. 3 (Part I) 1986, pp. 614–41; *Competition in Telecommunications*, Cambridge, MA, MIT Press, 2000.

4 J.J. Laffont and J. Tirole, 'The politics of government decision making: a theory of regulatory capture', *Quarterly Journal of Economics*, vol. 106, no. 4, 1991, pp. 1089–127.

5 A particularly extraordinary example of this is the £2 billion state guarantee given by the British government to the three French and Chinese companies—all of them nationalised corporations—building the Hinkley Point C nuclear power station. See https://www.gov.uk/government/news/2-billion-support-for-hinkley-point-c (accessed 22 October 2015).

6 For examples from the NHS, see J. Davis, J. Lister and D. Wrigley, *NHS for Sale: Myths, Lies and Deception*, London, Merlin Press, 2015, esp. pp 16–21.

7 Social Enterprise UK, *The Shadow State*, London, Social Enterprise UK, 2012.

8 For details of recent British cases, see C. Crouch, *The Knowledge Corrupters: Hidden Consequences of the Financial Takeover of Public Life*, Cambridge, Polity Press, 2015.

9 Social Enterprise UK, *The Shadow State*. It could be argued that such critics have a certain axe to grind, since they represent smaller firms that find it difficult to win contracts of this kind in the face of competition from the large corporations; but since the promotion of such competition was a key part of the original justification for outsourcing, it may be considered not an unreasonable case.

10 Crouch, *The Strange Non-Death of Neoliberalism*.

11 The British Conservative–Liberal Democrat coalition government of 2010–2015 established a 'strategic relations initiative' under which ministers developed special links with a selected set of seventy-six global corporations across a number of sectors, not just those involved in public contracting. See 'Buddy scheme to give multinationals more access to ministers', *The Guardian*, 18 January 2013, http://www.theguardian.com/politics/2013/jan/18/buddy-scheme-multinationals-access-ministers (accessed 22 October 2015).

12 In the event, a local campaign group to save Lewisham Hospital took the case to court, where it was ruled that the government lacked the power to make closures in that way. The government then prepared plans to change the law to enable them to do so in future. See https://www.gov.uk/government/groups/ukti-strategic-relations-team#supporting-the-uks-top-76-investors-and-exporters (accessed 22 October 2015).

13 Ibid.

14 R. H. Bork, *The Antitrust Paradox: A Policy at War with Itself*, New York, Free Press, 1993, 1st edn 1978; R. A. Posner, *Antitrust Law*, 2nd edn, Chicago, University of Chicago Press, 2001.

15 T. Cave and A. Rowell, *A Quiet Word: Lobbying, Crony Capitalism and Broken Politics in Britain*, London, Bodley Head, 2014.

16 Davis, Lister and Wrigley, *NHS for Sale*.

17 A helpful discussion of the various issues arising from the TTIP can be found in *Queries*, no. 6, Spring 2015, pp. 32–83, http://www.queries-feps.eu/PDF%20Complet%20-%20Queries%206.pdf (accessed 22 October 2015).

18 The most impressive example of this was R. A. Dahl's *Polyarchy, Participation and Opposition*, New Haven, CT, Yale University Press, 1971. However, already by the 1980s Dahl had become critical of his own position as a result of the corporate dominance of US politics: see Dahl, *Dilemmas of Pluralist Democracy: Autonomy Versus Control*, New Haven, CT, Yale University Press, 1982.

19 M. Förster, A. Llena-Nozal and V. Nafilyan, *Trends in Top Incomes and Their Taxation in OECD Countries*, OECD Society, Employment and Migration Working Papers 159, Paris, OECD, 2014; F. Bastagli, D. Coady and S. Gupta, *Income*

Inequality and Fiscal Policy, IMF Staff Discussion Note SDN/12/08, Washington, DC, IMF, 2012.

20 US Supreme Court, *Citizens United v. Federal Election Commission*, 08-205, Washington DC, US Supreme Court, 2010.

21 US Supreme Court, *McCutcheon v. Federal Election Commission*, 12-536, Washington DC, US Supreme Court, 2014.

22 P. Bump, 'Here's just how much the Koch Brothers are planning to spend on the 2016 election', *Washington Post*, 27 January 2015.

23 W. Merkel, 'Is capitalism compatible with democracy?', *Zeitschrift für Vergleichende Politikwissenschaft*, vol. 8, no. 2, 2014, pp. 109–28; W. Streeck, 'Comment on Wolfgang Merkel, "Is capitalism compatible with democracy?"', *Zeitschrift für Vergleichende Politikwissenschaft*, vol. 9, no. 1, 2015, pp. 49–60.

24 F. A. von Hayek, *The Road to Serfdom*, London, Routledge, 1944; *Individualism and Economic Order*, London, Routledge, 1948; *The Constitution of Liberty*, Chicago, IL, Chicago University Press, 1960. For detailed analyses of the anti-democratic tendencies in Hayek's thought, see Mirowski, *Never Let a Good Crisis Go to Waste*, and W. Streeck, *Gekaufte Zeit*, Berlin, Suhrkamp, 2013.

25 C. Crouch, *Post-democracy*, Cambridge, Polity Press, 2004.

26 C. Crouch, 'Can there be a normative theory of corporate political power?', in V. Schneider and B. Eberlein, eds., *Complex Democracy: Varieties, Crises, and Transformations*, Berlin, Springer, 2015, pp. 117–31.

10. Decarbonisation: Innovation and the Economics of Climate Change

DIMITRI ZENGHELIS

Introduction

CLIMATE CHANGE will alter the nature of our economies. The average global surface temperature of the Earth has now risen 1 degree Celsius above pre-industrial times, and the atmospheric concentration of the principal greenhouse gas carbon dioxide has reached more than 400 parts per million (ppm), rising at a rate of 2 ppm every year.[1] At around 450 ppm climate modelling indicates the likelihood that the average temperature rise will ultimately exceed 2°C, the level set by the international community as the threshold of 'dangerous' warming which should not be crossed. We are adding to the stock at a faster rate than ever before. Due to the time lag between greenhouse gas emissions and their impact on the temperature, the next ten to twenty years will be decisive in determining the course of climate change in the future. Unless stronger action is taken to curb and reverse rising emissions—not just of carbon dioxide, but also of methane, nitrous oxide and hydrofluorocarbons (HFCs)—the world is with high probability heading for warming beyond 2°C. On current trends, the temperature rise could exceed 4°C by the end of the century.[2]

The economic impacts of warming above 2°C would be profound. The Intergovernmental Panel on Climate Change (IPCC) has listed the likely impacts. These include a higher incidence of extreme weather events (such as flooding, storm surges and droughts), leading to the risk of a breakdown of infrastructure networks and critical services, particularly in coastal regions and cities; a heightened risk of food insecurity and breakdown of food systems resulting from changes in rainfall and reduced agricultural productivity; increased ill health and mortality from extreme heat events and food- and water-borne diseases; greater risks of displacement of peoples and conflict; and faster loss of terrestrial and marine ecosystems and species. These effects would not be distributed equally, with more severe impacts being experienced by poorer communities, and in particularly vulnerable countries and regions. Climate risks increase disproportionately as temperatures rise; above 3°C irreversible 'tipping points' may be reached such as the collapse of ice sheets and resulting sea-level rise, and substantial species extinctions.[3]

It is impossible to estimate accurately the economic costs of such effects, owing to many uncertainties. But even at 2°C of warming, the IPCC

Published by John Wiley & Sons Ltd, 9600 Garsington Road, Oxford OX4 2DQ, UK and 350 Main Street, Malden, MA 02148, USA

estimates the annual costs at 0.2–2.0 per cent of global GDP, even if strong measures are taken to adapt to such change.[4] Within GDP, much more economic output would need to be devoted to adaptation and defensive measures. In fact these are almost certainly under-estimates, both because the studies on which they are based are incomplete and because the impacts at higher temperatures are likely to be multiplicative. As Dietz and Stern have argued, climatic change is likely to undermine the core economic assets—particularly in infrastructure and natural and human capital—that drive growth and productivity. The economic costs are therefore likely to be much higher.[5]

So unchecked climate change would have severe consequences for our economic systems. But the challenge posed by global warming is in fact much greater than this, for, as we shall show in this chapter, controlling greenhouse gas emissions sufficiently to hold the temperature rise to 2°C will require a profound transformation in the ways in which goods and services are produced, distributed and consumed. The requirement radically to reduce carbon emissions means that the shape and structure of modern capitalism will have to be changed.

And in turn this will require a different approach to economics. Climate change has tended to be treated both by economists and policy-makers as an 'environmental issue', to which the orthodox tools of economic analysis and policy can be applied. But, as we shall show, it is a much deeper problem than that. Because tackling climate change will require such a major shift in economic systems, thinking about it requires a broader, more evolutionary perspective. It involves understanding the path-dependent nature of techno-logical change, rethinking the use and design of economic modelling and deploying a much wider range of economic instruments than the standard policy toolkit.

The challenge to capitalism

The reason why climate change presents such a challenge for modern capital-ism is that it is caused by carbon. Carbon—specifically, carbon from fossil sources—is the source of energy which powers most of the world's economic activity, and has done for more than 200 years, since the use of coal to fire steam engines first gave birth to the industrial revolution. It is not too much to say that capitalism was founded on carbon. Even though today we have other sources of energy—nuclear power, and renewables such as hydro, wind and solar—the global economy is still overwhelmingly dependent on oil, gas and coal, which make up almost 80 per cent of primary energy use.[6]

And the problem is that fossil carbon emissions have to be reduced to zero if global temperature is to be stabilised. This arises from the basic mechanism of the greenhouse effect. Greenhouse gases (GHGs) stay in the atmosphere for tens and in some cases hundreds of years. It is the stock of GHGs that drives temperature change, not the annual flows. So the key insight of climate science—which has often not been properly grasped—is that no matter what the temperature at which we seek to stabilise, whether two degrees warmer or six degrees, net GHG emissions must ultimately fall to zero. In other words, the global economy must decarbonise more or less completely. ('Net emissions' allows for the fact that some emissions can be sequestered, either through an increase in natural carbon sinks, such as forests, or through carbon capture and storage technologies. 'Geoengineering' techniques may also have the potential to offset some of the effects of global warming, but are untried, carry significant risks and do not address other impacts such as ocean acidification.) The IPCC's climate modelling shows that to have a likely chance of holding warming to 2°C, carbon emissions must be reduced to net zero by 2065–2085, and all GHGs by the end of the century.[7]

This will require a fundamental structural transformation in all economies. Though we obviously cannot foresee every technology or method which will be involved in the future, the outlines of how such a transformation could come about are already visible.[8] Fossil fuels for energy will have to be more or less phased out, to be replaced by nuclear and renewable energy combined with electricity storage (and some role for carbon capture and storage). In transport, this will mean almost complete electrification of vehicles, and/ or the widespread use of hydrogen fuel cells, both based on clean energy sources. To accommodate much higher energy demand, the efficiency of energy consumption in all its uses will have to increase dramatically. This will mean major shifts in patterns of production, distribution and consumption, using digital and information technologies to manage energy demand and 'dematerialise' economic output. The design and functioning of buildings and transport systems, and the patterns of towns and cities as a whole, will have to change very significantly. To reduce the demand for energy to extract and transport physical resources, in agriculture and in the manufacture and transport of industrial and consumer products, major changes will be needed in almost all sectors. As Carlota Perez argues in her chapter in this volume, all this will add up to a technological revolution on a par with those which have disrupted and transformed economic systems in the past.

Can this be done, and at the requisite speed? That is of course unknowable until it is attempted. It is not just a question of technological change. The political implications are far-reaching. Climate change is a collective action problem, a 'tragedy of the commons'. To decarbonise economies, nation-states and the private sector need to build new and in most cases currently more expensive energy, transport, industrial, agricultural and urban systems. In doing so they will inevitably cause current assets and activities based on fossil energy to decline in value and profitability. This will, equally inevitably, encounter resistance. Yet on their own none of these actions will be sufficient to address the global problem, since only if all act will the actions of any be effective. And in a context where most political and financial decision-makers have short-term outlooks, the major benefits will accrue to future generations—a disjuncture which has been aptly called 'the tragedy of the horizon'.[9] It means that all countries have incentives to limit domestic costs by 'free-riding' on the actions of others. It is a formidable set of obstacles.

The challenge to economics

So capitalism—and politics—are profoundly challenged by climate change.[10] But so is the discipline of economics, for climate change is not like most other environmental problems with which economics has learned to deal.

Contrary to widespread belief, orthodox economics has not ignored the environment. For a hundred years there has been a mainstream sub-discipline of environmental economics dealing both with resource scarcity (much of it based on the original work of Jevons and Hotelling), and with pollution (building on the work of Pigou).[11] Neoclassical economics recognises environmental problems as negative externalities of market transactions, a form of 'market failure'; so interventions to 'correct' the failures are needed. These could be regulations of various kinds (requiring behavioural changes in law), but economists have generally been able to show that often these will be less efficient than instruments which provide financial incentives for firms and consumers to change their behaviour, such as taxes or permit trading systems. A relatively simple static economics follows in which the optimal environmental outcome occurs where the marginal cost of abating pollution is equal to the benefit gained, and this is done most efficiently through some kind of market-based instrument.[12]

The orthodox economic approach to climate change has largely followed this approach. Global warming is a form of pollution, an externality of market transactions which generate greenhouse gases. As GHG emissions rise, warming increases, creating a 'damage function' measuring the 'social cost of carbon'. This cost can be internalised by pricing carbon (and potentially other GHGs): applying a carbon tax or establishing emissions trading schemes which provide incentives for economic actors to reduce the carbon dioxide they generate. When the tax rate equals the social cost of carbon, the optimal level of warming will be achieved. Of course no environmental economist thinks the real world is as simple as this, but the neoclassical framework provides a helpful set of conceptual tools to grapple with the problem, and carbon pricing remains the overwhelmingly favoured policy instrument among climate economists and businesses.[13]

But it's not enough. Pricing carbon is indeed a necessary policy for cost-effective emissions reductions. It is transparent and non-discriminatory, sending a price signal which allows the market to determine the most efficient form of short-term emissions reductions. With no price on a damaging activity, over-consumption is all but guaranteed. But pricing isn't sufficient to achieve on its own the scale and speed of decarbonisation required to stabilise global temperature at safe levels. This is because the extent to which

175

carbon is embedded in the economic system across a range of activities makes it a unique pollutant.

On the face of it, carbon is not unlike other pollutants. It is not a final good—a non-carbon 'green' electron is just as effective at providing energy as a polluting one. Renewable technologies suggest that carbon may ultimately prove no more essential to energy generation than lead was critical to petrol. But whereas the latter could be reduced or eliminated by changing one element of a production process, reducing carbon requires fundamental changes to an extensive and deeply entrenched global infrastructure. The pollutant sulphur dioxide (which caused 'acid rain') could be scrubbed from power stations without changing the core technologies and methods involved in generating electricity. But carbon dioxide is fundamental to the combustion process which powers more or less every economic activity in every sector throughout the global economy. So although carbon is in general substitutable, it is so effectively embedded in the fundamental physical structures of modern societies and their economies that the policy requirements to deliver change are significantly more complex. Carbon is globally pervasive on a scale quite unlike other pollutants.

Addressing it is therefore not a matter of marginalist economics in the neoclassical tradition. Eliminating carbon from capitalism is not about finding static equilibriums in markets corrected for minor failures. Because carbon is so central to capitalism it is a much larger task, involving a fundamental reshaping not just of individual technologies but of entire systems of production, distribution and consumption. For this we need to draw on much richer veins of evolutionary and institutional economic thought about the dynamics of change in economic systems. We need to understand the basis of growth in innovation, and the role of path-dependence in system transformation.

Innovation and growth

Technological innovation has long been recognised as one of the core drivers of economic growth, but in modern theories of endogenous growth it is given a pre-eminent role.[14] Investment in innovation—in human capital, research and development (R&D) and knowledge—is the key not just to productivity improvement but to an expansion in the ways in which value can be created.

This is crucial to solving the climate change problem. A long tradition in environmentalism has argued that the quest to remain within the planet's ecological limits must inevitably mean an end to growth. In 1798 Malthus posited that finite resources would quickly constrain humans' ability to supply rising demand. John Stuart Mill (1848) argued that the economy would eventually reach a stationary state. In the twentieth century the Club of Rome set out *The Limits to Growth* and predicted 'overshoot and collapse' in the economy, environment and population before 2070.[15] Yet since 1800 the world economy has grown by eighty times. The Malthusian mistake was to take the structure of the global economy as given. Malthus' model assumed that technologies and processes would remain broadly unchanged, meaning that the world would run low on resources in the face of growing population and demand. Yet it was human innovation that allowed agricultural yields to rocket and industrialisation to provide an unprecedented array of consumer possibilities. What Malthus and his later followers omitted to factor in was that every human mouth is born with a human brain: ingenuity and innovation in technologies, processes and institutions allows society to get ever more out of the resources it uses.

More recent critics of economic growth have argued that a continuous increase in economic output does not lead to a concomitant increase in human well-being, and is unsustainable within the finite biophysical boundaries of the planet.[16] But this is a contingent matter. It depends on the path of innovation: not just on how far new technologies and systems of production, distribution and consumption can raise output while reducing environmental impact, but on how far economic value can be created out of knowledge and information.

Unlike material resources, knowledge does not deplete. Indeed, knowledge builds on knowledge: one of the sources of endogenous growth is that constant or increasing returns to ideas can overcome diminishing returns to physical capital.[17] It is very hard to unlearn what has been learned and intellectual capital accumulates, so technical progress tends to push productivity ever upwards. As Isaac Newton famously acknowledged, he saw further only by 'standing on the shoulders of giants'. In a virtuous spiral, knowledge begets increased output and liberates resources for further investment. At the same time, as we have dramatically witnessed over recent decades, knowledge and information come to make up a larger and larger portion of GDP. It is not entirely true to say that knowledge is 'weightless', since it is created and disseminated by physical communications infrastructure which uses a great deal of resources and energy; but its growth in modern economies generates a radically reduced material throughput for each unit of GDP value created.[18]

So innovation offers the most important route out of the environmental problem. By harnessing non-carbon-based sources of energy—notably the earth's non-depleting abundance of solar and wind resources—and by shifting economies increasingly towards knowledge capital and information-based goods and services, decarbonisation becomes possible even while growth continues to occur. Proponents of such 'green growth' do not suggest that economic growth can defy the laws of thermodynamics. In the real world, of actual economic activity, the throughput of materials and energy and the resulting problem of waste disposal will remain central to the world's economic predicament. Rather, they note that technological progress can in principle support continued growth in value because the intellectual economy is unbounded. Even if the material economy must eventually attain a steady state in terms of the sustainable use of resources, economic development can continue to occur and humanity to prosper. Material growth, economic growth and human wellbeing can be decoupled.[19]

Path-dependence and innovation

But innovation does not happen in a vacuum. The downside to the propensity for knowledge to build upon knowledge is that it makes a radical shift in the course of technology and infrastructure much harder to achieve. Innovation is path-dependent: it is constrained by what has gone on before. Ideas and practices are sticky. Examples abound. It is generally believed that the ostensibly odd design of the QWERTY keyboard was to prevent English-language typewriters from jamming. Very few typewriters are still in use, but the world is stuck with the keyboard, irrespective of whether it now enhances writing productivity. London's city plan, including the shape and location of its new skyscrapers, is in part determined by Roman planning two millennia ago.

This is the phenomenon of 'lock-in': the ways in which existing infrastructure and ideas interact to set the course for future change. Any visitor to Copenhagen or Amsterdam will be struck by the popularity of cycling. When asked why this is so, people often point to the first-class cycle lanes. But the explanation given for these is the fact that so many people cycle. Such circularity is a feature of path-dependence, which by its nature leads to mutually reinforcing feedback mechanisms. Once set in train, behaviours, institutions and physical assets become hard to dislodge. The fossil fuel network, for example, incorporates not just mines, refineries, ports, pipelines, generation plants and filling stations, but also a vast reservoir of knowledge and wealth which allows oil and gas companies to hire top engineers to extract fuels from ever more inaccessible locations. They also have extensive lobbying power in various governments.

Yet these effects are largely ignored in conventional economic analysis, with its focus on static market failures. Urban policy provides a telling illustration. Over recent years multiple studies have shown how cities planned on a model of dense development with integrated public transport are much less carbon- and resource-intensive than cities based on a sprawling car-based model, even at the same levels of income.[20] At the same time, cities provide an extreme example of infrastructural and behavioural lock-in: once built, they are extremely hard to change retrospectively. It therefore matters hugely to the future course of climate change how the rapidly growing cities of the developing world are designed and built over the next three decades. Yet no mainstream quantitative assessment of climate change policy has so far managed to incorporate the impact of different urban forms. It isn't amenable to the standard market failure analysis, and carbon pricing is not the primary policy tool which will determine how cities are built.

Path-dependence increases the cost of radical change. To achieve the kind of transformation in our current fossil-fuel-based systems of production and distribution needed to slow global warming will therefore require strong government policy, which to begin with may be very expensive. European renewable energy policy provides a case in point. German subsidies for the installation of photovoltaic (PV) solar power, starting in the early 1990s, came initially at very high cost. But as demand rose, prices fell, and incentives were created for further technical advances. New firms entered the market, developing cheaper ways of manufacturing and installing the technology through 'learning by doing'. Mass manufacture—in China as well as Europe—pushed costs down further, leading to higher global demand. The result was a 90 per cent reduction in PV modules in just six years from 2009 to 2015, so that installed solar power is now at cost-parity with fossil fuels in many parts of the world, and close to it even in northern Europe. Consumer behaviour has changed, with solar power now a normal household investment. PV subsidies have radically declined, and are on their way to being unnecessary. At the same time, new lobbies for climate policy among both businesses and consumers have been created.

This is an example of how strong policy can overcome path-dependent inertia, and then set in train a new positive dynamic. (The EU in 2008 required all member states to adopt renewable energy targets amounting to 20 per cent of primary energy demand by 2020.) Positive feedback loops in the innovation chain interact across the economy, prompting institutional and behavioural change and the emergence of new scale economies. Without strong policy, innovation activity tends to be focused towards the incumbent, dominant technologies, where returns on incremental improvements are easily observed and understood. However, the alignment of expectations on the likely shape of future energy networks and innovations can lead to a 'tipping point' where the nature and direction of mainstream innovation activity can switch quickly. This can become self-reinforcing through new network effects. So long as one network technology is dominant, products and services linked to the use of that network will receive the bulk of innovation activity and there will be less effort committed to developing an alternative; but if a new technology network becomes dominant then innovation activity can shift quickly. The recent rapid development of energy storage technologies in the wake of the growth of renewables—storage being a principal means to cope with the intermittency of solar and wind power—provides a powerful example. The cost of lithium-ion batteries has fallen by more than 40 per cent in the past five years. This revolution has only just begun and has yet to play out.

One of the leading innovators in energy storage is the electric car manufacturer Tesla Motors. The company has adopted a radical approach to the problem of network lock-in.[21] In June 2014, Elon Musk, Tesla's founder, announced that his company would effectively make their electric vehicle patents public. But this was not technological altruism. In order to be able to

179

sell more of their electric vehicles Tesla simultaneously needs an entirely new vehicle-charging infrastructure. And for that to be built, the scale of the electric vehicle market needs to be greatly increased. Musk realised that fossil-driven networks are hard to dislodge given the vast existing network of petrol stations, and vested interests of car dealerships, that make driving a combustion-engine car so much the norm.[22] Rather than trying to win this battle alone, Tesla decided to expand the new market by stimulating the innovative resources of all car companies. Since the industrial revolution, firms have frequently exploited this path-dependence in technology adoption and network effects in order to diffuse their innovations and create new markets.[23] Toyota followed suit.

A striking finding of recent research is that the potential spillovers from low-carbon innovation to other sectors—one of the factors which helps to drive overall growth—may be higher than for other technologies.[24] Aghion et al. provide empirical evidence both for geographical knowledge spillovers (where a firm's choice of innovation path is influenced by the practice of the countries where its researchers are located) and for path-dependence (where firms tend to direct innovation towards what they are already good at).[25] Using data on 1 million patents and 3 million citations, Dechezleprêtre et al. suggest that spillovers from low-carbon innovation in the energy production and transportation sectors are more than 40 per cent greater than in conventional technologies.[26] At the same time Acemoglu et al. provide a powerful theoretical case to suggest that once systems of clean innovation have been started up, they may be more productive than conventional alternatives based on existing technologies.[27]

The lesson for policy-makers and economists here is an important one. As both Mariana Mazzucato and Carlota Perez note in their chapters in this volume, the direction of innovation is not pre-ordained. The challenge of shifting the fossil-fuel-based infrastructure of present production and consumption towards clean forms will require strong government policy with a clear goal of decarbonisation—what Mazzucato describes as 'mission-oriented'. In many cases this will need to overcome early high costs, which are likely to breed political resistance. But if a tipping point in investment and policy can be reached, feedback loops and network effects may kick in and accelerate the process of change, with positive spillovers to the rest of the economy. These mutually reinforcing mechanisms can lead to abrupt step-changes. Standard neoclassical economics, of the kind taught commonly in business schools, struggles to accommodate such dynamics. The long-run costs of global decarbonisation may therefore be far less, and indeed potentially negative.

Economic models

In assessing and determining policy options, governments use economic models. Most national policy frameworks are informed directly or indirectly by quantitative evaluation. In particular, national economic models allow specific and sectoral policies (such as carbon pricing and renewable energy subsidies) to be simulated, and their economy-wide effects on a range of macroeconomic indicators determined. By comparing the outcomes with those of a reference case ('business as usual') in which such policy is not carried out, its expected impacts can be identified. Integrated assessment models (IAMs) used to assess climate change policy include greenhouse gas emissions among their variables. These allow simulations to be performed which constrain emissions to a certain level in a certain time-period. The model can then show the least-cost pathway to meeting such emissions targets, and the macroeconomic outcomes which are projected to follow.[28]

But such an approach has severe limitations where long-run technological change is involved. The process of dynamic innovation, not just in technologies but inter-relatedly in policies and institutions, is very difficult to capture in standard economic modelling approaches.

An economic model is essentially a simplified framework for describing the workings of the economy. Based on data on how the economy has behaved in the past, it exerts the discipline of forcing the modeller to formally articulate assumptions and tease out the relationships behind them. Models are used for two main purposes: simulating (how would the world change relative to some counterfactual if we assume a marginal change in this or that variable?) and forecasting (how do we expect the whole economy to look in twelve months' time?) Economic models are powerful tools for understanding change in the short term. Simulations can cast helpful light on a question such as how an economy might respond to, say, an energy price spike, when the structure of the economy is assumed unchanged. Forecasting an economy a year ahead may be relatively unproblematic (so long as nothing unexpected happens in that period). But models are much less effective at providing forecasts in the medium to long term, precisely because the longer the period ahead, the less reasonable it is to take any aspect of the structure of the economy as given. The further out the period being considered, the larger the structural uncertainties, making model projections at best illustrative, at worst misleading. This is especially true when significant economic shifts are being projected, such as technological innovation and structural change, and where non-marginal impacts—such as those arising from climate change—are likely radically to alter the reference case.

To estimate the ways in which emissions can be reduced in a given economy, and the cost of doing so, most economic models use a version of a 'marginal abatement cost (MAC) curve'.[29] This shows the estimated incremental cost in a particular year (say, 2020) of abating an extra tonne of CO_2 through a specific technology or action, and the total technical abatement potential it offers. Pre-determined MAC curves therefore form one of the key behavioural drivers of economic models. In simulating the path of costs of each technique or action, most models assume a linear rate of technological and cost improvement.[30]

181

Yet we know this is not how technological change occurs. In reality, as we have seen, innovation is endogenous, and if sufficiently stimulated—whether by demand, policy, R&D spending or simply scientific advance—can be non-linear and discontinuous. Because innovation holds the key to our ability to decarbonise, this shortcoming is fatal. Modelling based on MAC curves risks missing or under-estimating the key changes which may occur in response to emissions targets or the use of specific policy instruments. In turn that means that such models are prone to over-estimate costs. The history of environmental policy is indeed littered with anticipated costs projected by economic models (often with accompanying warnings from vested interests) which have not in practice materialised once the policy was in place.[31] The huge divergence between the estimates of the future use of solar and wind power in International Energy Agency projections and the actual out-turn in such use provides a notable case in point.[32]

Models used by finance ministries, banks and central banks take the underlying structure of the economy as given and analyse perturbations on the margins through estimated behavioural equations.[33] Both 'new Keynesian' and computable general equilibrium (CGE) models rely on assumptions about pre-determined long-term trends or 'convexity' associated with diminishing marginal returns and diminishing marginal products, in order to converge on a steady state. Because they rarely look forward beyond a four-year horizon, such simplifying assumptions make for good approximations of short-term reality. But looking further out, the uncertainties grow and so do the chances that structural discontinuities will push the economy onto new paths, driven by new technologies, institutions and behaviours. Characterising key variables, like output, as reverting to a deterministic mean, or returns to investment as always diminishing, is convenient but unrealistic.

This causes problems for economic projections tasked with examining the impact of large transformative change such as transitioning to a decarbonised global economy over a longer period. The requirement that a model tends towards a steady-state equilibrium means many key dynamics are modelled as tendencies towards that equilibrium, rather than determinants of structural change. 'Change' is modelled as a transient state which self-corrects. Yet real-world growth is endogenous, subject to constant change originating within the system and characterised by often positively reinforcing feedback loops.

Economic factors that are subject to economies of scale, capital and institutional lock-in, irreversibilities, new networks and path-dependencies are particularly hard to estimate empirically. This is because in some cases they have not previously happened, so there is no data on which to base the relationships, and also because alternative equilibriums which would have resulted from alternate paths are not directly observable—the best we can say is that the world could have been very different. They are even harder to model, because of their non-linear dynamics. Shocks can have persistent effects and policy choices wide implications, making prediction increasingly difficult. It is well known that meteorological models make consistent and accurate forecasts over a two-week period, but then start to become less and less reliable as more chaotic effects emerge (the famous 'butterfly wing' effect). The same is true with economic models over long periods.

The problem is that the dynamics which are most pertinent and interesting when it comes to simulating the future in relation to climate change policy are those which are hardest to model. The result is that, more often than not, they are simply not modelled; and consequently the models tell us little about what such a future is likely to bring. They are especially unhelpful in projecting the long-run costs and benefits of policy. In its Fifth Assessment Report in 2014 the Intergovernmental Panel on Climate Change surveyed a range of integrated assessment models and pronounced that meeting the global temperature goal of no more than a two-degree warming would cost 2.9–11.4 per cent of global consumption in 2100.[34] This is absurd. Such models cannot provide any kind of rational description of what the economy will be like nearly a century ahead—either in the baseline (reference case) scenario or the climate policy scenario. No economic modeller has more than the faintest ability to predict the technologies which will be available for emissions reduction even forty years hence, let alone eighty; and even less their costs. Assuming that after eighty years of investing in and learning from technologies to harness and store renewable energies, it will still be cheaper to extract, transport and burn fossil fuels, is akin to predicting in 1900 that the costs of moving from the horse and cart to the combustion engine would be prohibitive, based on anticipated technologies at the time.

This does not imply jettisoning economic models altogether. Models are essential tools in helping us examine theoretical and empirical behavioural relationships, and thereby to articulate and understand the workings of a complex world. But their limitations for long-run analysis need to be properly acknowledged. Spurious precision needs to be avoided. And a much more sophisticated approach needs to be taken to integrating endogenous technological and institutional change within them. The modelling community could fruitfully focus attention on the economic processes which generate knowledge and drive innovation and systemic change. This could prove greatly valuable in designing effective policy.

Climate change policy

A range of policy instruments are required to cut greenhouse gas emissions. Michael Grubb has provided a helpful conceptual framework. He notes how regulatory measures (such as energy efficiency standards) are appropriate where economic activity is characterised by satisficing behaviour; market-based incentives (such as carbon pricing) in the domain of optimising behaviour; and innovation policy (such as deployment subsidies and R&D expenditure) where technological and structural transformation is required.[35]

Of these, innovation policy is the most complex, and the one where environmental economics has so far had least to say. As Mariana Mazzucato

183

notes in her chapter in this volume, the orthodox economic view has been that policy-makers should not seek to 'pick winners', since (it is claimed) they are likely to be poor at identifying technologies or companies which will be successful in the future. Yet as she also points out, in fact many of the most successful technologies of the modern age have been state-funded in their early development. If governments are to drive innovation in a low-carbon direction, they are going to need to support it through funding policy, both in R&D and in helping to finance deployment. (The evidence suggests in fact that the balance of funding may be too skewed towards deployment subsidies relative to early stage R&D. Fischer et al. estimate that the optimal ratio of deployment to R&D spending is around 1:2, while Zachmann et al. show that funding for deployment across twenty-eight countries is 150 times higher than for R&D.[36])

But successful climate policy-making is about more than particular policy instruments. Because decarbonisation requires structural change, wider considerations come into play. First, a general approach to economic policy which encourages flexibility is important. Open trade, strong competition policy and well-regulated labour markets facilitate the flow of resources from declining, high-carbon sectors to growing and more productive low-carbon activities more easily. Second, distributional issues are crucial. Structural change inevitably has adverse effects on particular industries, workers and communities—notably those in high-carbon fields such as coal mining, but also in sectors such as iron and steel and chemicals, which will need heavy investment to move towards lower-carbon production methods. Ensuring that transitional support is provided to enable investment in some cases, and the redeployment of labour to new sectors in others, will help smooth the transformation process, both economically and politically.[37]

Third, successful climate policy-making requires a willingness to take on entrenched interests. There is a well-established asymmetry in political economy which favours incumbents. The losers from any change, whether it is competition policy or climate policy, can readily identify the degree to which they stand to lose, and are well placed to lobby politicians to delay, limit or prevent policy which will adversely affect them. By contrast, the potential beneficiaries are often spread thinly and, in the case of nascent technologies and sectors, may still be relatively small or not yet even in existence.

Incumbents often claim, in particular, that stronger climate policy will put them at a competitive disadvantage relative to those in other countries, or even cause them to relocate elsewhere: the result, it is argued, will be 'carbon leakage', the transfer of emissions from the more strongly regulated economy to the weaker one, with therefore no net reduction in total. But the evidence does not support these fears. Recent studies of European climate policy, particularly of the EU emissions trading system, suggest that the impacts have thus far been small, whether in terms of carbon leakage, economic growth, employment or consumer prices, with only a few energy-intensive sectors at risk of significant adverse effects even if policy is strengthened.[38] Policy-makers should largely resist giving in to incumbent lobbies.

In fact policies and regulations which affected firms claim (*ex ante*) will damage them can turn out to incentivise innovation once implemented.[39] EU fuel efficiency targets for passenger cars, for example, have induced a series of technological improvements which have helped make European cars globally competitive. When in 2009 the EU introduced a fleet average target of 130 g/ km by 2015 it was widely opposed by the motor industry; but it was met two years early. In the US, by contrast, where gasoline taxation has long been kept low due to consumer and car-industry pressures, improvements in fuel efficiency have been far slower. As a consequence the US car industry was much less well placed to survive the combination of higher oil process and the global financial crisis, a key but largely unheralded factor in the bankruptcies of Chrysler and General Motors in 2009.[40] Economists have in general responded to the debate on climate policies and competitiveness by highlighting the effects of pricing carbon on fossil fuel dependent sectors, but less attention has been paid to the numerous opportunities associated with attracting and deploying new energy technologies. No doubt the latter is harder to quantify, but it also belies capitalism's inability to overcome vested interests and convey the advantages of transformational change to the population at large.

Perhaps the single most important feature of climate policy is consistency. Switching to lower-carbon forms of production requires investment; but this requires confidence on the part of businesses and investors that the policy framework will be sustained. When such confidence is absent, such investment is undermined.[41] It is not true that investment requires 'certainty'—no dynamic market can provide that. But there is now considerable evidence that environmental policy uncertainty is associated with negative effects at both firm level (lower investment and hiring) and country level (loss of GDP, unemployment).[42] Maintaining credible and consistent policy signals over time is therefore particularly important.

Climate policy-making is in this sense much to do with the creation and management of economic expectations. The greater the belief among economic actors that the world is shifting towards a low-carbon trajectory, the more likely it is to happen—and the more cost-effective it will be. Consider a business contemplating investment in, say, renewables or energy efficiency. Its anticipated returns will depend on its expectations about how others are going to behave. If few others are expected to invest likewise, the markets will be smaller, the technologies more expensive and the cost of capital higher.

But if on the other hand whole markets are expected to move at scale, then technology and financing costs will be expected to fall, and profits rise. Investment will breed investment; expectations will become self-fulfilling. A virtuous circle is therefore possible; but it requires policy-makers to show leadership, set clear goals and hold their nerve when immediate political resistance is encountered. Changing policy in response to events only increases risk and raises costs. None of these crucial dynamics which determine the viability of decarbonisation are captured in standard economic models.

Conclusion

Climate change poses a challenge to capitalism both from its consequences and its causes. If global warming is to be controlled at a safe level, net emissions will have to fall to zero within this century. Because of the centrality of carbon to our economies, this can only be done through a profound structural transformation—the decarbonisation of production, distribution and consumption systems.

Assessing whether this is achievable requires a form of economic analysis which focuses less on static market failures and more on the dynamic processes of innovation and structural change. Economic history provides a rich source of learning: Western economies have experienced a series of technological and socio-economic revolutions over the past 200 years. These Schumpeterian processes have demonstrated that path-dependence is powerful but it is not all-conquering.[43]

The task for policy-makers is therefore a much larger one than the neoclassical prospectus suggests. It is to steer a cost-effective transition to a decarbonised economy. This will require clear price signals and a credible set of mission-oriented goals and a focus on driving innovation in a low-carbon direction, overcoming the path-dependence of current high-carbon infrastructure and institutions. It means recognising how the costs of action fall as innovation occurs. Standard economic models and policy assessment techniques which do not account for this are therefore misleading, encouraging inertia and resistance to change. Policy-makers need courage to see policy through to the innovation and investment tipping points where feedback loops kick in and new technologies become competitive and are deployed at scale, into new networks, without the need for subsidy. They need to drive a shift in market expectations, and sustain investor confidence through consistent policy over time.

Is this possible? It may already be happening. Under the UN agreement achieved in Paris in December 2015 almost every country in the world has committed to cutting emissions over the coming ten to fifteen years, and accepted that the long-term path must be towards decarbonisation. The scale of investment in low-carbon energy that these plans will require is already shifting investor expectations, leading to predictions of further cost reductions as the scale of global markets expands and boosting the prospects of further technological innovation, for example in energy storage. The value of high-carbon assets, such as the stocks of coal mining companies, is already in decline, and investors are increasingly analysing the risks to such assets which further climate policy may bring.[44] Meanwhile, policy-makers are increasingly recognising the short-term benefits from effectively managing a low-carbon transition in terms of energy efficiency, energy security, urban pollution, congestion and generating innovation.[45] It is too early to say that a low-carbon transformation tipping point has been reached; but it is no longer fanciful to imagine it on the horizon. Indeed, the historic Paris Accord was as much a reflection as a cause of a fundamental change in perceptions about the economics of decarbonisation; one that has shifted from cost (and burdens to be shared) to opportunities and self-interest.

For the economics profession this brings new challenges. Conventional economics has had too little to say about how such change occurs. Too much focus has been placed on narrowly understood market failures, and on economic models based on static cost estimates and business-as-usual baselines which assume away the most interesting questions about how socio-technological transformation occurs. Economists must work harder to make their analyses fit for purpose. But the onus is also on leaders in business and government to understand how path-dependence places a premium on early and strong action. In the transition to a low-carbon future, it may prove easier to drive change than to predict it.

Notes

1 World Meteorological Organisation, *Greenhouse Gas Bulletin*, no. 11, 9 November 2015, http://library.wmo.int/pmb_ged/ghg-bulletin_11_en.pdf (accessed 14 April 2016).
2 IPCC, 'Summary for policymakers', in *Climate Change 2014: Impacts, Adaptation, and Vulnerability. Part A: Global and Sectoral Aspects. Contribution of Working Group II to the Fifth Assessment Report of the Intergovernmental Panel on Climate Change*, 2014, https://www.ipcc.ch/report/ar5/wg2/ (accessed 14 April 2016).
3 Ibid.
4 Ibid.
5 Dietz and Stern show that accounting for the endogeneity of growth leads to a much stronger case for climate policy action than indicated in standard economic models. In this chapter we extend this basic logic to argue that accounting for the drivers of growth and innovation affords the opportunity to dramatically lower the costs of reducing emissions. S. Dietz and N. Stern, 'Endogenous growth, convexity of damage and climate risk: how Nordhaus' framework supports deep cuts in carbon emissions', *The Economic Journal*, vol. 125, no. 583, 2015, pp. 574–620, doi: 10.1111/ecoj.12188, http://onlinelibrary.wiley.com/doi/10.1111/ecoj.12188/abstract (accessed 14 April, 2016).
6 *World Energy Outlook Special Report 2015: Energy and Climate Change*, Paris, International Energy Agency, 2015.
7 IPCC, 'Summary for policymakers'.
8 A useful account of some of the major transformations required can be found in Global Commission on the Economy and Climate, *Better Growth, Better Climate*, New Climate Economy, 2014, http://2015.newclimateeconomy.report/ (accessed 14 April 2016). See also *World Energy Outlook Special Report 2015*.
9 Mark Carney, governor of the Bank of England, coined this term in a speech on climate risk and the financial system in 2015: 'Breaking the tragedy of the horizon—climate change and financial stability', 29 September 2015,

http://www.bankofengland.co.uk/publications/Pages/speeches/2015/844.aspx (accessed 14 April 2016).

10 For useful discussions of the character of the problem, see D. Helm, *The Carbon Crunch: How We're Getting Climate Change Wrong—and How to Fix It*, New Haven, CT, Yale University Press, 2012; and also N. Stern, *Why Are We Waiting? The Logic, Urgency, and Promise of Tackling Climate Change*, Cambridge, MA, MIT Press, 2015.

11 For a survey, see D. Pearce, 'An intellectual history of environmental economics', *Annual Review of Energy and the Environment*, vol. 27, 2002, pp. 57–81, doi: 10.1146/annurev.energy.27.122001.083429.

12 R. Perman, Y. Ma, M. Common, D. Maddison and J. Mcgilvray, *Natural Resource and Environmental Economics*, London, Pearson Education, 2011.

13 See for example Global Commission on the Economy and Climate, *Better Growth, Better Climate*, and the conclusions of the Business and Climate Summit, May 2015, http://www.businessclimatesummit.com/wp-content/uploads/2015/05/Business-Climate-Summit-Press-release.pdf (accessed 14 April 2016).

14 See P. M. Romer, 'The origins of endogenous growth', *The Journal of Economic Perspectives*, vol. 8, no. 1, 1994, pp. 3–22, doi:10.1257/jep.8.1.3. JSTOR 2138148. See also D. Acemoglu, *Endogenous Technological Change. Introduction to Modern Economic Growth*, Princeton, NJ, Princeton University Press. pp. 411–533. Romer notes that it was intensive—not extensive—use of resources which drove economic output growth: 'We don't really produce anything. Everything was already here, so all we can ever do is rearrange things.' See D. Zenghelis, *The Economics of Network Powered Growth*, Cisco IBSG, 2011.

15 T. R. Malthus, *An Essay on the Principle of Population*, London, printed for J. Johnson, in St. Paul's Church-Yard, 1798; John Stuart Mill, *Principles of Political Economy*, London, Longmans, Green and Co., London; Longmans, Green and Co. 1848; D. H. Meadows, D. L. Meadows, J. Randers and W. W. Behrens III, *The Limits to Growth: A Report for the Club of Rome's Project on the Predicament of Mankind*, New York, Universe Books, 1972.

16 T. Jackson, *Prosperity without Growth: Economics for a Finite Planet*, London, Sterling, VA, Earthscan, 2001; H. Daly, *Beyond Growth: The Economics of Sustainable Development*, Sussex, UK, Beacon Press, 1996 Edward Elgar Publishing Limited. Cheltenham, UK. Northampton, MA, USA; H. Daly, 'Georgescu-Roegen versus Solow/Stiglitz', *Ecological Economics*, vol. 22, no. 3, 1997, pp. 261–66.

17 P. Aghion and P. W. Howitt, 'A model of growth through creative destruction', *Econometrica*, vol. 60, no. 2, 1992. pp. 323–51; G. Grossman and E. Helpman, *Innovation and Growth in the Global Economy*, London, MIT Press, 1991, p. 77; P. Romer, 'Endogenous technological change', *Journal of Political Economy*, vol. 98, no. 5, 1990, pp. S71–S102; R. M. Solow, 'Technical change and the aggregate production function', *Review of Economics and Statistics*, vol. 39, no. 3, 1957, pp. 312–20R; R. M. Solow, 1994, 'Perspectives on growth theory', *Journal of Economic Perspectives*, vol. 8, no. 1, 1994, pp. 45–54.

18 D. Quah, *The Weightless Economy in Economic Development*, Centre for Economic Performance Discussion Paper No. 417, London School of Economics and Political Science, March 1999; M. Weitzman, 'Hybridizing growth theory', *American Economic Review*, vol. 86, no. 2, 1996, pp. 207–12.

19 M. Jacobs, *The Green Economy*, London, Pluto Press, 1991; C. Hepburn and A. Bowen, 'Prosperity with growth: economic growth, climate change and environ-

mental limits', in R. Fouquet, ed., *Handbook of Energy and Climate Change*, Chelten-ham, Edward Elgar, 2013, pp. 617–38.

20 *Green Growth in Cities: Key Messages from the OECD*, OECD, http://www.oecd.org/gov/regional-policy/GGIC%20flyer_v4.pdf (accessed March 2015) and also *Cities and Climate Change: Key Messages from the OECD*, OECD, http://www.oecd.org/env/cc/44245217.pdf (both accessed 14 April 2016). See also Global Commission on the Economy and Climate, *Better Growth, Better Climate*.

21 U. Eberle and R. Von Helmolt, 'Sustainable transportation based on electric vehi-cle concepts: a brief overview', *Energy and Environmental Science*, vol. 3, 2010, pp. 689–99.

22 Incumbent networks of car dealers in certain US states are acting to effectively block the sale of Tesla cars and prevent the path-dependent feedbacks that might reduce the profits of traditional car manufacturers. See J. Surowiecki, 'Shut up and deal', *The New Yorker Blog*, 21 April 2014, http://www.newyorker.com/magazine/2014/04/21/shut-up-and-deal (accessed 14 April 2016).

23 J. Bessen, 'History backs up Tesla's patent sharing', *Harvard Business Review Blog*, 13 June 2014, http://blogs.hbr.org/2014/06/history-backs-up-teslas-patent-sharing/ (accessed 14 April 2016).

24 Smulders points out that growth and stable environmental quality can only be maintained if there are non-diminishing returns to investment in new (green) knowledge capital: see S. Smulders, 'Endogenous technological change, natural resources and growth', in R. S. Simpson, M. A. Toman and R. U. Ayres, eds., *Scarcity and Growth Revisited*, Chapter 8, Washington DC, Resources for the Future, 2005. Popp provides some evidence that these returns may be diminish-ing: D. Popp, 'Induced innovation and energy prices', *American Economic Review*, vol. 92, no. 1, 2002, pp. 160–80.

25 P. Aghion, J. Boulanger and E. Cohen, 'Rethinking industrial policy', *Breugel Pol-icy Brief* 04, June 2011.

26 A. Dechezleprêtre, R. Martin and M. Mohnen, *Knowledge Spillovers from Clean and Dirty Technologies: A Patent Citation Analysis*, Grantham Research Institute on Cli-mate Change and the Environment Working Paper no. 135, September 2013.

27 D. Acemoglu, P. Aghion, L. Bursztyn and D. Hemous, 'The environment and direc-ted technical change', *American Economic Review*, vol. 102, no. 1, 2012, pp. 131–66.

28 See IPCC, http://www.ipcc.ch/ipccreports/tar/wg2/index.php?idp=90 (accessed 14 April 2016).

29 McKinsey & Company, *Global GHG Abatement Cost Curve* Version 2.1, http://www.mckinsey.com/client_service/sustainability/latest_thinking/greenhouse_gas_abatement_cost_curves (accessed 14 April 2016).

30 Some models do incorporate learning and induced innovation, but only to a lim-ited extent. They do not encompass the full array of interrelated feedbacks which generate the kind of multiple equilibria that characterise the real world in order to retain computation stability and convergence. See for example the World Induced Technical Change Hybrid (WITCH) model: http://ledsgp.org/re-source/world-induced-technical-change-hybrid/ (accessed 14 April 2016).

31 M. Macleod, P. Ekins, R. Vanner and D. Moran, eds., *Understanding the Costs of Environmental Regulation in Europe*, Cheltenham, Edward Elgar, 2009.

32 M. Metayer, C. Breyer and H. J. Fell, *The Projections for the Future and Quality in the Past of the World Energy Outlook for Solar PV and Other Renewable Energy Technologies*, Energy Watch Group (Berlin) and Lappeenranta University of

Technology (Finland), 2015, http://energywatchgroup.org/wp-content/uploads/2015/09/EWG_WEO-Study_2015.pdf (accessed 14 April 2016). See also C. Candelise, M. Winskel and R. Gross, 'The dynamics of solar PV costs and prices as a challenge for technology forecasting', *Renewable and Sustainable Energy Reviews*, vol. 26, 2013, pp. 96–107.

33 The author was previously Head of Economic Forecasting at HM Treasury 1999–2003.

34 IPCC Fifth Assessment Report Working Group III, 'Summary for policymakers', p. 15, http://mitigation2014.org (accessed 14 April 2016).

35 M. Grubb, *Planetary Economics*, London, Routledge, 2013.

36 C. Fischer and R. Newell, 'Environmental and technology policies for climate mitigation', *Journal of Environmental Economics and Management*, vol. 55, no. 2 (March), 2008, pp. 142–62; G. Zachmann, A. Serwaah and M. Peruzzi, *When and How to Support Renewables? Letting the Data Speak*, Bruegel Working Paper, 2014/01, 2014.

37 The concept of a 'just transition' has been used to promote policies which will make decarbonisation more equitable for those sectors and communities adversely affected. See ITUC, 'What's Just Transition?' 8 September 2009, a flyer for explaining to decision-makers, interested organisations and the general public the rationale, meaning and examples of 'Just transition' policies, http://www.ituc-csi.org/what-s-just-transition?lang=en.

38 S. Bassi and D. Zenghelis, *Burden or Opportunity? How UK Emissions Reductions Policies Affect the Competitiveness of Businesses*, Policy Paper, Centre for Climate Change Economics and Policy & Grantham Research Institute on Climate Change and the Environment, 2014.

39 See B. Combes and D. Zenghelis, *Tough Love*, MacroPlus Comment, Llewellyn Consulting, 2014.

40 See Bassi and Zenghelis, *Burden or Opportunity?*

41 M. Romani, N. Stern and D. Zenghelis, *The Basic Economics of Low-carbon Growth in the UK*, Grantham Research Institute on Climate Change and the Environment and Centre for Climate Change Economics and Policy, LSE, 2011.

42 S. R. Baker, N. Bloom and S. J. Davis, *Measuring Economic Policy Uncertainty*, Working Paper, 2012. See also D. C. Etsy and M. E. Porter, *National Environmental Performance: An Empirical Analysis of Policy Results and Determinants*, New Haven, CT, Yale Law School, 2005.

43 C. Perez, *Technological Revolutions and Financial Capital: The Dynamics of Bubbles and Golden Ages*, Cheltenham, Edward Elgar Publishing, 2003.

44 See J. Leaton, N. Ranger, R. Ward, L. Sussams, M. Brown et al., *Unburnable Carbon 2013: Wasted Capital and Stranded Assets*, Carbon Tracker and Grantham Research Institute on Climate and the Environment, London School of Economics. See also A. Ansar, B. Caldecott and J. Tilbury, *Stranded Assets and the Fossil Fuel Divestment Campaign: What does Divestment Mean for the Valuation of Fossil Fuel Assets?*, Stranded Assets Programme, Smith School of Enterprise and the Environment, University of Oxford, October 2013.

45 Global Commission on the Economy and Climate, *Better Growth, Better Climate*.

11. Capitalism, Technology and a Green Global Golden Age: The Role of History in Helping to Shape the Future

CARLOTA PEREZ

Introduction: growth without technology or sustainability without growth?

THE INCREASED awareness of the role of technology and innovation in the economy has not yet found a clear expression in orthodox economic theory —or in the growth strategies being applied across most of the advanced world. There are currently widely divergent opinions on the likely impact of information technologies on growth and employment. While the optimists claim that these technologies, guided by the market, will eventually bring growth,[1] the naysayers counter with predictions of high unemployment and low growth.[2] At the same time, a significant proportion of the environmental movement has been calling for zero growth, 'de-growth' or similar, essentially blaming technology for climate change and other environmental and social ills.[3]

In this chapter, I shall argue that what all of these divergent views on technology and growth share is the absence of a proper historical understanding of innovation: of its nature, of the interactions it generates in the economy and of the regularity in the technological upheavals from which innovation has sprung since the first Industrial Revolution. Although it is difficult to find an economist today who will not accept that innovation is a key driver of economic growth, it remains almost impossible for them to express its impact adequately in orthodox models. Increases in labour productivity through the change in proportions of labour and capital do reflect *process* innovations, but the impact of radical *product* innovations can neither be expressed nor predicted. Such truly new capital goods and infrastructures as (historically) steamships, railways and computers, which cost less and less at the same time as their influence on growth and society becomes more and more powerful, are probably the most dynamic inducers of growth. The specific nature of these technologies is not easily measurable, and there are hardly any comparable statistics of such 'game-changers' across the past two centuries, so they are routinely ignored. Yet this oversight is a waste of one of the richest sources of knowledge about how growth comes about and how jobs are created and destroyed.

Published by John Wiley & Sons Ltd, 9600 Garsington Road, Oxford OX4 2DQ, UK and 350 Main Street, Malden, MA 02148, USA

Similar problems with measurement and analysis have led many economists and policy-makers to see a conflict between growth potential and environmental concerns. Orthodox economics has long struggled to deal appropriately with the role of natural resources in the economy. Decades of low and decreasing costs of energy and raw materials made it seem reasonable to ignore their impact, and thus both the concepts of output per hour and of the ambitiously named 'total factor productivity' fail to measure the productivity of resources. Nor have many attempts been made to incorporate the role of innovation in resource use. In 1956, Solow proposed that the nature of technology should be recognised as being wider than just the contributions of capital and labour, measuring its total contribution as the unexplained 'residual' after those had been taken into account.[4] Half a century later, with environmental and energy issues becoming pressing concerns, Ayers and colleagues suggested introducing the efficiency of energy into the models.[5] But such approaches do not go very far in analysing the role of concrete innovations in productivity and growth, much less in guiding growth and employment policy. Over recent years, as the high volatility and uncertainty of resource prices have become the 'new normal', energy and materials conservation and raising the productivity of resource use have increasingly become strategic business goals.[6] Yet such innovation is not taken into account in the usual analyses of growth. Instead, the environmental regulations that have prompted such innovations are often perceived as growth suppressors.[7]

Meanwhile, the calls for zero growth or de-growth coming from the environmental movement also stem from an incorrect assumption: that the only possible patterns of growth available are those of the resource-based forms of mass production which shaped most of the twentieth century. Both these opposing camps see a conflict between economic growth and environmental concerns. Yet both have largely ignored the evidence that new information and materials technologies, if well guided towards environmental ends, have the potential to radically reduce the material and energy content of consumption patterns and production methods. Such a direction for innovation can stimulate profitable investment, bring growth and allow millions of new consumers in the developing world to adopt highly satisfying lifestyles—albeit very different in kind to twentieth-century notions of good living. This possibility was identified as early as 1973 by Chris Freeman and other evolutionary economists at the University of Sussex, who argued that well-directed technological change could curb waste and excessive use of energy and resources without bringing growth to a halt.[8] Such studies have snowballed since, with 'green growth' analyses and associated policy proposals now beginning to emerge even from mainstream economic organisations such as the World Bank and OECD. The 2014 report of the Global Commission on the Economy and Climate, *Better Growth, Better Climate*, has been particularly influential.[9] Yet in wider economic and environmental debate the confusion persists. The need to understand the processes of technical change and the ways in which major new technologies have historically been assimilated and shaped since the Industrial Revolution is as urgent for the environmental movement as it is for orthodox economics.

This chapter therefore seeks to connect an understanding of innovation as an economic process with the possibility of enabling new patterns of growth in a global 'green' direction. It will show how, historically, the innovation potential of each major technological revolution has been shaped and steered by government, society and business in periods that are very similar to the present, when the recessions following major bubble collapses have led to widespread fears of joblessness and secular stagnation.[10] It will argue that this pessimism is a recurrent phenomenon based on the stalling of innovation, after major bubble collapses, in spite of the existence of plenty of technological possibilities.[11] It results from the decoupling of the financial sector from the production economy during the boom and its reluctance to take risks investing in the real economy after the experience of the crash. The necessary 'recoupling' has historically involved a paradigm shift in direction for the economy and society as a whole. The chapter will therefore argue that a radical change in policy is now needed to tilt the playing field strongly towards green growth and green innovation as the new direction for our age, and that such policies can bring back growth and jobs and reduce inequality.

Technological revolutions and economic development

The history of technological revolutions

Technological progress is commonly misperceived as continuous. Economists typically take the British Industrial Revolution of the 1770s as the start of the industrial age and the commencement of the process of constant 'development' and economic growth which has transformed the West and to which less developed countries aspire. Nevertheless, a number of analysts have recognised additional breaks or 'industrial revolutions' in the sequence, such as a second major leap forward in the late nineteenth century and, increasingly, the 'digital revolution' of the current times. On the other hand, a recent view holds the prospect of a significant reduction in technology-driven growth in the West, using the term 'secular stagnation' originally coined in the 1930s.[12] A closer analysis of past patterns of change reveals that these views are a simplification of the historical record.

My research, which builds on the work of Chris Freeman, Giovanni Dosi and other evolutionary economists,[13] confirms the view of Kondratiev and Schumpeter that there have been not one or three, but five distinct 'technological revolutions' since around 1770, driving what can be called successive 'great surges of development'. The first of these surges was indeed the Industrial Revolution. The introduction of mechanisation, the development of factories with water power and the associated network of canals radically changed ways of working and living and saw the ascendance of Britain as a world power. The second upheaval, from 1829, based on coal and steam, iron and railways, brought the rise of the educated and entrepreneurial middle class. Then, from 1875, the age of steel and heavy engineering (electrical, chemical, civil and naval) saw the proliferation of transnational railways and transcontinental steamships, enabling an intense development of international trade and the first 'globalisation'. That period witnessed the emergence of Germany and the US as challengers to British hegemony. In 1908, with the launch of Ford's Model-T, the age of the automobile and highways, of oil and plastics and of universal electricity and mass production shook up patterns of working and living once more. In this instance, the US led the way, harnessing the interrelated technologies and infrastructures to produce the great surge of development that created the mass-produced, suburban American dream. Most recently, in 1971, the year that Intel's microprocessor was launched, our current age of information and communication technologies (ICT) was initiated.

It is important to emphasise that, when identifying these shifts as 'revolutions', we are not referring only to the radical new technologies themselves. True, each of these technological leaps has brought with it a whole new set of interrelated innovations, industries and infrastructures. But it is the potential of these technologies to increase productivity across the *whole* economy that makes them truly revolutionary. Their propagation changes the relative cost structure of production in most sectors, by providing new powerful and cheap inputs (such as steel in the third shift, oil in the fourth and microelectronics in the current one). They unleash innovation potential that typically leads to synergistically connected chains of new products *and* to the renewal of mature industries. The new infrastructures—from canals to railways, to steamships, to highways and electricity, to the internet—allow wider and deeper market penetration at decreasing costs. And their application gradually transforms organisational models and the 'common sense' criteria for best practice in production and innovation across *all* industries. The result is what can be described as a 'techno-economic paradigm shift', which leads to a profound transformation in ways of working and consuming, changing lifestyles and aspirations across society.[14]

Perhaps the greatest of these technological upheavals was the one brought by mass production and the automobile in the first decades of the twentieth century. The major leap in manufacturing productivity made the so-called 'American Way of Life'—or a variation of it—accessible to the great majorities of people in the advanced nations. The transformation of agriculture, through mechanisation, petrochemical fertilisers and pesticides, increased food production enormously, while the introduction of cheap plastics to replace natural materials supported the mass consumption of low-cost appliances and clothing and the innovations of disposable packaging and bottling. It was a major shift from the world of paper and cardboard, horses, bicycles, trains and tramways, and it blurred the previously clear separation between city and countryside as the automobile enabled sub-urban sprawl.

A regular pattern of diffusion

Although each of these revolutions has been distinctly specific, due to its technical characteristics and also to historical, political and other contingent factors, certain features do recur each time. Such recurrence is explained by the fundamental ways in which the market economy and society generate and assimilate the paradigm-changing processes of technical change.[15] Every time, the great surge of development driven by each revolution has taken half a century or more to spread unevenly across the economy. And each has occurred in two distinct periods—installation and deployment—with a 'turning point' or transitional phase in the middle that has been marked by a bubble collapse and a shorter or longer recession (see Figure 1).

The first period, installation, is characterised by the turbulent times of Schumpeterian 'creative destruction'.[16] Financial capital drives the process, funding emerging entrepreneurs and innovators to explore the vast potential made possible by the new technologies. Historically, it is a time of ferocious competition, during which the ideology of *laissez-faire* tends to shape the behaviour of governments. This permits financial capital to override the

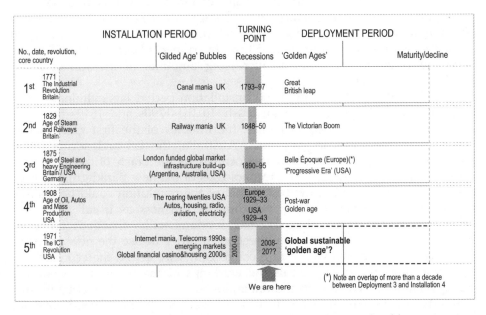

Figure 1: The historical record: bubble prosperities, recessions and golden ages
Source: Based on Perez 2002 and 2009

entrenched power of the production giants of the previous paradigm, enabling the modernisation (or destruction) of the mature industries and spreading a new 'common sense' across both the business world and society —turning to 'normal' many processes, practices and expectations that would have been inconceivable only decades before. This frenzy phase of extravagant *Great Gatsby*-esque prosperity also facilitates a necessary over-investment in the new infrastructures, in order that coverage (whether of canals, railways or the internet) is broad enough for widespread usage. This enables the paradigm to diffuse from niche to mainstream.

However, installation also involves painful social disruption and adaptation. The diffusion of the new paradigm leads to a massive displacement of old skills and to polarisation between new and old industries, regions and incomes. As the mature industries of the previous paradigm that do not manage to modernise decline and the new industries choose 'greenfield sites', major shifts occur in the location of jobs. The contrast between the bankruptcy of Detroit and the ascent of Silicon Valley is a dramatic example of this in the current shift away from the Age of Oil and the Automobile to that of ICT. At the same time, the free market ideology, which plays a role in encouraging the abandonment of the old way of doing things and of favouring the new, also leads to economic instability and, eventually, begins to stifle genuine growth rather than promote it. Unrestrained by regulation, financial capital becomes increasingly speculative, moving further and further away from investments in production until the paper economy of the stock market decouples from the 'real economy' of goods and services, taking off from the performance of the companies they represent. Thus, we see a flourishing of casino-like financial instruments, such as those that fuelled the sub-prime mortgage and toxic instruments boom in the US in the 2000s, in order to mobilise the increasing amounts of investment funds looking for easy gains.

Indeed, in the past, as now, every installation period has culminated in a major bubble followed by a major crash. In the 1790s and 1840s the canal and railway manias ended in panics; the bubbles of the first globalisation collapsed in the 1890s in Argentina, Australia, the US and several other countries; and the 'Roaring Twenties' ended in the crash of 1929. In each case, the basic infrastructure and technologies of the new paradigm had been installed so that the full growth potential of the revolution could be realised across the entire economy. Yet, reverting to 'business as usual' after such crashes does not work. Business has fundamentally changed; economic growth now requires a radical redirection in order to use the new potential for investment and innovation in a convergent way across the economy. At the same time, the crash reveals the workings of the financial casino, and this revelation, together with the unemployment and income inequality that regularly accompany it, have historically set the political conditions for unleashing a second period: that of deployment, which is characterised by more harmonious growth than in the bubble booms. But before this can occur, finance has typically been regulated and reoriented so that it serves the production economy once again. Immediately following the crash, private investors have become risk-averse and are not ready to fund the expansion. Thus, after the major collapses, the state has historically stepped in to play an active role in favour of investment and growth.[17]

Why we are now in the equivalent of the 1930s and 40s

What is critical to understand, first, is that the recessions that follow the mid-surge crash result not only from speculation and panic, as is commonly believed regarding the current economic crisis, but also from the structural changes brought about by the new paradigm itself. Each technological revolution is based on an interrelated set of new technologies, industries and infrastructure networks that develop in intense 'feedback loops', providing markets and suppliers for each other, lowering production costs and increasing profitability—in the way that computers generated markets for microchips, the internet for computers and both of them together for the iPhone.[18] It is these synergies between the new technologies, industries and infrastructures that are the hallmark of a technological revolution and the basis for its rapid growth in the initial decades of diffusion.

These revolutions also provide a new *potential* to transform and enable innovation in other industries. In the current shift, we have already seen the initial impact of creative destruction. ICT has transformed many pre-existing industries and opened the way to new opportunities, from turning tangible products into services to the creation of the home office and the globalisation of production and trade. It has also changed some of the patterns of consumption towards greater information intensity as well as towards more generalised innovativeness and entrepreneurship—individual and collective —using networks and platforms. But its transformative work is far from done. As has been the case with previous revolutions, the next few decades may be as different from the bubbles of the 1990s and 2000s and the recession of the 2010s as the golden age of the 1950s and 1960s differed from the Roaring Twenties and from the depression of the 1930s.

The second period in the diffusion of each revolution is 'context-dependent' deployment. The new set of possibilities is disparate and often unconnected. It is referred to as 'potential' precisely because it can be used and shaped in different ways and because profitability depends on relative costs, dynamic demand and the availability of synergies in terms of suppliers, skills, distribution networks and customer learning. Hence the potential inherent in each revolution requires the choice of a *direction* in order to come to fruition: in other words, an orientation for innovation is necessary, applicable across multiple and disparate industries, which can generate synergies advantageous to all of them.[19] For policy-makers the key insight is that this direction is neither pre-determined nor automatically defined by the technologies of the revolution. Rather, historically it has resulted from a

197

combination of factors: the constellation of lifestyle-shaping goods and services made possible by the technologies; the ability of investors, entrepreneurs and governments to recognise the potential of these products; the political ideologies of those with the power to affect their deployment; and the socio-historical context in which they emerge. Politicians and policy-makers in the past did not count on historical hindsight, so the successes or failures of deployment directions can be ascribed to the intuitive quality of the leadership and to the relative power of the various interests at play. At present, with a greater understanding of the processes at work, the direction can become a conscious socio-political choice. In order to visualise the breadth of the range available, suffice it to note the marked differences in the direction given to the potential of the mass production revolution by Hitler, Stalin and the Keynesian democracies of the West.

In the US, which was at the forefront of that revolution, the installation period began in 1908, bringing a new highway-based infrastructure, the spread of electricity, the communication device of the radio and the promise of aviation. Optimism—and investment—in this brave new world was high, accelerated by the World War I production boom. But, by the Roaring Twenties, investment had turned speculative; it was a bubble prosperity; a 'Gilded Age'.[20] The Great Depression that followed made it difficult to recognise the vast range of viable innovations and of potential mass markets connected with plastics, energy-intensive materials, electrical appliances and the personal automobile. At the time, assembly-line manufacturing and the mechanisation of agriculture generated the same fears of unemployment and 'secular stagnation' that globalisation, robotics and artificial intelligence do today.[21] Yet the greatest boom in history was just around the corner—a great surge of consumer-pulled growth, given direction by the practice of suburbanisation and the ideology of the American Dream. This consumerist way of life that went on to fuel economic expansion for decades was not merely the sum of the new products and infrastructures made possible by the mass production paradigm, but resulted from a synergistic combination of political and societal choices. It was the measures of the welfare state, such as free (or subsidised) education and healthcare, labour union-secured salaries and a progressive tax structure, along with complementary institutional innovations such as the credit system, unemployment insurance and mortgage guarantees, which made it possible for growing numbers of the population—including blue-collar workers—to aspire to a suburban home and the new lifestyle. Thus, the social safety net and suburbanisation, together with the Cold War, defined the optimal space for successful profitable innovation with dynamic, reliable and synergistic markets. On the global stage, complementary institutional innovations, such as the World Bank, the IMF, the GATT, the Bretton Woods agreement on the 'gold dollar', the UN (and, ironically, also the Cold War) stabilised international economies and trade, furthering the positive-sum game created between business and society.

A similar process of state-enabled convergence in innovation has occurred during every deployment period. Each technological revolution makes feasible a wide range of new interrelated infrastructures, production equipment and life-shaping goods and services. Yet it is in a process of socio-political choice that the specific set that will flourish from the new range of the possible is fully defined. Historically, that choice—particularly in the Western market societies—has not required coercion, but rather is driven by aspirations for the lifestyle that the new goods and services provide. The rich and educated tend to be the pioneering adopters, with increasing layers of society copying their example.

In the mid-nineteenth century, the age of steam, coal, iron and railways saw economies of scale in production and transport that led to the emergence of 'Victorian living'. The British middle classes established an industry-based urban lifestyle (different from that of the country-based aristocracy) which gradually spread to the new bourgeoisies in other countries. The age of steel and heavy engineering, which built the transcontinental and transoceanic infrastructure networks that led to the first wave of globalisation, similarly brought the cosmopolitan lifestyles of the *Belle Époque* to the European and American upper and middle classes, later spreading to the upper classes of the world. As with the 'American Way of Life' of the postwar period, each of these styles became the model of 'the good life' and, as such, shaped the consumption patterns and desires of the majority, provided secure growing markets and guided innovation trajectories.

We are now in a crucial moment in history similar to the 1930s, requiring thinking and measures as bold as those of Keynes, Roosevelt and Beveridge[22] and as ambitious as the Bretton Woods agreements. Unemployment and inequality are increasing due to globalisation, new technologies and the decoupling of finance from the economy during the prosperous bubble period. Critically, the 'American Way of Life' of the last paradigm brought patterns of consumerism, disposability and profligate use of energy and materials that now confront the world with major environmental challenges, not least that of climate change. Up until now the ICT revolution has done little to change this: mass use of computing technologies has rather added to global energy and materials demand. But our current information era is only halfway through its diffusion path. If history is a guide, it has twenty to thirty years of deployment ahead. We have indeed witnessed a rash of new products and increasingly changing consumption patterns over the past two decades due to the widespread installation of these 'general purpose' technologies, yet their capacity to transform every single industry and activity is only in its early stages. There is a huge potential for innovation that is technologically feasible but still risky and uncertain in terms of markets and profitability. What is lacking is a direction that responds appropriately to the current contextual conditions and the specific wide-ranging innovation potential now installed. The playing field needs to be tilted to achieve something similar to what suburbanisation did in the postwar boom. In the next section, it will be argued that a 'green' direction and full global development —together—form a direction that is capable of unleashing the vast potential available on a growth path that could lift all boats.

ICT and the green direction

What is the 'green direction', and how is it related to the present ICT paradigm? As noted in the introduction, both 'zero growth' environmentalists and those in favour of unfettered markets see a conflict between economic growth and environmental concerns, despite the mounting evidence to the contrary coming from successful sustainable business models.[23] This chapter argues that the ICT revolution has the capacity to facilitate wide-ranging sustainable innovations to radically reduce materials and energy consumption while stimulating the economy. It can significantly increase the proportion of services and intangibles in GDP as well as in lifestyles.

To understand the role of ICT in the green shift, it is important to clarify that, although many products and services will involve digital technologies, not all need to do so. Once you learn to network with computers and iPhones, you naturally network without them; once Spotify and Kindle teach you to access music and books from a shared source, rather than possess a collection of boxed CDs and a heavy-to-move library, you find it natural to share tools with your neighbours, and so on. That is what a paradigm shift is about: a new common sense for innovation and behaviour with or without the actual technologies. All those trends that involve reducing waste and responding to needs in intangible ways are going in the direction of 'green growth'.

A very broad definition of 'green growth'

Part of the difficulty in understanding the notion of green growth may be the 'green' tag itself, which typically refers to avoiding climate change by reducing CO_2 emissions through renewable energy or use of 'sustainable' products. Although renewable energies, resource-efficient innovations and new environmentally friendly materials are certainly key elements, they are not sufficiently far-reaching alone to revive growth. From a technological point of view, such product categories do not constitute a synergistic system, just as automobiles and plastics alone would not have been enough in the last technological revolution: they do not lead to sufficient technical convergence in equipment, engineering, skills or suppliers.[24] Rather, 'green' is one of the possible *directions of stimulus* for deployment of the general purpose technologies of ICT across every industry and sector in which challenges brought by globalisation and environmental degradation turn from obstacles to solutions. Thus, green growth should be seen as a 'mission-oriented' pathway to promote a major switch in production patterns and lifestyles, creating new sources of employment and well-being. It involves tilting the playing field in such a way that profitable innovation and investment opportunities will reinforce each other synergistically. This would create a positive-sum game between business, society and the planet capable of addressing not only environmental problems, but also (as will be discussed below) the issues of inequality and slow, jobless growth.

The previous section discussed *why* such a direction is needed to unleash innovation potential; but why should 'green' be seen as the most promising option? The massive technological transformations that occur across society with each major shift are contingent on context and conditions. The new potential changes the context for development and opens successive 'windows of opportunity', while closing old ones—generating different scenarios for business and social action.

Increasingly, the greatest window of opportunity of the present day is the possibility of overcoming the contextual legacy of the previous paradigm; in this case, the environmental degradation and resource scarcity brought about by the age of oil and mass production. At the most basic economic level, mass consumption combined with the new billions of middle-income consumers in the emerging world have led to fast-growing demand for materials, energy and food in the emerging countries, increasing overall demand, exhausting the most easily accessible sources and pushing up marginal costs. The impact of climate change is only intensifying that effect. While the availability of cheap oil in the 1990s and of cheap labour in Asia in the 2000s enabled the old path of disposability to be perpetuated, the growing reality of dwindling resources and violent price hikes and drops has led to a perceptible shift in market context. We are no longer in the postwar era of clearly defined national economies with energy and materials abundance; we are now in a globalised economy and we have only one planet.[25]

At the same time, the technologies of the ICT paradigm have been changing the context of what is possible. It is now infinitely easier to establish interactive local, regional and global networks for coordination of production and services. Where economies of scale once relied upon standardisation of both supply and demand, variety, specificity and adaptability are now handled easily with ICT. This is true not only in manufacturing; natural resources can be managed far more efficiently, with intelligent control systems being developed for everything from monitoring, extraction and irrigation to processing, sorting and distribution. Along with the organisational capacities brought by ICT, this is leading to the development of niche and custom markets and the hyper-segmentation of all markets, from produce, energy and materials through manufactured goods to services. And market access enabled by ICT is open to all, from traditional farmers to innovative high-tech companies, from organic vegetables to tailor-made alloys: consumer and supplier can locate each other directly.

A shift in consumer demand

Meanwhile, beginning with small-scale efforts by (mostly) non-profits, the concerns and values of the environmental movement have spread to a broader base of consumers and to larger and larger companies. As the negative impacts of climate change and environmental degradation have become more apparent, stock markets are increasingly acknowledging the risks and insurance companies are beginning to include it in their calculations.[26] Crucially, this shift in values, combined with the economic realities of the market and the innovations made possible by ICT, are redefining our concept of the 'good life', from one of standardised mass consumption to one that is custom-tailored and sustainable. The lifestyles of the wealthy and the educated younger generation reflect this already: a preference for organic, locally sourced fresh foods rather than highly processed ones; for natural materials and sustainable design; for cycling, car-sharing and recycling; for experiential rather than passive entertainment. It is a 'good life' that promotes high-quality individual health, which in turn is seen as dependent on environmental health—what might be called a 'green good life'.

Such a change in the shape of consumer demand opens up even further the potential synergies across industries inherent in what the ICT paradigm has made technologically feasible. Stimulated by a 'green' direction and underpinned by the model of a green good life, the transformative nature of ICT is capable of enabling innovation across the whole production spectrum, from the extraction of natural resources to manufacturing, distribution, logistics and reuse, and in the ways of organising production and consumption in multiple interrelated industries and societal applications. Each innovation brings with it a set of new 'problems', stimulating further innovation (in materials, equipment, processes, distribution and so on), which spur investments and can lead to entire new industries. This clustering of interdependent users and producers and of self-reinforcing capabilities results in synergies and support networks that make further innovations easier and profitable, as well as less risky.[27]

In essence this is about achieving growth and well-being across society by increasing the proportion of services and intangibles, both in GDP and in the individual satisfaction of needs. Product innovation trends are already visible: custom-designed eco-friendly materials, conservation, recycling, reduction of material content per product and designing for durability and zero-waste. The notion of a 'circular economy' has entered the mainstream, with global corporations such as Philips and Unilever championing the process. This promotes the gradual replacement of 'products' with 'services', particularly in the replacement of possession with renting. From commercial lighting systems and airplane engines to jeans, carpets and cars, the question has become: why buy when you have the option of 'renting' a product that is upgradeable, maintained and available on demand? There is increasing innovation towards making cities more liveable and less polluting, with the revamping of transport systems and the built environment and the promotion of the 'sharing economy', in which ICT-enabled communication allows citizens to share goods, either through a centralised, fee-paying service, such as a car club, or using direct peer-to-peer exchange for such items as household tools and garden equipment. And lifestyle aspirations are stimulating industries in the areas of personal health and individual fulfilment—from innovations in local food networks to high-tech ICT and bio-science-driven preventive and personalised medicine, and the championing of the 'collaborative' and 'creative' economies. Some of these socially driven processes could become an enriching complement to the traditional profit-driven economy, while enhancing the quality of life of the participants.

Thus 'green' as a direction is not about sustainability *versus* growth; instead, it turns the environmental crisis from an economic problem into an economic opportunity. In that sense it can be seen as a 'mission orientation' for investment across mutually reinforcing industries, in the same way that World War II, the Cold War and the 'American Way of Life' drove technological investment in the past. But it also involves multiple smaller innovations that are increasingly seen simply as lifestyle choices rather than 'green' issues, encompassing a wide range of changes in production and consumption that would stimulate growth, business creation and employment right across the economy. Such a direction would not only reduce carbon emissions and strengthen environmental sustainability, but could allow millions of new consumers in the developing world to share in good, healthy and creative lives. Indeed, in the same way that the boom of the previous lifestyle shift relied upon enabling the working classes of the advanced nations to benefit from the material comforts of suburbanisation, full global development is not only a desirable but a necessary condition for a return to economic health today. It is to this that we shall turn next.

'Green growth', development, jobs and inequality

The green direction has to be a global issue. This is so for technological, environmental and economic reasons. ICT has made national borders invisible to all trade in intangible services and information, in particular to finance. Resource scarcity and climate change are planetary problems, both in the short term—a poor harvest in Kenya affects the consumer price index in the UK, for example—and in the long-term prognosis for overall environmental health. As already noted, it is not feasible for China, India and the developing world to grow along the old mass consumption model; a 'green' direction is a necessity in a situation where new millions are striving for the good life while facing finite resources and the threat of pollution and global warming. Finally, globalisation is an economic necessity: in order for the potential inherent in the current paradigm to be fully realised in this period of deployment, there needs to be demand on a global scale.

The quality and profile of domestic and global demand

In economic terms, any new 'direction' will only work successfully if the appropriate volume of demand is forthcoming. In the 1930s, Keynes wrote to Roosevelt that 'putting most of your eggs in [the housing] basket' was 'by far the best aid to recovery because of the large and continuing scale of potential demand; because of the wide geographical distribution of this demand; and because the sources of its finance are largely independent of the stock exchanges'. He added: 'there are few more proper objects for [direct subsidies] than working-class houses'.[28] For that period, it was a good prescription, and was at the core of postwar economic success. It was in the nature of the main organisational innovation of that particular era—mass production—to reduce prices and increase profits the higher the volume of *identical* products. Therefore, the institutional innovations influenced by Keynes' advice—such as mortgages, loans, unemployment insurance and pensions—brought stable purchasing power to the working class and provided a specific demand-pull associated with a standardised model of home life.

Today, the flexible production methods enabled by the ICT revolution allow for market segmentation and, in doing so, make differentiated products more profitable than highly standardised versions, which have in fact become low-price 'commodities' with narrow profit margins. Furthermore, Keynes was dealing with what were—and more intensely became—national economies with clear borders separating domestic from export markets. Globalisation changes all this: taxes can be avoided because payments can cross invisible frontiers; interest rate changes can encourage finance to move masses of money from one foreign affiliate to another; and domestic income distribution can end up creating demand in and stimulating the economy of another country.

Meanwhile, the ICT revolution has brought a new potential for growth in the developing world, as shown by the enormous success of Asia and the gradual rise of Africa and Latin America as exporters and innovators.[29] Cheap and ubiquitous internet access is already bringing education, services (such as mobile banking) and the opportunity to enter the global marketplace to corners of the world that did not have the infrastructure to fully participate in the previous paradigm. ICT-enabled innovations in the natural resource industries, from monitoring and extraction to the fabrication and niche sales of sustainable goods, promise an area of development for all resource-rich nations.[30] Facilitating and funding investment in the lagging countries of the developing world would create markets for green engineering, infrastructural and equipment technologies from the advanced world. The process would provide dynamic demand for both capital equipment and consumer goods between advanced, emerging and advancing countries. At the same time, through job creation in both the producer and user countries, it would not only lift many millions into better lives and reduce

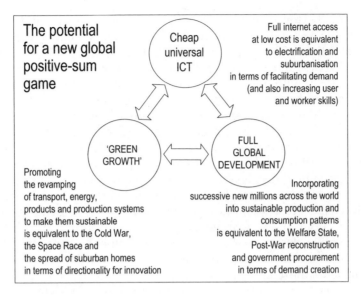

Figure 2: Conditions for a sustainable global golden age
Source: C. Perez 2012[31]

migratory pressures by creating jobs 'at home', but would incorporate new consumers and generate new trade flows for all (see Figure 2).

New sources of employment growth

Once green growth is increasingly defined as a general direction for innovating across the global economy and for weaving a coherent fabric of producers, suppliers, services and skills, it is easier to see how it can become a solid route to jobs and growth. As noted, the green direction implies redesigning existing products and equipment as well as revamping buildings and infrastructures. This is a challenge for engineering that would open opportunities for high-tech reindustrialisation in the West. At the same time as this retrofitting effort, another major job-creating and export-promoting route is the design of sustainable production equipment and infrastructure adequate to the specific climatic and other conditions of the developing world, where in the past standardised equipment and processes—with inadequate scale and characteristics—have been adopted.

'Green growth' also supposes the return—and heightened importance—of product durability, accompanied by maintenance as a key service. Planned obsolescence and disposability were strategies for demand expansion in the face of saturated markets. The growth of the global middle classes, and of the wealthy (who buy luxury products), can amply compensate for a drop in the sales of lower-quality, disposable products, while also countering what would otherwise be an uncontrollable rise in the cost of materials.

Producing for the top of the range with the most advanced and safest technology possible and with high niche market profits is a better strategy under the new conditions. This could then lead to a very active rental sector for organising second-, third- and Nth-hand markets in each country and across the world, along with the growth of disassembly, remanufacturing, recycling, reusing and other materials-saving processes. Information for 3-D printing replacement parts and the provision of regular upgrades for the maintenance of products could become standard practice. This would create a business model in which repair and reuse would take the place of planned obsolescence. With the 'internet of things', chips can be put on each product to provide usage histories, enabling a thriving rental and maintenance industry to assign adequate prices. In the advanced world, such a business strategy would create great quantities of jobs for displaced assembly workers in maintenance, upgrading, warehousing, parts 'printing', distribution and installation, while design, redesign and many other creative industries and services would employ university graduates. A 'green mission' would thus be equivalent to the combination of postwar reconstruction, the Cold War and suburbanisation in terms of demand creation, employment and directionality for innovation.

Pendular shifts in income distribution

In addition to the creation of jobs, a green direction is also a path towards reducing income inequality, which is rightly a current source of economic and social concern. The history of technological revolutions shows us that this is nothing new. During the 'bubble' phase of each great surge, the new industries (such as those of Silicon Valley pre-crash) and the financial world 'decouple' from the sluggish mature economy, and the extraordinary profits and capital gains that ensue lead both to highly unbalanced regional growth and to a concentration of income towards the top of the scale, particularly among those benefiting from the easy millions made in finance.

Thomas Piketty's work with Saez on inequality allows us to plot the changing distribution of income in the US over the past hundred years against the recurring diffusion pattern of two technological revolutions (Figure 3).[32] This shows the polarisation that occurred in the bubble prosperity of the Roaring Twenties, its reversal in the golden age of the 1950s and 1960s and then the renewed polarisation during the installation period and the bubble collapses of the current ICT revolution. Figure 3 shows that there was indeed a pendular movement in inequality: the share of US taxpayers' income going to the top 10 per cent of the population in the two installation periods rises to 50 per cent, whereas in the deployment period of the postwar decades it comes down to less than 35 per cent. Equivalent differences apply to the top 1 per cent.

It is notable that the historical golden ages, so-called because they spread prosperity across a much wider range of society, have occurred after each

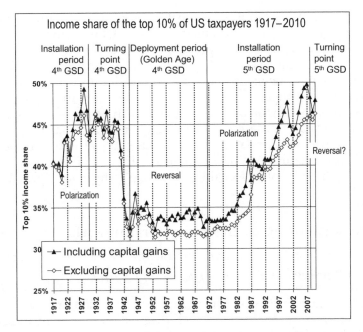

Figure 3: Pendular movement in the polarisation of income along each great surge of technological development in capitalism

Source: Perez, 2012, using data and basic graph from Piketty and Saez (see endnote 31), with our period indications

major bubble collapse, overcoming the resulting recession and tending to reverse the revealed income polarisation. The Victorian Boom, for example, saw reductions in hours of work, increases in wages and the provision of relatively decent workers' housing.[33] In the *Belle Époque*, new welfare policies were applied in Europe based on increases in taxes on the wealthy, including the spread of Bismarckian social insurance from Germany across most of the continent, such as that of Lloyd George's 'People's Budget' in the UK.[34] Much more far-reaching was the reversal in inequality engineered in the postwar welfare state of the advanced Western nations: the innovations in social institutions discussed above encouraged a clear direction in production and lifestyles.

Now, following a century in which consumer demand has become a significant driver of the economy and in which democracy has brought the whole of the adult population of the West into the political process, comparably explicit measures towards overcoming polarisation are in order. The current welfare state—what has survived of it—was designed in a world of 'jobs-for-life'. That is no longer the case for the majority of workers; this paradigm involves continuous change, flexibility and adaptability. Social expectations—and the ease with which the lives and riches of others can now be observed thanks to ICT technologies—mean that the current genera-tions will not easily accept a declining level of welfare, either for themselves or for their children. As during previous post-bubble collapses, the expres-sion of such frustrations can be seen in the rise of xenophobic and anti-immigrant movements, in the attraction of disaffected youth to extreme fascist/religious groups and equally in the growth of extreme left movements and in various bursts of protest such as those of Occupy or the *indignados*. Obstinate austerity policies that make the majorities suffer the consequences of the financial casino and the national debt will do nothing but exacerbate the anger. Only a radical shift in policies can bring back healthy growth and stable societies. Providing criteria for doing that is the object of the final section.

A radical reshaping of the policy framework

This chapter has presented a dynamic picture of the context facing econo-mists, environmentalists and, especially, policy-makers. It has explained how the context changes with each successive technological revolution and along its diffusion path. Schumpeter did not exaggerate when he referred to those processes as 'creative destruction'. Such destruction and renovation occur in the technologies and the economy and they also need to happen in the organisational, institutional and policy spaces.

A mental paradigm shift

For a company or for a society to get the most out of the potential offered by the new technologies of one of those upheavals, it has to assume that the way things were and the way we thought they should be are both obsolete until proven contrary. A new understanding and fresh thinking is required.

Yet the mass production revolution is still with us in its patterns of resource use, in its wasteful mode of consumption and in many of its pro-duction models. It is being copied in the emerging economies and aspired to in the developing ones; it is hankered after by the layers of impoverished unemployed in the advanced world and rightly made the main target of attack by the environmentalists. The ICT industries, whose strategies origi-nally evolved in the boom of the 1990s, found oil at its lowest price and abundant, extremely low-cost labour available in Asia. Unthinkingly, they were led to adopt the planned obsolescence model generalised in the 1960s to overcome the limits posed by the saturation of markets. Thus the intangi-ble nature of information technologies did not express itself in imaginative strategies encouraging minimal use of materials and maximum upgradeabil-ity. Fortunately, that is now beginning to happen, alongside innovation in the reduction of energy use.

At the same time, these new technologies have transformed the structure and organisational model of most of the surviving corporations. Over the past thirty years, these have shifted from bureaucratic command-and-control pyramids to flexible networks spanning the globe, incorporating widely differentiated units in complex value-chains with varying degrees of competence and autonomy. Meanwhile, consumer behaviour, although still primarily oriented to the 'consumerist' mode, has been gradually moving away from the accumulation of products and towards personalised services, enabled by the use of computers, software and especially the smart phone.

The two areas affecting the economy where sufficient change has clearly not occurred are government and economics. In policy-making, instead of moving from the intelligent Keynesian way of intervening appropriate to mass production in a national context, to another intelligent way of doing so, suited to a world of globalised flexible information-intensive production, most politicians in power decided that the state should get out of the way to let markets decide. Fortunately for them and unfortunately for society, the fact that there was a new technological revolution to propagate did allow markets to be hugely successful in the 1990s and 2000s—until the two bubbles that resulted from the installation of the internet and the invention of new financial instruments collapsed. In spite of the high cost of rescuing the banks and the rising inequality across society revealed by the recession, the shrinking of the state has continued, led by the vain hope that markets will find a way of bringing a miraculous revival if left to themselves. History has shown that this is the wrong moment for that. Yet the current economic orthodoxy, incapable of explaining the crashes, holds on to an interpretation of how the economy functions that ignores the role of technology and the accumulated learning of the other social sciences. It has taken refuge in increasingly complex mathematical models, as if economics were more closely akin to physics. Worse still, these economists and many of their critics are still waging the ideological battles of the 1960s and 1980s, without realising that we are now in a completely different context—one that has more in common with the 1930s.

Economics needs to be truly evolutionary. If it wants to use models, it has to learn to represent structural change. At the same time, instead of pretending it can be a hard science, it needs to develop qualitative thinking and engage in 'appreciative theorising'[35] to enrich its quantitative methods and bring them closer to the changing social reality. It is interesting to note that practically all the macroeconomic tools and concepts that are being used today—from GDP to the natural rate of growth—were developed during the 1930s and 1940s in the context of mass production, the war effort and the development of the national welfare state.

According to the dogmas of the current orthodoxy, the credit crunch should not have happened, quantitative easing should have led to inflation and increasingly unfettered markets (without any 'crowding out' from the government) should have already achieved strong growth. Their recommended austerity policies have now gone on for eight years with feeble to appalling results; any CEO of a serious corporation with an equivalent failure rate would have been replaced years ago.

It is often said that one should never let a good crisis go to waste. We are now in the midst of what can be considered a crisis in terms of a deeply unbalanced global economy that is wasting a huge innovation potential. The battle is not between state and markets; it is between policies that will maintain uncertain growth and increasing income inequality and a direction that can bring a sustainable global golden age that can lift all boats. We could now use the existing transformative power of the new technologies in a direction that will turn environmental challenges into a solution to various social and economic ills.

Policy-making in the deployment period

One of the main differences between the installation and the deployment periods of each technological revolution is the source of dynamism. Installation is supply-driven; the new technologies are self-propelled and mutually reinforcing. Deployment is mainly demand-pulled; but not just by the quantity of demand, but also by its profile and dynamism. That is why it is not possible to apply the Keynesian recipes, which worked for mass production and in the context of relatively closed national economies, to countries operating in globalised conditions, with flexible production technologies and with growing intangible trade and financial flows across the internet.

The best pre-condition for successful policy-making is having a correct interpretation of the nature of the changing context being faced. If the historical recurrence discussed in this chapter is correct, the relevant parallel is not the Thatcher–Reagan model applied in the 1980s, when the wealth-creating and productivity-enhancing powers of the mass production revolution were exhausted, but rather the policies applied when that revolution was installed after the Roaring Twenties and was ready to be unleashed across the whole economy. Keynesianism and Bretton Woods were the transformative set of policies that created the new context to achieve both better business and better lives for all, through a sort of covenant between government, business and society, where all benefited. An equivalent covenant is needed at this time, with as many adequate norms, policies and institutions as were set up then.

Recent and current conditions are not a good basis for judging future scenarios. It would have been nearly impossible for people in the mid-1930s to imagine that those bedraggled, hungry, unemployed workers queuing at the soup kitchens could seriously aspire, just over a decade later, to a suburban home full of electrical appliances with a car at the door. It was also difficult to imagine that widespread decolonisation would become the norm—be it through peaceful or violent means—when empires seemed stable and Germany was preparing to expand by force and change the maps of Europe and Africa. These are not times for maintaining the status quo or for trying to return to recent conditions. If the advanced world governments stay on the current austerity path, they will wait forever for the market to do the right thing for growth and social well-being. These are times to be as imaginative and bold as Keynes and Roosevelt and Beveridge, but in full awareness of the specific nature of the current technological potential and of the opportunities it opens and closes.

There can be no return to the centralised bureaucracies of the 1950s and 1960s, however successful they may have been during mass production times, but neither is it possible to bring back the unfettered market booms of the 1990s and 2000s. Free-wheeling finance was successful at the turn of the century because it first had a technological revolution to install and then had to spread the new economy across the globe. Both tasks were hugely profitable but are now basically complete. In the process, as has happened in previous equivalent bubbles, finance learned to make doubtful innovations that do not create wealth but merely lead to differential inflation, where financial assets increase their value faster than salaries, to the detriment of workers and small productive businesses. Massive bailouts have allowed finance to remain unscathed and focused on short-term speculation, expecting high returns from such activities. That context is also encompassing the behaviour of production companies, many of which have acquired the short-term profit expectations of the bubble years and are more engaged in stock buybacks, cost cutting, tax avoidance and quick deals than in R&D, training or other innovative activities with a longer-term horizon.[36] As a result, massive amounts of money are sitting idle in the corporate world, in banks, financial companies and production ones. The longer this situation lasts, the harder and deeper the negative consequences on the economy and society.

History shows that capitalism is capable of reversing some of the worst ills it creates, but only after experiencing a crisis. Financial collapses, wars, prolonged recessions and/or major social unrest have played that role.

A wave of green innovation enabled by ICT is possible, but unless it happens in a convergent way across most industries and countries, the potential innovations will remain risky and the market will not engage. Only a strong tilting of the playing field in favour of sustainable investment, with policies that are credible, consensual and likely to remain stable in time, will move finance from internally oriented speculation to investment in the production economy.

A clear socio-political choice

Capitalism is only legitimate when enabling the successful ambitions of the few to benefit the many. Globalisation has improved the lot of many millions in the old 'third and second worlds', but by reducing many of the gains of the welfare state in what was called the 'first world'. The policy changes required are as bold, systemic and wide-ranging as the Keynesian policies, the welfare state and the Bretton Woods agreements were in the previous similar moment. They will need to achieve a positive-sum game between business and society but this time at a global scale, that is, between advanced, emerging and developing countries. The breadth and depth of the changes brought about by the spread of each technological revolution require an equivalent redesign of the institutional framework in order to unleash their full transformative potential. The best pre-condition for policy-making is a powerful interpretation of the present moment; with such an understanding, it becomes easier to also imagine a new powerful set of policies to address the new times. The following are some of the types of policies which might be introduced.

- *Don't tax labour; tax energy and materials.* Redesigning the tax system (using digital databases) to tax 'bads' rather than 'goods'—for example, taxing resource and energy use instead of labour and consumption—would stimulate saving of materials and energy and encourage employment and consumer spending on intangibles.
- *Regulate for durability and maintenance.* Making producers responsible for the entire lifespan of their products would encourage the circular economy and manufacturing durability, as well as stimulating the growth of a rental and maintenance economy.
- *Redesign the metrics with which to measure wealth production.* As numerous studies have shown in recent years, GDP has very limited meaning and is even distorting in the knowledge economy. New metrics need to be designed to account for the use of energy and materials and to measure the various ways in which value is now created and well-being enhanced.
- *Facilitate the sharing and collaborative economies.* The proliferation of free internet-based services has inspired many to innovate in networks of sharing access to possessions, exchanging time and collaborating in creative projects. This is one of the routes along which ICT enables a green economy grounded in sustainability and focused on services and personal care.
- *Move towards some form of basic income.* Providing a minimum income in the advanced countries—such as the universal basic income currently being trialled in Finland, a negative income tax and/or workfare for community projects and services—is the necessary platform for encouraging the sharing and collaborative economies, the growth of voluntary organisations and of creative endeavours that could contribute to the quality of life both at the community level and through participation in global networks. In the 'green good life', well-being would increasingly be measured not by possessions, but by positive experiences of healthy living, community sharing and creative involvement in networking and group activities. Any of the chosen systems of basic income distribution, plus additional support for special cases, can take advantage of ICT and the debit card systems for its administration.
- *Skill and reskill at the global level.* Widespread agreement on the importance of education and skills needs to translate into a central part of a 'new new

deal'[37] across the world, taking intelligent advantage of the power of ICT, including the increasing value of so-called 'Massive Online Open Courses' (MOOCs) and lifelong education. Increasing the creative capabilities of the population of developing countries would improve their life chances, reduce migratory pressures and increase trade.

- *Support development across the lagging countries.* Just as the Marshall Plan aided the reconstruction of Europe while increasing transatlantic trade, the international community needs to implement new and effective ways of giving support to development, recognising the new possibilities opened by ICT and globalisation.[38] As discussed above, the rise of these countries would benefit advanced, emerging and developing nations, creating new and important trade flows in all directions.
- *Reorient finance* not by controls but by taxing short-term gains highly and lowering the rate with time, thus making it more profitable to invest in the real economy and to do so long-term. In addition, public investment in green research, development and market creation,[39] in revamping the built environment and in funding private green projects is necessary to provide support for the riskier innovations in the green direction and to increase the synergies for others to invest.

This list is far from complete—but it is a list that is grounded not only in the historical discussion above, but also in examples already being tried out and explored in villages, towns, cities and nations around the world. Yet for such a radical shift to occur, it is important to go beyond the listing of potential policies and to examine both the process by which such policies are designed[40] and the type of organisations that are to implement them.[41]

- *Modernise government itself.* Abandoning the 'command-and-control' model of organisation has been part of the modernising paradigm shift experienced by companies in recent decades; little beyond the introduction of computers has taken place in governments in this respect. Instead, following a neoliberal recipe, the primary 'new' practice has been to outsource public services or to establish so-called 'public–private partnerships'. This has been done in the name of efficiency, and under the assumption that the private sector knows best and will save the state money. In most cases, as Colin Crouch shows in his chapter in this volume, such expectations have not been fulfilled.[42] The worst consequence has been the weakening of public sector skills and the avoidance of necessary modernisation, which in turn has reduced the attractiveness of public service as a career for the most talented. Making the move towards creativity and flexibility for agile and knowledgeable government institutions is essential if economies are to be led to powerful and synergistic growth with increasing social benefits.[43]
- *Consensus-building for policy design.* The old mode of policy change has been for governments (typically one party) to introduce a new policy that

213

elicits enormous resistance, encouraging lobbying, efforts at finding avoid-ance loopholes and even corruption. This will not work in the current globalised economy. New institutional mechanisms are needed to ensure positive-sum outcomes by working with all the stakeholders, from busi-ness to civil society. The process of policy design matters more and more.[44]

- *Devolution of national power.* In a globalised world, it seems increasingly necessary to consider devolving part of national power, both down, to local governments, cities and regions, and up, to supranational entities. This is a daunting task, and one that confronts huge political hurdles. But when globalisation and differentiation have radically altered the condi-tions under which finance and the whole economy operate (illustrated by the ease of tax avoidance), supranational institutions with enforcing power will prove unavoidable.

What is clear is that the old recipes will not work now and have not worked in recent times. Neither will the simple austerity recipe of getting govern-ment out of the way and expecting markets to do it all without a clearly defined context with a certain and stable direction. We need serious rethink-ing, intense consensus-building, global negotiations and determined leader-ship. The technologies capable of driving a sustainable global golden age are available; unleashing them successfully requires an understanding of the historical moment and the willingness to make a clear socio-political choice.

Acknowledgements

I am grateful to Anthemis (UK) Ltd for financial support for the work on this chapter and to Tamsin Murray-Leach for her collaboration in research, writing and editing.

Notes

1 See for example R. D. Atkinson, 'How certain are you that robots won't create as many jobs as they displace?', *The Christian Science Monitor*, 3 December 2015, http://www.csmonitor.com/Technology/Breakthroughs-Voices/2015/1203/How-certain-are-you-that-robots-won-t-create-as-many-jobs-as-they-displace (accessed 29 December 2015); E. Brynjolfsson and A. McAfee, *Race Against the Machine: How the Digital Revolution is Accelerating Innovation, Driving Productivity, and Irre-versibly Transforming Employment and the Economy*, Lexington, MA, Digital Frontier Press, 2011.

2 R. Gordon, *Is U.S Economic Growth Over? Faltering Innovation Confronts The Six Headwinds*, Working Paper 18315, National Bureau of Economic Research, August 2012, http://www.nber.org/papers/w18315 (accessed 29 December 2015); T. Cowen, *The Great Stagnation: How America Ate All the Low-Hanging Fruit of Modern History, Got Sick, and Will (Eventually) Feel Better*, New York, Dutton, 2011.

3 For example, T. Jackson, *Prosperity Without Growth*, London, Earthscan, 2009; S. Latouche, *Farewell to Growth*, London, Polity Press, 2010.

4 R. M. Solow, 'A contribution to the theory of economic growth', *Quarterly Journal of Economics*, vol. 70, no. 1, 1956, pp. 65–94.

5 R. U. Ayres, L. W. Ayres and B. Warr, *Energy, Power and Work in the U. S. Economy 1900–1998*, Insead's Center For the Management of Environmental Resources, 2002/52/EPS/CMER, 2002.

6 R. Dobbs, J. Oppenheim, F. Thompson, M. Brinkman and M. Zornes, *Resource Revolution: Meeting the World's Energy, Materials, Food, and Water Needs*, McKinsey Global Institute report, 2011, http://www.mckinsey.com/business-functions/sustainability-and-resource-productivity/our-insights/resource-revolution (accessed 29 December 2015).

7 See for example G. B. Christiansen and R. H. Haveman, 'The contribution of environmental regulations to the slowdown in productivity growth', *Journal of Environmental Economics and Management*, vol. 8, no. 4, 1981, pp. 381–90; K. Palmer, W. E. Oates and P. R. Portney, 'Tightening environmental standards: the benefit-cost or the no-cost paradigm?', *Journal of Economic Perspectives*, vol. 9, no. 4, 1995, pp. 119–32.

8 H. S. D. Cole, C. Freeman, M. Jahoda and K. Pavitt, *Models of Doom: A Critique of the Limits to Growth*, New York, Universe, 1973; C. Freeman and M. Jahoda, *World Futures*, London, Martin Robertson, 1978.

9 Global Commission on the Economy and Climate, *The New Climate Economy*, report for the Global Commission on the Economy and Climate, 2014, http://2014.newclimateeconomy.report/ (accessed 29 December 2015). See also M. Jacobs, *Green Growth: Economic Theory and Political Discourse*, Working Paper 92, Grantham Institute, 2012.

10 In 1934, Hansen's 'Capital goods and the restoration of purchasing power', *Proceedings of the Academy of Political Science*, vol. 16, no. 1, Money and Credit in the Recovery Program (April), pp. 11–19, and in 2014 L. H. Summers's 'Reflections on the "new secular stagnation hypothesis"', in C. Teulings and R. Baldwin, eds, *Secular Stagnation: Facts, Causes and Cures*, London, CEPR Press, pp. 27–38.

11 Brynjolfsson and McAfee, *Race Against the Machine*; E. Brynjolfsson and A. McAfee, *The Second Machine Age*, London, W. W. Norton & Co, 2014.

12 See particularly Gordon, *Is U.S. Economic Growth Over?* ch. 4.

13 J. A. Schumpeter, *Business Cycles: A Theoretical, Historical, and Statistical Analysis of the Capitalist Process*, New York, McGraw-Hill, 1939; N. Kondratieff, *The Major Economic Cycles*, 1922, published in English in G. Daniels (trans.) *Long Wave Cycle*, New York, E.P. Dutton, 1984; G. Dosi, C. Freeman, R. Nelson, G. Silverberg and L. Soete, *Technical Change and Economic Theory*, London, Pinter Publishers, 1988.

14 See C. Perez, *Technological Revolutions and Finance Capital: The Dynamics of Bubbles and Golden Ages*, Cheltenham, Edward Elgar, 2002, particularly ch. 2; 'The double bubble at the turn of the century: technological roots and structural implications', *Cambridge Journal of Economics*, vol. 33, no. 4, 2009, pp. 779–805.

15 See Perez, *Technological Revolutions*, chs 4–5.

16 J. A. Schumpeter, *Capitalism, Socialism and Democracy*, London, Routledge, 1994 [1942].

17 A fuller account of these processes can be found in Perez, *Technological Revolutions*.

18 C. Freeman and F. Louçã, *As Time Goes By: From the Industrial Revolutions to the Information Revolution*, Oxford, Oxford University Press, 2001.

19 M. Mazzucato and C. Perez, 'Innovation as growth policy: the challenge for Europe', in J. Fagerberg, S. Laestadius and B. R. Martin eds, *The Triple Challenge for Europe: Economic Development, Climate Change and Governance*, Oxford, Oxford University Press, 2015, ch. 9.

20 M. Twain and C. D. Warner, *The Gilded Age: A Tale of Today*, Hartford, CT, The American Publishing Co., 1873.

21 Brynjolfsson and McAfee, *The Second Machine Age*.

22 Even bolder were the creators of the Swedish model, Rehn and Meidner, whose model of cooperation between business government and trade unions brought the country to the first ranks in productivity, competitiveness, skills and well-being. That model became inadequate once the mass production revolution approached exhaustion, as happened with the orthodox Keynesian recipes across the rest of the advanced world. R. Meidner and G. Rehn, *The Trade Union Movement and Full Employment. Report to the LO Congress in 1951*, Stockholm, The Swedish Confederation of Trade Unions (LO), 1951.

23 Ellen MacArthur Foundation, *Towards A Circular Economy: Business Rationale For An Accelerated Transition*, Report, 2 December 2015, https://www.ellenmacarthurfoundation.org/publications/towards-a-circular-economy-business-rationale-for-an-accelerated-transition (accessed 29 December 2015); Ellen MacArthur Foundation, *Growth Within: A Circular Economy Vision For A Competitive Europe*, Report, 25 July 2015, http://www.ellenmacarthurfoundation.org/assets/downloads/publications/EllenMacArthurFoundation_Growth-Within_July15.pdf (accessed 29 December 2015).

24 C. Freeman, *Systems of Innovation: Selected Essays in Evolutionary Economics*, Cheltenham, Edward Elgar, 2008.

25 World Wildlife Fund and SustainAbility, *One Planet Business: Creating Value Within Planetary Limits*, Report, WWF-UK, 2007, http://assets.wwf.org.uk/downloads/one_planet_business_first_report.pdf (accessed 29 December 2015).

26 See, for example, for the former, the FTSE's ESG (Environmental, Social and Governance) series of indexes, including the FTSE Environmental Opportunities Index Series and the FTSE4Good Environmental Leaders Europe 40 Index; more at http://www.ftse.com/analytics/factsheets?allproducts=RESPINV&Category=Go (accessed 29 December 2015); and for the latter, the speech by the Govenor of the Bank of England Ref to Lloyds of London insurance undertakers: M. Carney, 'Breaking the tragedy of the horizon—climate change and financial stability', speech delivered at Lloyd's of London on 29 September 2015, http://www.bankofengland.co.uk/publications/Documents/speeches/2015/speech844.pdf (accessed 29 December 2015).

27 B. Å. Lundvall, ed., *National Innovation Systems: Towards a Theory of Innovation and Interactive Learning*, London, Pinter Publishers, 1992.

28 J. M. Keynes, 'Private letter to Franklin Delano Roosevelt,' 1 February 1938, in D. E. Moggridge, *Maynard Keynes: An Economist's Biography*, London, Routledge, 1992.

29 R. Kaplinsky, 'Schumacher meets Schumpeter: appropriate technology below the radar', *Research Policy*, vol. 40, no. 2, 2011, pp. 193–203.

30 R. Kaplinsky, *Globalization, Poverty and Inequality: Between a Rock and a Hard Place*, Cambridge, Polity Press, 2005; C. Perez, 'Technological dynamism and social inclusion in Latin America: a resource-based production development strategy', *CEPAL Review N° 100*, 2010, pp. 121–41; A. Marin, L. Navas-Alemán and

C. Perez, 'Natural resource industries as a platform for the development of knowledge intensive industries', *Tijdschrift Voor Economische en Sociale Geografie*, vol. 106, no. 2, 2015, pp. 154–68.

31 C. Perez, 'Why IT and the green economy are the real answer to the financial crisis', Green Alliance Blog, 2012, http://greenallianceblog.org.uk/2012/03/19/why-it-and-the-green-economy-are-the-real-answer-to-the-financial-crisis/ (accessed 29 December 2015).

32 T. Piketty and E. Saez, 'Income inequality in the United States, 1913–1998', *The Quarterly Journal of Economics*, vol. 115, no. 1, 2010, pp. 1–39.

33 M. A. Bienfeld, *Working Hours in British Industry: An Economic History*, London, London School of Economics and Political Science/Weidenfeld and Nicholson, 1972.

34 G. Bruun, *Nineteenth Century European Civilisation 1815–1914*, London, Oxford University Press, 1990 [1955].

35 R. Nelson and S. Winter, *An Evolutionary Theory of Economic Change*, Cambridge, MA, Belknap Press, 1982. See also Freeman and Louçã, *As Time Goes By*, ch. 2.

36 W. Lazonick, 'From innovation to financialization: how shareholder value ideology is destroying the US economy', in G. Epstein and M. H. Wolfson, eds, *The Handbook of the Political Economy of Financial Crises*, Oxford, Oxford University Press, 2013, pp. 491–511.

37 B. A. Lundvall, 'Innovation and democracy in the Learning Economy: the "New New Deal" as response to the crisis'. Memorandum for 10 Downing Street Policy Seminar *Industrial Activism, Market Regulation and the Transition to a Low Carbon Economy*, 2009.

38 See Perez, 'Technological dynamism', CEPAL Review N 100, 2010, pp. 121–41; and Marin et al. 'Natural resource industries'.

39 M. Mazzucato, *The Entrepreneurial State*, London, Anthem, 2013; 'Serious innovation requires serious state support', *Financial Times*, 4 December 2013, http://www.ft.com/cms/s/0/f017a3c4-4e1b-11e3-8fa5-00144feabdc0.html#axzz2tbj5RZ76 (accessed 29 December 2015).

40 D. Rodrik, *Industrial Policy for the Twenty-first Century*, CEPR Discussion Paper 4767, London, CEPR, 2004, http://papers.ssrn.com/sol3/papers.cfm?abstract_id=617544 (accessed 29 December 2015).

41 E. Karo and R. Kattel, (2015) *Innovation Bureaucracy: Does the Organization of Government Matter when Promoting Innovation?* CIRCLE WP 2015/38, Lund University, 2015.

42 See also W. Drechsler and T. Randma-Liiv, 'The new public management then and now: lessons from the transition in Central and Eastern Europe', in M. de Vries and J. Nemec, eds, *Implementation of New Public Management Tools. Experiences from Transition and Emerging Countries*, Brussels, Bruylant, 2014, pp. 33–49.

43 The title of Lou Gerstner's account of turning the huge IBM bureaucracy into a gigantic, agile organisation can be a mirror for what can be done in governments. See L. Gerstner, *Who Says Elephants Can't Dance?* New York, Harper Business, 2002.

44 See Rodrik, *Industrial Policy*.

Index

Note: page numbers in italics refer to tables and diagrams; alphabetical arrangement is word-by-word.